CONTENTS

Before Words   vii

PART ONE
Managing the Future

1. Welcome to the Future!   3
   How to Manage the Business That Is There Instead of the One That Is Here

2. How to Make Money by Watching the News   19
   The Future is Taking Place Right Now — In the News Media

3. Managing Yourself   33
   How to Get More from Your Most Important Asset

4. The Power of Your Presence   57
   Leadership for Small Companies

5. What Makes Marketing Work?   77
   Products, Problems, and Possibilities

6. Managing Inventory   91
   Converting Inputs to Outputs — With Less in Between

PART TWO
Improving Business Performance

7	Who Cares? *How to Improve the Way Your Customers Are Treated*	111
8	Competing in the Service Economy *How to Position a Firm Whose Product Is Service*	129
9	What Causes Underperformance? *Is the System Working Against Your People?*	149
10	Winning Together *Sharing the Gains of Improved Business Performance*	173
11	What's the Competition Up To? *How to Collect and Use Competitor Intelligence*	187
12	Upping the Stakes *Fighting Back When the Competition Gets Tough*	201
13	The Gathering Storm *How to Get Through the Coming Recession*	215
	After Words	235

BEFORE WORDS

This Isn't a Preface Because Nobody Reads Them

Unlike the author of a book I recently read whose Preface breathlessly stated, that "this was the book I always wanted to write . . ."—I didn't. The essays that appear in this book were originally presented to groups of small business owners as a series of Breakfast Briefings under the general title of New Ideas for Small Companies, a program sponsored by the Ramsey Chair of Private Enterprise and the Small Business Development Center of Georgia State University in Atlanta. Since the program began in the fall of 1985, it has been our custom to meet monthly at a local hotel for breakfast; and precisely at 8:00 A.M., I rose to wax eloquent on a topic on which I had chosen to speak for sixty minutes. I could have gone longer, but my audience always left. Small business owners always seem to be in a hurry to be somewhere else.

As good as my notes were (to permit compliance with the rigid time allocation), they were cryptic lecture notes—neither something I could read to the audience, nor suitable for an article outline. So, while I was flattered by requests for a copy of my "speech," I held forth little hope that I would be converting my notes to a more intelligible form. That would require one heck of a lot of work, and I knew from past experiences that it was almost impossible to preserve in written form the informal spontaneity characteristic of remarks delivered as the spoken word. Nevertheless, I usually left each meeting with a handful of business cards—in case I changed my mind.

My most notable recollection is a dear elderly lady with blue hair who wagged her finger at me with a parental air: "You'll be sorry some day that you didn't preserve these talks of yours." Preserve them? I thought "preserve" was something one did to a frog in a jar of alcohol or last year's peach crop leftovers. But her admonition began to germinate. After all, I had at that time collected over thirty months' worth of these "ghosts of speeches past," and while I occasionally repackage bits and pieces of them in the fifty-odd talks I give each year to other small business groups, maybe there could be a higher calling for these words grown cold than collecting dust in my archival files.

On a cold December week day when a rare snowfall made a media event of two inches of frozen precipitation, liberating my three children from school to test the limits of hypothermia, I retreated to the sanctity of my study to begin the experiment: could I really capture the essence of three recently delivered Breakfast Briefings *sans* the audience that is such an essential part of the electricity I experience when I step before a live audience?

Nope. How could it take four to eight hours to dictate what I had easily delivered in sixty minutes? Why does the first typed draft sound like a eulogy for something that had died? My worst suspicions were confirmed. There was a heck of a lot of work required to write with the spontaneity of a presentation that was originally delivered in a different medium—a speech presented before a live audience—something my editors call "voice." Only after many revisions was I able to get these written versions to read more or less as I hope I sounded when I originally gave these topics as speeches.

In the nearly three years since the Breakfast Briefings began, about five hundred people have attended them, though not at one time. I would guess that our average audience ranged between thirty and fifty. The choice of topics and the content of their presentation was solely mine, and it was determined by several influences. To begin with, I am a microwave engineer by education whose first ten years out of college were spent with Scientific-Atlanta, at that time a small high-tech business that has since grown to international proportions. Thus, I have an engineer's curiosity about learning new things but a very practical perspective about applying knowledge—if I can't tell you something that will change the way you work in your business tomorrow morning, it probably isn't worth knowing. Nothing raises my blood pressure faster than to have someone say, "Franklin, that may be a good academic theory, but . . ." Theories, in my judgment, are intellectual oddities, and whether technical or business, their place is in a museum.

Second, while I was with Scientific-Atlanta, I worked not only in several technical capacities but also in virtually all of the business functions— marketing, production, finance, and various levels of management. Upon leaving the company, these experiences stood me in good stead to start several small businesses of my own and to participate with other people in business start-ups. So, like many of you, I've engaged in hand-to-hand combat with banks and the SBA, sweated out payroll time, hired employees that flunked out on the job, fought competitors for customers, had partners that I had to divorce, and cursed the government and the IRS for causing recessions. I am still active in several small businesses—not in their details, but in their direction—and I think there is very little about business that I haven't experienced firsthand, including many mistakes. Experience, it's been said, is not what happens to you, but what you do with what happens to you, and I believe I've been a good student.

Finally, for over a decade and a half, I've conducted seminars devoted to the problems of managing a small business, spoken to small business trade associations, and consulted with small business clients in almost every industry and every kind of business— manufacturing, distribution, retail, personal services, and even medical, accounting, and legal practices. I believe I understand entrepreneurs and their struggle to become business managers as well or better than most advisers, particularly since I "grew up" in a small business and have owned several. Consulting with them has been fun for me and, I believe, helpful for them.

The choice of Breakfast Briefing topics, then, flowed out of this diversity of personal experiences, and frequently it was an opportunity to talk about a problem I had recently encountered in working with a client. This book consists of thirteen of these topics. There may be subsequent volumes, covering another series of topics, but the market (that means you) will determine if that happens.

Undoubtedly by now the elderly lady with the blue hair has been received into the bosom of her Eternal Reward, but I think if she knew that she was influential in my getting at least thirteen of these presentations "preserved," it would do her proud.

Abe Lincoln supposedly said that a lawyer who represents himself in court has a fool for a client. Similarly, an author who critiques his own work isn't likely to produce a good work, no matter how broad his experience or fine-tuned his communication skills. So, I asked a long-time friend and business associate, Willis Cook, to read and critically comment on each chapter of this book. Willis and I share clients, coach youth soccer together, and have worked on many joint projects. He has insights I don't possess, so I believe his suggestions were helpful in bringing out other perspectives related to points I have made, as well as clarifying cloudy clauses.

And now for the other accolades. My thanks to:

Mike Mescon, former Dean of the College of Business Administration, Georgia State University, and the holder of the Bernard B. and Eugenia A. Ramsey Chair of Private Enterprise, which has sponsored the series of Breakfast Briefings in New Ideas for Small Companies.

Lee Quarterman, who directs the Georgia State University Small Business Development Center that co-sponsored the series and coordinated the logistical activities associated with each presentation.

Tom Clark, Chairman of the Management Department in which I teach as a faculty member of Georgia State University and who was one of the louder voices "bugging me" to write these speeches out.

Loyce McCarter my principal manuscript typist, who endured unreasonable turnaround times and endless revisions. She strokes the "fastest word processor in the East."

Cary Bynum, Director; Margaret F. Stanley, Editing and Production Manager; Edith F. Kilgo, Assistant Editor; and the staff of the Georgia State University Business Press. Cary claimed I had "made his day" when I informed him that after talking about this project for nearly a year, I was finally going to give him a draft of three topics.

And finally, the community of small business owners who have gathered each month for over three years now to see if I had anything new to say and to whom this volume is most appreciatively dedicated.

Willaim H. Franklin
Atlanta, Georgia

PART ONE
Managing the Future

CHAPTER ONE

WELCOME TO THE FUTURE!

How to Manage the Business That Is There Instead of the One That Is Here

When the Duc de la Rochefoucault informed King Louis XVI of France that the royal troops had defected in the face of a popular uprising and the Bastille had fallen, the startled king cried, "It is a revolt!" To which the Duc replied, "No, Sire, it is a revolution." The Duc apparently sensed what the bewildered king and his entourage didn't: this was not another one of those isolated riots that had pestered the royal families of Europe and England for centuries, with the multitudes charging the palace or the castle gates to reach for the royal throats. No, this uprising was different. This one had the marks of an event that could end *l'ancien regime*—the old way—and establish a new order. And it did.

I can imagine what poor King Louis said on receiving the news: "My problem these days is, the future isn't what it used to be . . . things are changing too fast." Louis' real problem, of course, was in not paying attention to the future, and it swept him away. The French Revolution occurred over two hundred years ago, but the premature arrival of the future, to borrow a phrase from Alvin Toffler's *Future Shock*, is still a problem, particularly when managing a business. Did you know, for example, that most of the so-called "excellent" companies extolled in Tom Peters' *In Search of Excellence* (Harper & Row, 1982) have since experienced problems, some quite serious? In fact, his most recent book proclaims triumphantly, "There are no excellent companies!"

That's no surprise, Tom. Look at the way most companies manage their affairs—they *clean up* what's already happened; they manage the aftermath of business and economic events, something over which they have no control. What managers ought to be doing is managing what hasn't happened, that is, managing their future while there is still something to control. Otherwise, they will continue to make the mistake King Louis made by ignoring the future and perhaps end up with a twentieth-century version of his demise.

Now, lest you think I've blown a circuit with all this talk of managing the future, let me ask you to think on these questions. What are you doing when you draw up a will? Take out insurance? Create a business buy/sell agreement? You're managing the consequences of events that have not yet occurred—yep, you're managing the future. But if you wait 'til you're dead, or your place burns down, or your partner wants out, you'll be managing the aftermath. In the first case, then, you're managing while there is still something to manage. In the second case, you're "managing" the cleanup—which is unmanageable.

BACK FROM THE FUTURE

Small business owners are particularly inclined to manage the aftermath. Why? Because they are trapped by their view of time in "tenses"—they, like all people, see time in the past tense, the present tense, and the future tense. But, being practical types, they work in the here and now, the present tense. After all, that's where all the action is, isn't it? The past tense is history, and the future tense—well, it's still "out there," somewhere. But today was yesterday's future. And because today was viewed yesterday as being "out there," I'll bet a lot of small business owners today will be spending their time cleaning up the aftermath of yesterday, choppin' with no chips flyin', wrestling with problems over which they have no control—or problems that are out of control—like poor King Louis. How about you?

There's really only one solution. If you want to avoid management by cleaning up, you must stop thinking of the future as being "out there." Like the Michael J. Fox movie of several years ago, you must manage your business back from the future. Here's an example of what I mean:

Creative problem solvers invariably begin by "seeing" the solution as a *fait accompli*. They then work back to discover the intermediate steps that will produce that solution. When those steps have been discovered, the problem has been solved, even though the solution hasn't yet occurred and may not occur for months or years. There's a difference between solving a problem and the solution occurring.

We use this kind of logic in many other ways. How can a person know that he is a success?* — *when* all of life's goals are achieved, or *while* those goals are being achieved? If the answer is "when," then success can only be ascertained when that person is dead! People will look down at his casket and say, "Ah, he was a success. Too bad he couldn't have stuck around and enjoyed it." Obviously, success and failure in life and business is determined "while," not "when." The journey, not the destination, is success. And the first step on that journey isn't a step *toward* success — implying that success is in the future — the first step *is* success, and that step is its own evidence.

In the same way, success in business isn't located in the future. To be sure, you must manage the future of your business — the consequences of events that have not yet occurred — because that is all you can control today. But the way you act today, determines your future. Like the creative problem solver, you must start at the end — in the future — and discover the events that produce that future. When you do that, the future is now. Like solving a problem before the solution occurs.

As a practical example, the process starts with a vision of your future business. A vision is not a hallucination or a daydream. It's not

---

*I want to go on record that I'm not a male chauvinist. But there's got to be a better way to demonstrate that than peppering speaking or writing with "he or she" when referring to a person in the singular. Unlike Greek, which uses *anthropos* for a person of no gender, *aner* for a person of male gender, and *gune* for a person of female gender, English has limits. This is one of them. I will continue to use "he" to mean people of both sexes, and I hope people (of both sexes) will tolerate this idiosyncrasy and read on.

hokey, or magic, or the power of positive thinking. A vision is a picture—a clear picture. What will your business look like in, say, five years? How will it "end up"? Now that's controllable—because it hasn't occurred. That picture shouldn't be a linear extrapolation of your business today. Your business today is the aftermath of yesterday. And that's not controllable—because today has already occurred. Visualize your company five years out—free-floating, disconnected, nonlinear. Choose your vision! If you can do that, knowledgeable people can chart a course back from that picture and fill in the blanks to determine the intermediate actions that will create the picture.

What kind of organizational structure is required to run the business you created five years out? What kind of people are working in it? How does it market its products and services? What are those products and services? What kinds of systems and procedures are being used to get the work out? Who are the company's managers and what do they control? Ah, now you're getting somewhere. You're no longer stuck in the present tense. You no longer have the baggage of the aftermath—all your yesterdays—to drag forward into the future. If you can answer these questions—if you can fill in the blanks in detail—that business already exists! All that remains is to chip away what is hiding the business that is there. Just as a gemologist removes material to free the gemstone that he sees is there, or a painter applies colors so others can see the picture that he has seen all along, you can now chip away every obstacle, seize every opportunity, to get at the business that you see.

In other words, begin to eliminate the products and services that won't be sold by your business five years from now—and begin to create the ones that will. You can then revise your marketing approach, install the new systems and procedures that will be required to do the work, recruit the people who will be needed by this new business, and eliminate the ones that won't. Now, that won't happen overnight. You still have the aftermath of yesterday to clean up, and that takes time to chip away too.

"Well, all of this sounds great," you say, "but how do I really do it?" I can tell you. But it's been said that brains, like bad soup, are best left unstirred. Nevertheless, in order to tell you how to do it, I've got to stir your brains a bit. So stay with me.

VISUALIZING FUTURE IMAGES

All successful people see themselves as having achieved their goals long before they literally accomplish them. Not surprisingly, failures also see themselves failing before failure is an accomplished fact. Perhaps you should know the story of Karl Wallenda. He had been a high-wire walker his entire life, and his feats included walking between tall buildings and even across Tallulah Gorge in North Georgia. In the last weeks of his life, his wife said he began to talk about falling. It seemed to be on his mind all the time. When he prepared to do a high-wire walk, he checked and rechecked the safety lines. He changed the size of the rope he was to walk on. It was clear that "falling" was on his mind. And finally he fell to his death, fulfilling what he had been thinking about, the picture in his mind.

Since small businesses are simply the extension of the entrepreneur, small business success or failure is really personal success or failure. The future images of success in business, therefore, exist in the mind of the business owner before they exist in the marketplace. Those images are progressively filled in, enhanced, and made more vivid with each rethinking of the image.

Not long ago I was in the office of an entrepreneur who was talking about a new business opportunity that he had been mulling over. In the space of thirty minutes, he must have said, "I can see it; I can see it," at least a dozen times. He was saying a fact, he really did see it. And the more he talked about it, the more detail he was able to flesh out, and the more vivid the picture became in his mind. I'd bet a dollar against a dime that he will pull it off, because that business already exists, the implementation is all that is lacking.

If you are still skeptical, let me tell you that there is a scientific basis for future images becoming realized accomplishments. After all, what is reality? What is The Truth? These are important questions because all people act in accordance with The Truth as they believe it to exist. The future economic climate of this country, for example, will not occur autonomously as if it had a mind of its own or was guided by some unseen intelligence. It will occur because we make it occur. And the first evidence of the future is the collective expectations of the American people.

Do you want to know the future? Then find out a way to determine what people are collectively believing to be The Truth.** I have done that on a small scale through surveys of small business owners' opinions. In a survey, I am interested in the expectations that small business owners hold about the future economic climate of this country in terms of when they think the next recession will occur, how long it will last, and a number of other things. Why? Because these collective expectations, if held on a wide scale, will produce the future—the expectations become a self-fulfilling prophesy.

What people *think* will happen affects what they will *do* today, and what they *do* creates the future—at least for a little while. The reason the future isn't fixed, is that the present isn't fixed. As time passes, expectations may be confirmed, or they may be changed. If expectations are changed, people will act differently today, so the future changes accordingly. What people think will happen is heavily influenced by their recognition of patterns of past events, which are then tied together to create present action. In essence, people ask themselves, "Have I ever seen anything like this before?" "Where is this leading ?" And when they think they recognize what's happening, they take action.

On an individual scale, a person creates his future within the future created by society's collective expectations. An individual future begins with images that are enhanced by rethinking. Now I wish I could tell you that you've just heard an original idea. But you haven't. The late Maxwell Maltz, the author of the book *Psycho-Cybernetics*, was a physician and a plastic surgeon. He discovered a number of things about how the mind works. For one thing, he came to realize that people see themselves as ugly when there are no serious facial abnormalities. It has to do with their self-image. He also discovered that the mind can't tell the difference between an actual occurrence and a thought occurrence. If something happens once, I regard it casually. If it happens many times, I regard it as reality—The Truth. If I think of something once—so what? But, if I think about it many times—ah! The Truth.

Why do people get nervous about giving a speech? Because they gave one hundred of them and became unglued each time? Nope.

**To a great extent, The Truth is what's reported as "news." See next chapter, "How to Make Money by Watching the News."

Because they gave one nervous speech and thought about it one hundred times. Their experience with speech-making is now one hundred bad experiences, one of which really occurred and the rest of which occurred in their minds. And that one hundred rethinkings of a single experience creates a reality to them—The Truth—mainly, giving a speech is bad news.

As I've said before, every successful business owner sees his success in his head long before he sees it in the marketplace. Many unexpected things may happen, but the picture in the head becomes reality. For example, Jim Hindman, the founder of Jiffy Lube, saw in his mind the number of units he would have in operation in a particular year that was then several years in the future. Unfortunately, Old Court Savings & Loan Association collapsed unexpectedly, cutting off his supply of funds to keep projects that were under construction going. Now, if you know anything about the construction business, you know a construction project that is shut down doesn't retain its condition. It goes backward. So Hindman knew it was necessary to continue those projects, but his problem was how to get the funds he needed. Nonetheless, his vision of a certain number of units by a certain year in the future persisted—and it was a vision also held by his employees and franchisees. To make a long story short, the franchisees and his employees made available over $1 million to Hindman with no papers signed, no promise to repay, no interest rate—the loan was simply their vision of the future, their trust in him, and a way to solve the problem. So, like a salmon swimming upstream, you also will have unexpected problems that will catch you off guard and temporarily block your vision for your business, but like all tough people, you've got to hitch up your pants and keep going.

Because they can see how their businesses end up, successful entrepreneurs, like Jim Hindman, always seem to be able to find the missing puzzle pieces. Let me explain. It would be difficult for you to put a puzzle together if you didn't know how it would look in completed form. But knowing the completed picture, you are able to make a start at finding and piecing together the puzzle parts—to begin fleshing out the picture. Invariably, you will have to skip over some places and leave them blank because you can't find the missing puzzle piece. But when it is found, you say, "Aha, that's the piece I was looking for!" In the same way, knowing how your business looks when it ends up allows you to spot the missing puzzle pieces—the unseen opportunities—as they come along. It's not magic. If you're not able to see how it ends up, you can't recognize a piece when it does come along.

It's a lot like a friend of mine who decided after an automobile accident that she would purchase a Mercedes. After she "saw herself" owning a Mercedes (even though it hadn't been purchased), she remarked how amazed she was to see how many Mercedes were on the road. The fact is, they were there all along, but her sensory blocking mechanism prevented her from noticing them. The picture of your future business is what enables you to overcome these sensory blocking mechanisms and seize opportunities as you recognize them.

Once you have envisioned the future image of your company, your job as its "future manager" is to engage in the actions that are necessary for your business to be ready for the arrival of the future—in other words, the arrival of a self-fulfilling prophecy. That's why I said if you can see the future business in your mind, it already exists.

But other people in your company must also be able to see the future business—see the future vision. Sharing that vision is one of your most important acts of leadership. Let me give you an example. I am a soccer coach for eight- and nine-year-old boys. For the most part, they're average kids, but we have won several division championships. Whenever we get ready to play an upcoming game, I always ask my players, "By how many points will we win?" I don't ask, "Will we win or lose?" I don't want them thinking about losing. I want winning to be a foregone conclusion with the only issue being by how much will we win.

There's a lesson here. People shouldn't think about what they don't want to happen; they should think about what they do want to happen. I have seen my guys come from behind, being down two points with five minutes left, and win the game. Why? Because they had already won the game in their minds, so they ignored the score at any point in the game and did what was already done in their heads—win. During one particular season, the team had scored thirty-seven points on opponents, but they had allowed only one point to be scored by opponents. As the season neared its end, an opponent scored only the second point to be scored that season. My goalie was in shock. He said, "I can't believe it!" This is a nine-year-old speaking! More than believing that he was invincible, he had seen something that defied The Truth, at least as far as he was concerned. We nonetheless went on to win the game.

Now I have some good soccer players, but no more than any other team in the league, because all of them came out of a draft pool. Although I've never played soccer myself, I think I've recognized and applied something to soccer that works as well as it does in personal and professional lives. The other coaches, all of whom have good players and some of whom have played the game themselves, believe that soccer is played with the feet, not the head. I believe the reverse to be true. Here's how.

An eight- or nine-year-old has trouble projecting himself into a future game to be played. The reason for this is that imaging mechanisms are not yet part of a child's concept skills—which is why they don't get nervous before public speaking. They can't project past "nervous" experiences into an upcoming event easily. So, I tape all of the games, make copies of those videotapes, and thus allow the boys to see themselves playing. With the help of a VCR, they now have a physical picture into which they can project themselves. I believe that this is the reason we progressively win more resoundingly as a season goes on.

So what's the point here? Like these young soccer players, your people must be able to project themselves into the future vision of your company. It's not enough that *you* are able to see it—they must be able to see it and see themselves in that picture. Most don't. And because they aren't in the picture, they engage in a struggle to get in the picture. This means that things are being done that wouldn't be done if they saw themselves in the picture. And, it means that things aren't being done that would be done if they saw themselves in the picture. But if eight- and nine-year-olds can be taught to put themselves in the picture and come from behind to win, your people can do likewise if you'll share your vision with them.

Consider this. People will act differently if they collapse the future into the present and then act on the future as if it is an accomplished fact. Otherwise, everything lags. There is cyclical behavior in economics and institutions because trends are not perceived as they are occurring. They are perceived after they have occurred. Then there is a decision lag ("Is this trend something I should be concerned with?") and an execution lag (the time it takes to implement an action). And the result? Reacting to fix the aftermath.

As I've said before, you create the future image of your business within the context of the future created by society's collective expectations. I can't say that I know with certainty what those collective expectations are at all times, but I believe that the successful small firms of the future will possess three important qualities that will enable them to do well in good times or bad. So, as you create the future image of your business and rethink that image repeatedly until it becomes The Truth and reality to you, here are three important blanks that must be addressed regardless of society's economic expectations:

- Value creation
- Smart systems
- Customerizing

VALUE CREATION

Perhaps you know the definition of *value-added*, but if you don't, it can be expressed this way:

Value-added = Revenues − Outside purchases

As you can see, if your product sold for one hundred dollars and consumed forty dollars of outside purchases (material, contract labor, and other paid-out expenses associated with the product), you would have created sixty dollars of "value added." In the future, your business must be a high value-added business for two reasons: first, value-added is the only source of permanent funding for your business other than equity; second, value-added will be increasingly a critical-to-survival factor for businesses in the future, as I will show shortly. Creating higher customer values increases value-added, because people will pay higher prices for your product or service.

I've talked about the importance of getting your employees into your future picture of the business. But, you must also get your customers into the picture if you are to create a future that includes customer value enhancement. That's what Dr. Edwin Land did with the Polaroid camera—he expanded the role of the customer and enabled the customer to get a developed picture in almost zero time instead of the usual one or two weeks turnaround time from a film processor. That's what Tom Monaghan did with Domino's Pizza—delivery in thirty minutes or it's free. (The franchised stores offer a discount if late; whereas, company-owned stores currently give the pizza to customers.) By putting the customer in the picture, Monaghan took a commodity—a pizza—and created customer value through home delivery.

That's also what self-service banking did with the automatic teller machines (ATMs)—the ATMs provide round-the-clock, instant access to your money. Years ago, banking hours were from 9:00 A.M. to 2:00 P.M. That eventually lengthened to 5:00 P.M., then drive-through windows appeared. Saturday hours came next. Then the ATMs appeared. Eventually, debit cards will replace credit cards. When you make a purchase with the card, your account will receive a purchase debit and the seller's bank account will receive a purchase credit. Result: instant cash for the seller, and you won't need to write checks at the end of the month for credit card purchases.

Each of these examples was conceived by first visualizing the customers in the picture, and then figuring out how to get them in the picture *practically* via a system, a procedure, or a technology. In other words, the business ignored the "how to" part of the solution until the customers were put into the picture, and that was shown to add value. In most cases, this involves challenging the conventional wisdom of the industry and/or looking at things from a different perspective. A chicken is an egg's way of making another egg—at least from the egg's perspective. So, by challenging the conventional perspective and asking, "How can the customer play a role in the delivery or consumption of my product?" you may discover an opportunity that has been heretofore ignored.

This much I can say: future pictures that exclude the customer from the picture are selfish—the business owner is thinking of his own needs outside of the customer's needs. Don't make that mistake. Thinking of the future only in terms of your firm's products or services instead of considering the future problems that those products and services must solve for the customer isn't really the future picture of a viable business, it's a future fantasy, and it will never get off the ground. Live realistically in the future tense — not the present tense extrapolated into the future!

SMART SYSTEMS

In the mid-1970s the chairman of the board of AT & T was John DeButts. I recall a television commercial in which he walked toward the TV camera through two rows of logos, representing all of the AT & T operating companies. As he stopped before the camera, he paused, pointed toward the logos, and said, "The system is the solution." It's a good point. Smart systems make everyone with access to the system smart. And every indication is that the focus of business in America in the future will be information access. We were once an industrial economy; in the mid-1950s we became a service economy. Now we are passing into the next economy — an information economy.

When we have smart systems, individual skills are less important than the system's skills. The individual will not need to know something if the system knows it. For example, 1–800 hotlines were created by manufacturers to allow customers to call if they had a question about the use of their products. A smart system (or 1–800 number) made the manufacturer's know-how available to a customer without the know-how. Another example: I recently read of a database company in New York whose customers pay a monthly subscription fee and a retrieval fee for answers to virtually any question that can be asked. How many Eskimos live in Alaska? How many red Fords are registered in DeKalb County, Georgia? How many women bankers are married and over the age of forty? Amazingly, these answers can often be retrieved in hours, and the company boasts that 90 percent of its inquiries can be answered by the next day. How? Because the information already exists — it simply doesn't have a way to get to the people who need it. This retrieval company is a smart system connecting people to the information.

I'm sure most of you are familiar with the concept of the present value of money. The same concept can be applied to information — there is present value in information. In other words, the longer one must wait to get information, the less value it has. Remember my earlier comment regarding cyclical behavior, that it is caused by a reaction lag whenever information is not available in realtime but, rather, arrives after the fact? Eliminate information lags and you'll be able to act in real-time. Computer trading programs, for example, enable their users to possess virtually *perfect knowledge*. Perfect knowledge is a principle that says a person will not pay $1.88 a pound for steak in one grocery store if it is known the same kind of steak can be purchased for $1.77 per pound in a nearby store. People pay higher prices because they don't possess perfect knowledge. So, computer trading programs spot trends quickly and execute trades to preserve profits.

Stock price arbitrage also depends on access to information that approaches perfect knowledge. Surrounded by terminals fed by data banks, a trader can spot a security that is selling at a higher price in one market than it is in another market. This enables him to buy in the low-price market and sell in the high-price market. Smart systems not only provide users with access to information, but also provide information quickly so that it approaches perfect knowledge.

Connectivity is a requirement of any advanced economy. Everything is connected to everything. Recently, the primary air traffic control computer in O'Hare International Airport in Chicago went down, forcing controllers to use a secondary computer. This delayed flights into and out of O'Hare for up to three hours. However, delays at O'Hare also delayed flights in Atlanta, Denver, Dallas, and Los Angeles, — none of which had computers down, — because O'Hare's problems backed up through the system as a result of air route connectivity.

If you want to possess perfect knowledge, information connectivity will provide you or your people with instant access to information needed to manage a business well. But too often information has to "get around" the organization to be available to its people. In other words, the organization is an obstruction. Future businesses will find ways to "lay cable" to every brain — connect everything to everything. Today, information must be asked for; in tomorrow's businesses, information will look for us — prompted by advanced cues such as "I want to know anything that . . . " Trend consultants essentially provide that service now, albeit inefficiently.

Smart systems reduce the hierarchy of management levels in a business. It's accepted folklore that the span of management is somewhere between five and seven people. When this is exceeded, another level of management is created, and when its span of management is exceeded, yet another level is created. What do all these levels of management do? For one thing, they simply watch other people work—they add questionable value; but whatever value exists serves primarily as an information switch. Information is collected and dispatched around the organization by these intermediate managers. By connecting everything to everything, intermediate levels of management "switches" can be eliminated. In fact major companies are now using connectivity to downsize their middle-management staffs.

I know of a company that has developed a product to connect computers that talk at different speeds in different formats and in different languages. This prevents the obsolescence of otherwise unintelligent computer systems that can't talk to each other and, consequently, require either human intermediaries or widespread replacement of equipment. An otherwise unintelligent system is converted into a smart system by allowing computers to have access to all the information each contains.

Smart systems connect workers to customers in ways that improve quality and customer satisfaction. That's what Domino's did. They eliminated intermediaries such as restaurant facilities and waiters, allowing the company to downsize their facilities by focusing on home delivery. The "software" in Domino's system is fast home delivery and the "hardware"—the pizza—is a commodity.

Smart systems increase the revenue per employee by using outsiders to sell, service, or support certain business needs. The ADP company built a business on this principle. By pooling the payroll requirements of many companies, they were able to achieve economies of scale that allow them to provide payroll services to their clients at a cost lower than if the work were performed in-house. By contracting for outside services, fewer employees are needed to prepare the payroll, so revenue per employee increases.

Smart systems also eliminate breakdowns and bottlenecks. McDonald's and other fast-food restaurants have virtually automated the production of their products. The food is portion-controlled, and the cooking processes are virtually fail-safe. In fact, the only way a McDonald's restaurant can mess up a hamburger or fries is to cook the food early so that it is no longer warm or fresh when purchased. But what's the biggest headache for fast-food restaurants?—employees. Employee turnover is abysmal—about 500 percent per year. Replacement employees are hard to find, and as you've probably noticed, many do their jobs with remarkable indifference. So, since people are the biggest problem in the system, McDonald's is experimenting with a smart system that virtually eliminates employees and allows the product to be cooked and distributed to customers with much more control over production, quality, and customer service level.

What's the point here? The future image of your company should not be a bigger company, but rather a smarter company. A smarter company with fewer, smarter employees who conduct the business. I know of a company that does $10 million in sales with only twelve employees, resulting in an unheard of revenue of more than $800,000 per employee. The design work for products is contracted to outside sources, the products are made by groups outside the company, the sales force consists of independent sales representatives who don't work for the company, leaving the smart things to the twelve in-house employees—coordinating the business, invoicing the customers, and collecting payments.

CUSTOMERIZING

It should come as no great surprise to anyone that "mass markets" no longer exist. The trend away from mass markets began in the late 1950s. *Customizing* will give way in the future to *customerizing*. Be ready for it. Customizing means that a product or service is essentially uniform for all customers, but cosmetic changes are made to suit the product to customer tastes. Customerizing takes this even further by essentially treating each customer as a market. Customers will be able to purchase the basic elements of a product and configure them to do things that are unique to their individual requirements. Today, for example, a user can program or reprogram some computer software products to perform whatever functions are required. Customerizing. Each software customer now becomes a unique market. In an early but primitive attempt, Burger King's advertising boasted that "you can have it your way." However mundane this example may be, it is a sign of the times—customers will increasingly have more control over the design of the products they purchase.

IN CLOSING . . .

Let me remind you again that you create the future of your business by seeing it in your mind. And if you can fill in the blanks in detail, that business already exists. The future, not the present, is all you can manage in your business. But as you visualize these future images, remember: trends indicate that successful companies of the future will be high value-added businesses that put the customer in the picture; employ smart systems, giving employees access to information immediately by connecting everything to everything; and provide more freedom for their customers to customerize their products and services—to have it their way.

I've talked a lot about managing the future rather than the present by getting away from managing the aftermath—the consequences of events over which you now exercise no control. By creating your future business in your mind, all that remains is to chip away whatever hides the business that is there. Here's an example of what I mean.

There's a story about two businessmen who were riding in a cab down Constitution Avenue in Washington, D.C. They were admiring the government buildings and reading the inscriptions engraved on many of the facades. As they passed the National Archives Building, they noticed its engraved motto: "The Past is Prologue."

"Hm, 'The Past is Prologue,' I wonder what that means?" remarked one of the businessmen.

From the front seat, the cabby answered, "I'll tell you what it means . . . It means, 'You ain't seen nuthin' yet!'" That's a rather apt description for the endlessly changing and often disruptive economic climate in which we must now operate—and the best reason I can offer for managing the business that is *there,* not the one that is *here.*

CHAPTER
T W O

HOW TO MAKE MONEY BY WATCHING THE NEWS

*The Future Is Taking Place Right Now —
In the News Media*

What's the value of information? I can best demonstrate the answer to that by asking more questions. How much would you pay for next month's *Wall Street Journal*? Next year's *Wall Street Journal*? A bundle! As I mentioned in the last chapter, information, like money, has present value. The longer it takes to see that a trend or change or whatever is under way, the less value there is in what you see. But, you don't need next month's or next year's *Wall Street Journal* to spot a trend. The future is taking place now — and it's being reported in the news media.

In 1967 Keuffel & Esser issued a report predicting what life would be like in the year 2067 — one hundred years from then — three-dimensional television, domed cities, computerized traffic management, and so on. But the report failed to predict that a cheap pocket calculator would, within five years, make an antique of Keuffel & Esser's most famous product — the slide rule! And Swiss watch manufacturers failed to read the same trend in digital electronics — so digital and electric watches replaced their industry.

Failure to spot change and respond to it can be hazardous to your economic health. The future is indeed taking place right now, and it can be predicted with reasonable accuracy. Prediction requires being a news monitor, not a historic trend watcher — there has to be a trend to be a trend watcher. News creates trends. So look in the correct direction — forward. History looks backwards.

In the field of statistics there is a concept called a "naive model." Basically it extrapolates a historic trend into the future — linearly. Its naiveté is based on the fact that what has happened will happen again. Plain foolishness. But the same naiveté infects some pretty sophisticated people like a virus. Prior to the October 1987 stock market crash, one market guru was predicting a 3000 Dow Jones based on his studies of the Elliott Wave Theory. The Elliott Wave Theory assumes that economic cycles repeat themselves. Does history repeat itself? Do people collectively react to the same stimuli in the same way? Every time? Are we that robotic? Foolishness.

The October 1987 market meltdown occurred on the heels of widely reported events. In December 1986 the Dow Jones hit 2000 — a nervous milestone. In January 1987, the dollar plunged in a free-fall that had everyone with lots of dollars biting their fingernails. In February 1987, Brazil repudiated interest on its debt — primarily debt to the United States. Throughout the summer of 1987, news reporters began to compare the euphoric market run-up with the Crash of '29. Two books were published and widely discussed, each of which predicted a worldwide depression that would be worse than that of the 1930s. Ninety days before October 19, a spate of negative news reports appeared in the print and broadcast media.

I remember one in particular. It was a three-part series in *The Atlanta Constitution* that, using the Kondratieff Cycle, predicted economic disaster for the world. In that same series, John Kenneth Galbraith, the noted liberal economist who is never at a loss for words of gloom and despair, voiced his concern for the American economy. Galbraith was also interviewed in *The New York Times* and *The Washington Post* — both respectable papers. You can go to the library and prove it to yourself: during the ninety days prior to October 19, 1987, negative news in the print media and on television (you'll have to take my word for it regarding television) reached new highs. In fact, the cover of the September 28 *Fortune* magazine featured the question, "Are Stocks Too High?" Ironically, it also pictured an individual, characterized as "Wall Street's Most Successful Investor," who thought the volatile market would climb a lot more—despite, I might add, the fact that it had been flat for a couple of months.

I picked up the October issue of *The Atlantic* magazine, which was on the newsstands in mid-September, because its cover headlines struck me: "The Morning After—America is About to Wake Up to a Painful New Economic Reality, Following the Biggest Binge of Borrowing and Spending in the History of the Nation." You wouldn't pass up a title like that, would you? When we're nervous, don't we want to confirm our concerns that we ought to be more nervous? So, predictably, after a steady diet of bad news, the stock market collapsed like an anchor, dropping 600 points in two trading days. Just as the news had predicted. Or had the news caused it?

Most people would agree that the market was overpriced after it had reached a Dow Jones of 2000—which occurred in December 1986. Why didn't it crash in March, when the market was 2300? Or in July, when it was 2500? Or in August and September, when it stalled at 2600? I think the answer to those questions is this: the public hadn't ingested enough bad news. When the market began to stall, negative news was begetting negative news and the accumulated effect caused the market to cave in. In the late summer of 1989, by contrast, the market was above 2700 and was predicted to go to 3200. But the nervousness of '87 was conspicuously absent in the news.

In 1979, I read a newspaper article entitled, "How to Make a Million Dollars by Watching the Six O'Clock News." The content was simplistic, but the concept was very interesting. I began watching and reading news from an additional perspective. What was the general tone of the news? How did it mirror people's concerns? How would people likely react to the news I was reading or seeing? I came to an interesting conclusion. If I could: listen and read every news item in every newspaper, magazine, and TV or radio news program, encode those news items into categories, and count the volume of news on every subject, I'd have to conclude that those news stories receiving the greatest volume of news were the major issues of the day.

Not a startling conclusion. But, these major issues represent pressure points for potential change, trends, and opportunities. I became much more of a news scanner than a news consumer. I looked for clues about the future and the dangers and opportunities that were potentially there. The fact that I hadn't come up with a new idea was demonstrated dramatically in the summer of 1983 when I bought a copy of *Megatrends* (Warner, 1982). I must confess I haven't yet read it completely. But I did read John Naisbitt's methodology.

Naisbitt monitored 6,000 newspapers monthly to discover what was being written about. In every print and broadcast medium, there is a "news hole." In other words, if you were to monitor two or three months of any newspaper or news magazine, the number of column inches of news reported is essentially the same—the news hole. If you monitor television and radio broadcasts, the amount of time devoted to news is about the same each day. Some newspaper issues are fatter than others but on balance, there is a fixed amount of space either in the print media or broadcast media that is devoted to reporting the news. This is an important point because if something forces its way into the news, something is forced out of the news.

In a fixed news system like this (fixed in terms of the number of pages or the number of air-time minutes), issues rise and fall like pistons in an engine. An issue that continues to be reported time after time is a key issue, perhaps even a trend. It has outcompeted all other issues that could have been reported in order for it to be reported in the medium in which it appears. And why would it be reported time after time? Because it's important to the consumers of news.

Now, I can't track news with the sophisticated methods that Naisbitt does, nor can you. But I can give you some ideas that will make you a better business manager by becoming a better news monitor. Hence the title of this chapter: How to Make Money by Watching the News.

I make no apologies for using news to make money. Nor should you. We're all interested in profiting by the risks we take, and the score card is money. I've certainly never met a successful person who was interested in losing money. And we can make money or avoid losses—which is the same thing—by spotting trends, opportunities, and dangers before other people do. Because when other people do, the "window of opportunity" has closed.

I don't expect to see a trend for a critical issue years before others do, but if I can see it six months—maybe even less—before others, I can get a jump that can be a sufficient advantage. So can you. Woody

Allen said that if aliens ever visited this planet, he wasn't worried about a civilization that was a thousand years ahead of us, or one that was a hundred years ahead of us, he was worried about one that was fifteen minutes ahead of us, because it would be first in line at the movies and never late for an appointment with the boss.

Here are some ideas that will help you use the news as a window on the future—not just the present—and be fifteen minutes ahead of the competition.

NEWS IS MARKETED, NOT REPORTED

Do you care to know how many bowling alleys there are in this country? Probably not. Are you interested in knowing that Sally Smith will marry Bobby Jones next Saturday at the Lawrenceville Baptist Church? Probably not. Do you want to know what's being done by the state and federal government to preserve salt marshes? Not really. These "news" items aren't reported because there's no interest in them. If I, as a reporter, thought you ought to know about the state of salt marshes, and if I wrote on these and other issues outside of your interests and concerns, I'd get fired.

Media compete for mind share just as companies compete for market share. Company A competes against Company B for its share of the consumer dollar. In the same way, Media A competes against Media B for its share of the consumer's mind. In fact, the mind *is* the market for news. So news focuses on what people want to know—or the news doesn't sell. How do news reporters find out what people want to know? By asking. Through interviews and polls. By listening (Letters to the Editor, for example). By watching the frequency of news that's *being* reported in other media. By monitoring social and economic changes.

Example. People began paying more attention to fitness and their health when articles began to appear in the media regarding the benefits of jogging and other aerobic exercise. Ken Cooper led the way, and Jim Fixx wrote a best-seller on running. Once the news-consumers became concerned about their personal health, they complained about inhaling other people's cigarette smoke because of the Surgeon General's warnings about smoke and lung disease. The results? Numerous articles on the effect of second-hand smoke, the establishment of smoke-free workplaces and smoke-free airplane flights, changes in smoking trends among the young, the diversification of tobacco companies into other businesses, the development of smokeless cigarettes, and on, and on, and on. The news produced change, change produced more news, and more change, and more news, and more change—do you get the point? Twenty years ago, smoking was a non-issue. So there was no news on it. Had there been news on smoking, it wouldn't have sold. But had you been monitoring the news volume on smoking, you would have predicted smoke-free work areas, smoke-free flights, and smoke-free restaurant spaces—and the decline of the tobacco industry. Not a place to invest money.

A newspaper reporter interviewed me when he learned that I was to speak on the topic of "How to Make Money By Watching the News." He didn't particularly like being told he was in the marketing business. But I told him to think about what he was doing right then—as he was interviewing me. He was conducting market research. He was interviewing me to see if I had anything to say, and he was determining whether my topic would allow him to write an article that would sell to others. The "others" were his editor, who would have to make a decision regarding the news hole (whether the article would make it or not), and assuming that the article made it into the newspaper (which it did), he would be reporting this news to the readership. A news editor is a critical element in the news marketing process because, given newspaper space limitations, if the reporter who interviewed me consistently misses the news hole, he's gone.

My monthly Breakfast Briefings seminar, out of which this book evolved, is fundamentally marketing. I could talk on the use of quantitative methods in making business decisions (a topic that I think business owners *need* to know about, but I doubt that they *want* to know about it). And if I advertised the fact that I was going to speak on the topic of quantitative methods in business decision making, I doubt that the "product" would sell. People wouldn't come to hear me speak or read what I might write on that topic. And if I had consistently picked the wrong topics, the Breakfast Briefings, and this book, would have been unwritten history.

So, the first step in spotting trends, changes, opportunities, and dangers—and benefiting from what you spot—is to recognize that news is marketed, it is not reported. News sells, because it is what people want to know more about.

THE DOG THAT DOESN'T BARK

In one of Sir Arthur Conan Doyle's tales of Sherlock Holmes, the great detective was asked, "Is there any other point to which you wish to draw my attention?"

"To the curious incident of the dog in the nighttime," said Holmes.

"The dog did nothing in the nighttime," came the response.

"That was the curious incident," remarked Sherlock Holmes.

The absence of a bark can be as significant as the presence of a bark. Similarly, the absence of news tells what the public doesn't know—probably what it doesn't care to know. For example, the nuclear accident at Chernobyl occurred in the spring of 1986. It was much in the news for several months. There was international concern about the potential for similar accidents and nuclear safety in general. Two-and-a-half years later, it's no longer in the news. Why? No interest.

As a news monitor, you must pay attention to news that isn't news—that is, news that isn't reported . . . if it isn't there, it won't change anything. News that disappears and then reappears after having been absent for some time must also be monitored. In other words, you must learn to listen for the "dog that doesn't bark." What's the biggest economic concern of the American people right now? The deficit. How could you know? It's often in the news. What is one of the lesser concerns of the American people? Unemployment. How could you know? It's rarely in the news. The news hole is fixed, so the fact that five million people want a job and can't find one isn't reported—it's the dog that doesn't bark. But during the Carter years, it was a hot topic.

What is an issue of growing concern? Inflation and interest rates. How could you know? Because the number of news stories on inflation and interest rates has been increasing since the spring of 1988, when interest rates began climbing. The Federal Funds Rate during most of 1988 rose from a rate of 7 percent and is currently over 9 percent—almost a 30 percent increase—which leads to my next point.

EVIDENCE THAT A TREND IS UNDERWAY IS LONG-STANDING

The future doesn't explode onto the present scene—it evolves. News is reported in snatches. And these news snatches, when reported frequently, are clues to the future. But the volume of news in the snatches is also important. For example, the number of column inches of help wanted ads is an economic indicator of future job trends. As another example, the number of column inches or the amount of broadcast time devoted to health care cost containment will likely affect prospects for selling the new Photoelectro Tomography (PET) machines that are technically superior to Magnetic Resonance Imaging and CAT scanners. The PET machine allows doctors to examine organs in three dimensions dynamically (as opposed to the static CAT scan) and allows non-invasive exploration of body organs. But with the amount of negative news regarding health care costs, it is likely that technological improvements in health care equipment will face a tough market, so future research and development may decline.

News becomes especially important when it represents a departure from a historic norm. For example, *The Wall Street Journal* recently reported that factory output was down *again* for three months in a row. Down again—a departure from the norm. Repetitive news on an issue reflects the growing concern of news consumers. Otherwise, there would be no repetitive news. Politicians try to discover these growing concerns, and then rely on "spin doctors," who manipulate media reporting and sound bites to position their response to those concerns. Frequently reported news builds into a force for change or for the maintenance of status quo. For instance, the controversial *Roe vs. Wade* abortion decision by the Supreme Court in 1973 may be reviewed if more and more news is devoted to abortion protests. Both the volume and the frequency of news will build a force for change—a departure from the current norm. In fact, in the 1988 election, voters in three states approved referenda related to the elimination of funding for abortions, a departure from a norm that would have been unheard of a decade ago in the era of "women's liberation." That era appears past. Why? No news on it. So, the Court will respond to the public's concern—"the will of the people"—and will learn of those concerns through the news.

NEGATIVE NEWS CREATES NEGATIVE VIEWS

Have you ever noticed that our ears pick up negative news faster than positive news? Negative news piques our concerns for stability and security. Thus, while Dukakis probably lost the 1988 election for a number of reasons, it seems clear that he wasn't able to shake off the negative news regarding his stand on the Pledge of Allegiance, his alleged softness on defense, and his image of not being tough enough on criminals. The negative news created negative views of him that amplified his phlegmatic demeanor on television and his mishandling of the "What if Kitty was raped . . . ?" question. And in general, people paid more attention to every nuance of his campaign because of their initial negative views. Bush, by contrast, was able to shake his "wimp" label with his speech at the Republican convention. His ratings soared. The press reported news about the new, more confident Bush, and that's what the news consumer saw.

Another important point. Negative news causes more negative news. The concerns that are mirrored in the news demand that more information be reported in order to confirm the legitimacy of those concerns. Newspeople accommodate us by providing what we want. Negative news sensitizes. Positive news assures. But we don't need assurances as much as we need information that tells us how concerned we should become on a negative issue. So, negative news is more powerful in getting through to the consumer.

How can you use these ideas in a specific way to watch the news to your benefit? Here are six recommendations.

DETERMINE WHAT YOU WANT TO KNOW

People read news with different interests. What are yours? I have clients in several areas of:
- Medicine and health care.
- Construction and construction-related industries.
- Software development.
- Retailing.
- Manufacturing.
- Distribution.
- Finance and financial products.

These clients operate in over ten regional economies around the United States and Canada. In addition, my work with small companies and my own personal business and investment interests require me to monitor news regarding the general economy. So I suspect my needs with regards to the news are broader than yours. Quite likely, your needs are industry- and region-specific — perhaps also specific to your city's economy — but you must be able to complete the sentence, "I'd like to know more about _____."

IDENTIFY EVERYTHING THAT AFFECTS AND IS AFFECTED BY YOUR INTERESTS

In other words, you've got to look out the front door and the back door for news. What will affect you as a business owner? What does your business or industry do that will affect others?

Remember earlier I said that if I could read everything and encode it into categories, I could spot dangers, opportunities, and trends by watching the news volume in each category? By having specific objectives, you don't have to read every news item. Nor do you need to monitor every news medium. By knowing what affects and is affected by your business, you can establish "watch" categories. For example, one of my clients is NTW, an Atlanta tire retailer. Its owner's watch categories would be:

- U.S. economic outlook, employment, interest rates, inflation, and other news regarding the general economic climate.
- Atlanta economy.
- Retailing trends/news.
- Tire industry news.
- Automotive aftercare trends.
- Consumer spending news.
- Competitor news.

As time goes on, once you have defined certain watch categories, refine those categories into subcategories and add categories you hadn't thought of originally. The more specific you can be about categories and subcategories, the more discriminating you can be as a news monitor.

SCAN SELECTED MEDIA

As a news monitor, you are looking for dangers, opportunities, and trends. So the content of news is secondary; the subject of the news is paramount. The media you use will be specific to your interests.

But, as a business owner, I believe a daily scan of *The Wall Street Journal* is imperative. You should also scan the business section of your city's paper—for example, I live in Atlanta, so I scan *The Atlanta Journal/Constitution* daily and the *Atlanta Business Chronicle* (a weekly), both of which give a sense of the local Atlanta business environment. If you're affected by consumer markets, scan *USA Today* daily. If you're affected by regional and other local economies, scan the preeminent newspapers and business chronicles in those markets. Scan *Business Week*. Scan one or two industry-specific publications.

Vital Speeches of the Day will help you to determine what important opinion setters are talking about. Obviously, knowledgeable people are invited to speak on topics that relate to current audience concerns. *Vital Speeches of the Day* (P.O. Box 1247, Mt. Pleasant, SC 29464, telephone 803-881-8733) is a digest of these key speeches.

The *Utne Reader* (2732 West 43rd, Minneapolis, MN 55410, telephone 612-929-2670) is a reader's digest of trendy issues. *American Demographics* (P.O. Box 58184 Boulder, CO 80322, telephone 1-800-828-1133) analyzes hot spots in consumer markets, trends that are shaping consumer behavior, and other important consumer information.

Although television is the most influential medium for news, not much of that news is devoted to business, therefore, I personally do not monitor it. I do watch television news, but my motive is primarily to remain informed on world and local events.

KEEP A SCORE CARD

Ideally you should determine the percent of the news hole that is filled with information devoted to topics you're monitoring. But that can be considerably time consuming. Recognize also that monitoring the number of articles written about topics in which you have interest doesn't distinguish between a three-column-inch news report and a twenty-five-column inch news report. So you need to track the volume of news in terms of the number of column inches or the number of words written on the subject. Since typeface doesn't change from issue to issue in newspapers and magazines, count the average number of words in one column inch for each print medium you are monitoring. Then measure the number of column inches devoted to the article. Convert this to words. Keep a record of the number of words written over a period time in your news-watch category or subcategory. The more that is written, the more important the issue is. If in doubt about the category, choose only one. If you file the reported words in two categories, you would double-count the news, distorting your impressions of the news volume produced for a category.

Of course, a PC would help your record keeping, but if you don't have one, don't be discouraged by having to keep the records manually. Also, graphing the monthly or quarterly words written on a subject will spot trends. Remember, a trend is a departure from the volume of news that has been historically reported on a topic. Trend spotting is essentially what Naisbitt did to provide fodder for his book *Megatrends*.

While I think there is great value if you do the news monitoring yourself, because it helps you develop a pulse for the news, you can delegate the monitoring and classifying of news to a staff employee, or you can have that person clip articles for you. This is essentially what a clipping service does for clients.

UNDERSTAND WHY THINGS ARE CHANGING

As I said before, look for departures from the norm — the volume of news that has been historically reported on a subject. What's driving the departure? Is it affecting or being affected by another category you're monitoring? If not, should you begin monitoring other related categories?

Somehow, you must make sense out of what you're monitoring; otherwise there is no value in monitoring it. I classify positive news differently from negative news to make it easier to distinguish the direction of trends. And I try to determine how news in a watch category mirrors both broader and narrower concerns of the news consumer. This brings me to my final point.

TRANSLATE THE NEWS
INTO AN OPPORTUNITY PROFILE

Avoiding being blindsided by a trend is an opportunity. Monitoring news for dangers, opportunities, and trends is the payoff. So reports that housing starts are off for the fourth month in a row — down 20 percent from last year's average — might signal a major homebuilder to scale back. But concurrent news that overbuilding in commercial construction is driving down lease rates, enticing major lessees to relocate within the overbuilt city or accelerating their plans to do so, might signal the same homebuilder to stay the course. Particularly with accompanying news that a *Fortune* 500 company is relocating its headquarters to that city.

News of the growing popularity of fax machines in replacing in-city couriers might encourage a courier service owner to accept a recent offer to sell out while there's still a market for selling out. News that car owners are keeping their vehicles longer and driving them more miles per year, might encourage someone in the automotive aftercare market to expand business and promotion. And there are many other examples. The point is this: somehow you must translate the news into an opportunity profile in order to make money by watching the news.

An important point to remember is this: information changes the receiver of that information. Figure out what the masses will do when a trend, opportunity, or threat becomes obvious. You may choose to be a "contrarian" and do the opposite. As I mentioned in the previous chapter, a three-part article appeared in *The Atlanta Constitution* during August 1987, comparing the market run-up and general economic conditions to the conditions preexisting the 1929 stock-market crash. I didn't buy the writer's implications or conclusions. But I certainly thought others would, and that motivated me to make substantial changes in my stock market investments — just in case. And, as you know, the "just in case" happened on October 19.

BEFORE CLOSING . . .

For millennia, mankind has been using oracles, prophets, and signs to answer the question "What's going to happen?" For example, Shakespeare's worried Macbeth was told by a witch that "no man born of woman" would harm him and that he would never be vanquished until "Great Birnam wood to high Dunsinane hill shall come against him" — both unlikely events. Except that the attack was led by Macduff, a man born by Caesarian section, who used the camouflage of Birnam wood to cover the advance of his troops on Dunsinane hill, fulfilling the prophecy.

Monitoring the news is a sure way to answer, "What's going to happen?" And it's more reliable than listening to a bunch of witches. E. B. White, the American writer, said, "The only sense that is common in the long run is the sense of change . . . and we all instinctively avoid it." Don't whistle in the graveyard or put your head in the sand when the news signals a new direction, even one contrary to your own personal beliefs. Society learns through the news, and eventually changes occur. Anticipate the change, and, as Woody Allen feared, with fifteen minutes advance notice, you can be first in line.

CHAPTER
THREE

MANAGING YOURSELF

How to Get More From Your Most Important Asset

John Ruskin said, "The highest reward for a person's toil is not what they get for it, but what they become by it." This is why owners of small companies are unique. They're shaped by experiences that executives are insulated from in large companies. Most have never worked for any company other than their own. From time to time owners of small companies feel inadequate and need a "sounding board" who can be trusted to be constructively critical of them so they can become better at managing themselves. In most cases that comes in the form of personal advice — anecdotal experiences from one businessman to another. And the business owners who succeed on a grand scale are like sponges — life-long learners who absorb new ideas about how to get more from their company's most important asset: themselves.

"It's lonely at the top" is a somewhat trite expression, but it's often true. Who does the owner talk to when he's having a bad day? How does he deal with a situation when he doubts his own objectivity? When I think back over the incidental personal conversations I've had with clients in these situations — sometimes late at night, or in the back of a cab, or over a meal — I realize my advice reflects my own personal values and attitudes in coping with difficult, ambiguous, and often stressful times, and I frequently am reminded of Hamlet's warning to Shakespeare's Horatio:

There are more things in Heaven and Earth, Horatio, than are dreamt of in your philosophy.

In no sense do I present the following ideas as prescriptions. They probably qualify more as ruminations than polished themes that have evolved from thoughtful reexaminations. But I've spoken many times to business groups on the subject of managing yourself, and most of the ideas that I've given to clients have forced their way back into my lecture notes on each occasion. If that is any justification, it's time to write them out.

THE LONGEST JOURNEY

Dag Hammarskjold, the late Secretary General of the United Nations, once wrote, "The longest journey is the journey inward." Hammarskjold was as much a philosopher as he was a diplomat, so he realized the importance of self-knowledge, self-scrutiny, and realistic insight. It's not narcissistic to have a heightened sense of self, and that can only be gained by an unending reevaluation of your values, assets, and aspirations.

A business, after all, is a reflection of its owner's hopes and dreams—which are not always rational. In fact, I think it is safe to say that rational people don't start companies, if you take into account that 90 percent of them ultimately fail, and four out of five of those failures occur before the company's fifth birthday. With odds like that, a person would have to have the mentality of a kamikaze pilot to start the business that pays his paycheck. But the heightened sense of self—self-knowledge, insight, and the irrational belief that the odds can be beaten—is what creates a Federal Express, or an Apple Computer, or an MCI.

This, then, is the beginning of managing yourself. To be able to look inward frequently and know in new detail what you're trying to become. Your business is the vehicle for that.

DUCKS WERE MADE FOR SWIMMING

I read a story once about a duck, a rabbit, and an eagle who decided to learn each other's skills. The duck, of course, was an excellent swimmer, but it had a terrible time flying and wasn't so hot at running either. In fact, the duck spent so much time trying to fly and run that it sprained its wings and ruined its feet. Then it was no longer good at swimming. Similar problems occurred with the rabbit and the eagle.

The moral of the story is clear. No one can be good at everything, but everyone can be good at something. And when we take time away from developing our strengths in order to patch up our weaknesses, we eventually achieve mediocrity in everything. Build on strength, but recognize your short suits. Then surround yourself with people and advisers who can help you cover all bets. It's been said that if you hire people who are smarter than you are, you prove that you are smarter than they are. Get better at what you're good at. In the future you'll be farther along at any point in time than you would be by trying to get good at what you're not.

Businesses are started by people who know how to make things, sell things, or solve some sort of problem. They're basically technical people, not business managers. I've never known anyone who started a business so he would have something to manage. But because entrepreneurs are so good at what they do, their endeavors turn into businesses that must be managed. This problem invariably hangs a business owner on the horns of a dilemma. If more and more time is spent conducting the affairs of the business, the owner may be making the same mistake that the duck made. Ducks were made for swimming—not running or flying. On the other hand, the owner's ego may not permit what ought to be done—hiring someone to run the business and cutting that person in on the action.

Beyond the start-up phase, your job is more like an orchestra conductor than a bus driver. The critical task is to assemble a Superbowl team and then go to glory together. Calvin Klein never really made it big until he hired an old high school chum to run his business. Similarly, Mitch Kapor hired a business manager for Lotus Development Corporation and progressively turned the reins over to him. In fact, look at every small business that made it big, and I'll bet you'll see that an entrepreneurial team—a balance between business and technical skills—was responsible for it. Peak performers focus on their natural abilities and then buy what's missing.

THE OTHER GUYS

In the early 1970s, I was on the dissertation committee of a woman whose doctoral dissertation dealt with an investigation of recidivism among people who are sent to prison. Since she was a career and vocational development major, she believed that poor education caused released or paroled prisoners to commit crimes that would result in their being returned to prison. As part of her research, she interviewed a number of prisoners, and not surprisingly, she found that none of them deserved to be imprisoned. They had been apprehended by mistake because the crimes they supposedly committed were actually committed by "some other guy." The real reason for recidivism is a prisoner's failure to take responsibility for his crime. He blames others, the system, the lawyer, the judge—everyone but himself. Rehabilitation will never occur until the prisoner sees himself as "the other guy."

I had a student who was chronically late to class. Each time I spoke with him about it he would say, "I can't help it"; to which I'd say, "Then point out to me the person in this room whose fault it is so I can correct him." He blamed traffic, the bus driver, and other causes—all conveniently outside his control. Like the prisoners, this student wouldn't accept responsibility for causing something to go wrong, and until he did, he would never get it corrected. The displacement of responsibility prevents a student or a business owner or, for that matter, anyone from getting better.

There is a concept in understanding human behavior called locus of control. *Locus* is the Latin word for *place*, thus, "the place of control." People are said to have an internal locus of control or an external locus of control. People with an internal locus of control believe they are in control of what happens to them, whereas, people with an external locus of control believe they are controlled by events and other people. Things just happen to them. I believe in all of us there resides a tendency to displace responsibility—"everything I eat turns to fat" (though I never knew of anyone who ate something accidentally). Examine yourself when things go haywire. What could you have done differently to prevent this? In other words, there needs to be a sense of responsibility that is punctuated by "I" rather than "the other guys" — the government, taxes, inflation, interest, competition, or the system.

I was with a business owner who had recently fired two salesmen and was now having problems with his controller. He said to me, "What's wrong with me? . . . This is the third bad hire I've made." You see, he was taking responsibility for having hired the wrong people, rather than blaming other people, even though the bad hires very definitely were responsible for their poor performance. He was taking responsibility and looking for answers — not blaming the guys he hired.

In another instance, a client had hired a general manager who was to free the business owner from day-to-day management so the owner could pursue and develop other opportunities in the marketplace — something he was really good at doing. After seventeen months, it was obvious that the general manager wasn't cutting it, and he was terminated. We met to talk about the problem. "What could I have done to have prevented this from happening?" the client said. Only by accepting the responsibility was he able to see that delegating the search and screening to an objective third party and using psychological evaluations could have prevented a hasty hire.

Experience doesn't come from what happens to you, but rather from what you do with what happens to you. You can learn from your wins and losses, but it is your responsibility to do that. I have never met a successful person with an external locus of control. It would be impossible for such a person to succeed. When the inevitable obstacles and setbacks occur, that person would be looking in the wrong place for the answer.

ONCE-BORN, TWICE-BORN

In William James' book, *The Varieties of Religious Experience*, he discusses a concept for which he identifies "once-born" people and "twice-born" people. The once-born people are those whose lives have been easy — everything seems to go well for them and there are few, if any, setbacks. The twice-born people, on the other hand, have had difficult lives, scarred with setbacks and defeats. James described these contrasting personalities from the standpoint of their religious mental health, that is, he believed some people are reborn through the tragedies of their lives.

I believe there is a further application of these contrasting character types. There are lessons to be learned with your nose bloodied, your teeth loosened, and your eyes blackened, that you could learn no other way. People whose lives are too pat, too unscarred, may have difficulties in coming back from personal or business reversals because they haven't developed the toughness to do so. None of us wants to walk through the "valley of the shadow of death," but I have, and I'll bet you have, and it never seems as dark the second and third trips through.

Early in the Civil War, Lincoln relieved General George B. McClellan as commander of the Army of the Potomac. McClellan was a man of small stature, ambitious, egocentric, and contemptuous of Lincoln. But Lincoln was used to commanders with big egos. He relieved McClellan for failing to aggressively pursue General Lee after the Battle of Antietam. McClellan was well-liked by his army and was the darling of polite society, so, predictably, many people intervened to get Lincoln to change his mind. To one of them he said, "I cannot bore with an auger too dull to take hold." Then Lincoln went on to say something that showed real insight into McClellan's profound battlefield conservatism: "He would have been a better general if he had suffered some humbling reverses early in his career."

How you react to disappointments, setbacks, and reversals has a direct impact on how successful you'll be. The inability to cope with setbacks or the unwillingness to expose yourself to the risk that setbacks will occur creates rigid behavior patterns. I've seen it happen. In one instance, the owner of a small manufacturing company became a virtual prisoner to himself. After a disastrous business failure that led to the failure of his marriage, he wouldn't make the necessary emotional investment in developing another venture that could be another potential failure (in his way of thinking), preferring to work alone in a small machine shop, content to eke out a living well below the standard he had previously produced.

When James Forrestal fell out of favor with Harry Truman, he was replaced as Secretary of Defense after Truman's reelection in 1948. Forrestal, like McClellan, was an extremely ambitious person, but once relieved from public power, he couldn't cope with political impotence, fell ill, and took his life. By contrast, Winston Churchill, booted from office after the British calamity at Gallipoli, went on to become Prime Minister and a great leader in World War II. In the latter conflict, he was able to cope with setbacks and failures because he had reacted to the Gallipoli experience in a positive way, helped by his writing and a supportive wife.

This brings up another interesting point. A study of successful businessmen was conducted using the graduates of Harvard University for the years 1942 through 1944. The study found that the successful graduates had harmonized their career with their personal lives, had better relations with their wives and children, socialized more with friends, and engaged in more public-spirited activities than their unsuccessful counterparts.

While many entrepreneurs achieve success at the expense of personal, family, and social lives, they also lose the emotional support needed to cope with the pressure and the stress of their jobs—and this can only be found in intimate relationships and diversions. The idea that success in small business accrues only to workaholics who sacrifice their marriages and their relationships with their children is a myth. While business or economic conditions may require a Herculean effort from the business owner, it need only be for a time. Those who make that a permanent work practice are deluding themselves, losing balance in their lives, and risking the loss of an important support system that will be needed to deal with inevitable downturns.

A client and friend suffered an unexpected rejection of an almost certain business loan application that his company desperately needed. Predictably, he went through a period of mourning, followed by periods of self-examination, followed by attempts to learn something from this experience, but he bounced back. He was a survivor because this was not his first setback, although it was his worst. And he had the support of his wife and friends.

The pattern of avoiding or dealing poorly with disappointment is usually developed early, in most cases during childhood. Stress always accompanies setbacks. Flights into activity or denial simply postpone the "payment" and miss the opportunity to raise one's tolerance for future adversity, which is the positive side of being "twice born." I've suffered through disappointments personally, and I've never said,

"Someday I'll look back on this and laugh." It wasn't funny then, and it isn't funny today. I've also suffered through setbacks with clients. I help them as much as I can to recognize that mourning and self-examination are necessary steps in learning something from the experience and that bouncing back is insurance against being crushed by a future disappointment.

CHANGE MAKES FOOLS OF US ALL

In Greek mythology Procrustes was a giant highwayman who would capture travelers and tie them to his bed. If the captive was too short, the victim would be stretched to fit the bed; if he was too long, his legs would be cut off to fit the bed. Nice guy. Procrustean behavior is rigid conformity—we make things fit our predispositions and our programs. The tragedy of the British commander played by Alec Guinness in the movie *Bridge on the River Kwai* was his procrustean behavior. As a Japanese prisoner, and faced with a new set of circumstances—one that called for innovative behavior and thinking—the commander responded with the rigid behavior instilled by years of garrison duty, and he built a better bridge for the Japanese than they could have built for themselves.

Procrustean thinking allows opportunities to slip by unnoticed. For example, did you know that Velcro™ wasn't invented, it was discovered? Its discoverer had taken a walk in a field while he was wearing woolen trousers. Returning to his house, the bottoms of his trouser legs were covered with "hitchhikers"— those prickly little seed pods that all of us have encountered. To us their removal is a nuisance, to him it was a discovery. By observing how the seed pods hooked into the soft material, the idea came to him that two pieces of materials could be fastened together, replacing a zipper or fastener. Thus, Velcro.

Human beings develop habits so they don't have to remember how to think or act in certain situations. Habits are good in the sense that they avoid the consumption of mental energy and allow us to act automatically. Imagine how long it would take to grocery shop if brand selections, package sizes, and even the basic grocery list had to be rethought every week before acting. But habits are bad in the sense that they create blind spots. Undetected change occurs, not because we can't see changed conditions, but rather because we won't see—we choose not to see.

A good deal of research has been conducted to study why businesses decline. The results overwhelmingly identify the principal cause as failure of management to respond to change—change, in many cases, that was recognized by outsiders who warned that the company's procrustean management was headed for trouble. I have worked with three different companies that faced disruptive change, whose owners engaged in activities that could best be described as tidying up the ice floe. They refused to act on fundamental changes in their industry, which even they acknowledged were occurring.

Why is this? Why does a person engage in self-destructive behavior? Why do people hold on to declining stocks? Why do people remain in jobs they despise? I don't claim to have all the answers, but I know that people get into comfort zones, and they are terribly resistant to pressures to step out of them. Commission salespeople limit the amount of money they could make because they become comfortable with what they do make. Making more money would get them out of their comfort zone. Even when people are unhappy with their business or personal circumstances, they fail to recognize they have imprisoned themselves. I heard it best described this way: "The certainty of misery is preferable to the misery of uncertainty." Maybe so.

But one of the fun things about my work with small companies is their general willingness to experiment and change. It is the basis of their competitive edge—a hungry fighter is hard to beat. But the farther a company gets from its start-up phase, the more tolerant its owner is likely to become of himself and the way the company functions. That's a dangerous mindset if you recognize that every business exists in an environment that is chronically changing.

Recognizing that change makes fools of us all, the truly effective small business executives make a practice of inspecting what they may be taking for granted and challenging the status quo. They value outsider advisers, recognizing that outsiders have skills that small businesses cannot afford on a permanent basis, and that outsiders don't have the same blind spots that owners do. Listen to your advisers, or engage some if you don't currently use them. Make a list of the fundamental changes occurring in your industry and your customer group. How are you responding to these changes? In the same procrustean way you've acted in the past? Unless you force yourself out of your comfort zones and see changes *as* they are occurring rather than *after* they have occurred, you may be tidying up the ice floe.

FLEETING THOUGHTS

I went to a military high school where I was blessed to have a literature teacher who really loved his subject and loved teaching it even more. He could bring a poem or short story alive by telling us the circumstances surrounding the composition of the work. That sure beat the heck out of simply reciting assignments. The story surrounding the poem "Kubla Khan" is one of my favorites. "Kubla Khan" was composed by Samuel Taylor Coleridge in an opium dream. When he awoke, Coleridge rushed to his desk to begin writing down the two hundred to three hundred lines of poetry he had composed while it was fresh on his mind. Unfortunately, a neighbor—described by Coleridge only as "a person from Porlock"—dropped by for a chat, and an hour later when Coleridge got back to his task, he found to his bitter disappointment that the remaining lines of poetry had slipped from his memory.

There's a lesson in Coleridge's experience. Important thoughts come to us fleetingly, and if not captured, they are later lost or, if resurrected, seem wooden at best. The more creative the activity you are pondering, the more important it is to capture flashes of insight and record them as you think of them. For that reason, I always carry with me a small microcassette recorder. I find it superior to writing down notes to myself because the tape recorder encourages me to flesh out more detail and can get it down as a stream of consciousness—something that can't be done by fragmentary notes.

All of us have a peak energy cycle. I am a morning person; therefore, early in the day is when I can most expect those fleeting thoughts. But they can come at any moment, so my recorder is always nearby. I spend a lot of time in a car, and I rarely turn on the radio. I think. Or I let my mind wander—to go where it wants to go. You see, like the Velcro discovery, all of us observe things that, when allowed to incubate—to simply rattle around in our heads—will frequently materialize into a solid idea. When pondering a problem, I will think on it just so long, then I drop it. It rattles around sometimes for days or weeks and then pops up as a fleeting thought that I quickly get down on my recorder.

I have a friend who heard me speak on capturing fleeting thoughts. He is a building contractor who must travel from one job site to another all day. He threw away his notepad and now talks to himself about new ideas—with a recorder. It is his verbal notepad. My oldest daughter's soccer coach carries a microcassette recorder in his hip pocket, and during a game he makes verbal notes about things he sees in the game that must be practiced in the next practice session. Try it. You'll be surprised at how many really good ideas pass through your head every day. Instead of letting those ideas go nowhere, let them go down on magnetic tape.

$1 MILLION AND A FATAL DISEASE

I have an exercise that I use in seminars for small business owners. I first ask them to imagine that they have inherited $1 million, and I ask them to write down ten things that they will do now that their new wealth makes them economically secure. Next, I ask them to imagine that they have learned they will die in six months from a terminal disease. Preparations for their funeral and estate matters have been completed. Now I ask them to write down ten things that they would do in the remaining six months of their lives.

Obviously, both lists contain things that are important to the people in the seminar. But invariably the first list contains items that don't require wealth to do them. The second list doesn't require urgency to act on every item either. So I ask them, "What are you waiting for?" And I ask you the same thing—what are you waiting for? Abe Lincoln said it best, "Things may come to those who wait, but only the things left by those who hustle."

All of us get fooled by our activity-orientation. We want to be doing something, but the "something" we do is not always the right thing. People, like businesses, succeed not because they do things right, but because they do the right things. Doing the wrong things as well as they can be done isn't a formula for effectiveness. Yet there is something about all of us that makes us drive faster when we've lost our way. A fanatic is a person who, having lost his purpose, redoubles his effort.

Most of us carry "to do" lists. But fewer of us make the distinction that some of the items on that list are of top priority, some of mid-priority, and some of low-priority. Even fewer of us work on the right things—the top priority first. The low-priority "to dos" are easier, faster, and more numerous, and at the end of the day, we can look at all those low-priority accomplishments and pat ourselves on the back for how hard we worked.

It makes little sense to work on a project due Friday if you've not completed one due Wednesday. Think of the future as an assembly line—a conveyor belt on which priority is the sequence of the tasks coming toward you. Also imagine that new top-priority tasks push past the low-priority tasks on the conveyor belt—so you may never get to work on low priorities. This would prevent you from engaging in "creative avoidance"— excuses for not working on the right thing, such as you don't have enough time, or you don't have the right information, or you're waiting for someone else to do something. The best remedy for creative avoidance is a heavy dose of "get started." Time expert Alan Lakein suggests an alternate remedy. Throughout the day, ask yourself, "What's the best use of my time right now?"

Peter Ilyich Tchaikovsky, the renowned nineteenth century Russian composer, said, "I have all of this music in me . . . I must write it down before I die." Don't die with your music in you. Successful lives are made up of successful days. If you succeed every day, you're succeeding in life. The way to succeed every day is to do the right things. And "the right things" are what's important to you. You don't need a million dollars or a fatal disease to discover that.

WHAT WOULD IT LOOK LIKE WITHOUT THE PROBLEM?

I was sitting in the office of a client's marketing manager. The marketing manager had struggled with the problem of declining sales without an answer until it had become some sort of mental Gordian knot. I knew that his job was on the line, though he didn't at the time. As I posed various solutions to him, he would in turn put each one of them down by saying something like, "Yes, but if we tried that . . . " After about forty-five minutes we had gotten nowhere, and it suddenly dawned on me we that were playing a game.

Many years ago I read a book by the noted psychotherapist Eric Berne, entitled, *Games People Play* (Ballantine, 1978). Berne can probably be credited with the creation of transactional analysis, which is the study of the psychology of human relationships as people interact with each other. Berne's psychotherapy patients named the games he described in his book, and the one the marketing manager was unwittingly playing is called "Why don't you . . . yes, but." The game starts by someone posing a problem to a person or a group of people who suggest possible solutions by saying, "Why don't you . . . ?" This is put down by, "Yes, but . . . " The game can go on indefinitely, but a good player can hold off everyone by putting down their recommendations until finally they give up. Whereupon the person with the problem wins. Except, he loses. Like the marketing manager—who was fired within months.

The marketing manager had a problem-fixation—he couldn't see any potential solutions because of his preoccupation with the problem. Once he identified declining sales as The Problem, his tendency was to focus all of his energy there. What happens with problem-fixation is a sort of means/ends inversion—the *way* something is to be solved gets tangled up in what the solution looks like. Most disputes, for example, are disagreements over solution *methods* rather than solution *outcomes*. In one last desperate attempt, I said to the marketing manager, "Dave (not his real name), what would your situation look like without the problem?" I asked for details—How much will each salesman sell? What is the average account size? What is the inventory turnover? How many calls per day would each salesman make? He looked at me like I was crazy and said, "If I knew the answers to those questions, I wouldn't have a sales problem!" At that point, I knew that the problem Tar Baby had him stuck, and nothing I could do would get him unstuck. Problems and obstacles are what we see when we can't see a solution as a *fait accompli*. We must be able to figuratively look around the obstacles in order to see what the solution looks like. As mentioned before, creative problem solvers invariably start with the solution and work backward through the intermediate actions that will produce that solution. The solution is an *output* and the intermediate actions are *inputs*. Not surprisingly, when people go through that process, they often discover that their inputs—the activities in which they've been engaging—don't lead to "that solution."

If your salesmen don't make enough calls or your average account size is too small, then your sales—the desired solution—will fall. As I said in the first chapter of this book, today is the aftermath of yesterday. Today, therefore, is uncontrollable. Sales today are the consequences of actions taken yesterday. If we continue to take those same actions, they will most likely produce the same result in the future. If we want something different to happen, we must see a new future. In order to do that, the question that must be asked is, "What would things look like without the problem?" Then we must manage the inputs to the future.

ONCE UPON A TIME

The lieutenant says, "When I get to be colonel, I'm going to change this situation." But when the lieutenant does become a colonel, he's forgotten what it's like to be a lieutenant. Or worse, he remembers things "as they were"—not "as they are."

Example: I was meeting with a client who had serious operational problems in his branches. The company had grown very rapidly, exceeding the owner's expectations. I had been in the branch offices and didn't see a single branch manager who wasn't putting out 110 percent. So I asked the owner, "Is the branch manager's job a doable job?" "Sure it is," he said, "I did it!" (Five years ago.) Nothing is static. And I can assure you the way he operated a branch "five years ago" was a lot different than the way they were functioning "today."

When I began consulting, I was fascinated when a business owner would tell me how something is done, only to find that out in the branches or stores or departments in question, it wasn't done that way at all. It no longer fascinates me; I expect it. Over time, employees make hundreds if not thousands of adjustments in procedures, of which the boss knows nothing. When the owner ran a branch, the "branch" was the business! And as the number of branches grew, the owner placed demands on branch managers in terms of paperwork and meetings that he never had to contend with, because he was the boss.

This is why I recommend that business owners make sales calls from time to time with their salespeople. They should ride in the delivery trucks, run a store or branch for a day, purchase and receive inventory, work the receptionist desk for an hour or two—in short do things to stay in touch. Because, as the company grows, the boss is drawn farther and farther away from the way things are, so that he makes decisions the way they were—once upon a time.

KEEP YOUR OPTIONS OPEN

If there is a single piece of advice I give repeatedly, it's to leave your options open. Activity-oriented bosses often do things quickly in order to close them out and move on to the next task. In so doing, they prematurely shut down options that may subsequently be needed.

I have a friend who was given an attractive offer to teach at another university. He announced his intentions to the department chairman without formally resigning, put his house on the market, and began looking for a house in the city where he would teach. As it turned out, his house wouldn't sell, so the entire deal fell through. Because he left his options open by not resigning prematurely and, consequently, having his plans formally announced to his colleagues in the college administration, he was able to carry on "business as usual" in the fall quarter with all but a few no wiser.

I don't believe in giving up an option until it hampers further progress. Burn your bridges at the last minute. For example, notify suppliers that you're canceling their product line only when a competing line is clearly a success—preferably when the supplier has discovered the decline in sales and can't retaliate. Don't terminate that manager you've been dissatisfied with until his replacement has been recruited. It may take months longer than you think. Leave your options open. It's a simple rule, but often violated. Ask yourself: "Have I shut down an option that I now wish was open *and* it could have been?"

CONSTRUCTIVE INTOLERANCE

I once worked with a person who would go to the mat on every issue. I don't believe he was indifferent about anything. When things went haywire, he reacted with the same intensity regardless of the importance of what had gone haywire. He and I were friends, and I was concerned that he was losing his effectiveness, so I told him that if he continued to mount a soapbox on every issue, no one would take him seriously. He continued, and they didn't.

Everyone wants things to go right. I can't imagine an effective business owner being tolerant of things gone wrong. But the degree of intolerance should be measured. The more important the deviation is, the more intolerant of it you should be; the less important it is, the less intolerant you should be. For example, you should raise a terrible fuss if an employee leaves a front door open all night, subjecting your inventory to theft. You should also be unhappy that the lights have been left on all night, wasting energy and dollars. You should say something about the light, but with a lot less intensity than your comments about the open door.

One of the most important attributes you can possess as a boss is to be predictable. If something was unacceptable yesterday, it will be unacceptable today, and it will be unacceptable in the future. The fuss you raised about something gone haywire in the past is the same fuss you should raise about it if it goes haywire today. I had a client several years ago who didn't do that. On some occasions he would go through the roof when an employee had done something improperly, and on other occasions he would ignore the same error. Needless to say, the company could never figure out what was important to him, because his actions were so variable. This caused him and the employees to experience a good deal of stress.

Mounting a soapbox on some issues and not on others is a way of communicating what's important. Being very angry on some matters and not as angry on others is a way of communicating your priorities. Anger and intolerance are effective management tools as long as they are controlled and consistent. But anger should be focused on the problem not the person. "Bugs Burger," the owner of a Miami-based pest extermination company, tells his service representatives to blow the whistle on themselves if they make a mistake in servicing a customer. If they do this, the mistake can be rectified with no real harm. But heaven help the person who claims to have serviced an account fully if he didn't. As "Bugs" himself says, "Mistakes are forgiven, liars aren't."

DON'T PRACTICE LIVE

Small company owners go live with their ideas prematurely—before they have debugged them through planning and experimentation. The only surprises you should encounter in the marketplace are those that couldn't possibly have been known otherwise. Something as simple as a procedure change should be worked out in your mind and then on paper before it is implemented in fact. And if possible, it should be progressively implemented, so that if problems are discovered, their damage can be contained.

I helped a client develop a new work procedure to allow him to raise the service level for his customers. Considerable time was spent developing the new procedure and looking for everything that could go wrong. Having found no problems, the procedure was ready to be introduced. Nevertheless, we resisted installing the procedure in all fifteen stores scattered about the state. Whatever could be learned in fifteen stores, could be learned in one. As it turned out, only minor problems were encountered. But several opportunities to significantly improve the procedure were discovered, and these were tested in the controlled environment of the test store. Once perfected, the program was rolled out companywide without a hitch.

Another example. When a client decides to purchase or upgrade a computer system—particularly when it's a small system, like a PC network—one of the hardest things I must do is get the client to write a requirements document, even if it's only one page. It takes money and time to write one, and the bigger the system, the more money and time it takes. If I prevail, I'm often the one to write the requirements document. By interviewing the system users and the boss, and by observing the procedures currently used, I'm able to write a description of the system, files, records, and the fields that each record will carry. But when draft copies of the requirements document are distributed to the boss and system users, invariably they will say, "That's not what we want." Nevertheless, that's what they said they wanted. When confronted with a hard copy of the system they described, they discover that each had seen a somewhat different system. At this point, it's not difficult to make changes. But imagine what the changes would be like with hardware on the floor and several thousand lines of custom code on hand. Then we would be practicing live.

In almost everything you plan to do, you can practice "off-line" by having meetings and discussions, by working it out on paper or on a computer, or by testing it in a corner of your business under very controlled circumstances. All of this is a form of practice. But you can also practice live rather than off-line. That's what you're doing when you operate your company without a business plan that becomes a governing document. That's what you're doing when you introduce a new procedure without testing the first draft under controlled conditions. That's what you're doing when you open a branch office or a store in a new location without first serving that market, albeit inefficiently, from existing locations to determine that there's enough of a market there to justify a branch or store. There will be lots of surprises, most of which could have been discovered by searching for them off-line. In other words, the "liveness" of your practice added no value to your discovery process, but it sure added a lot of cost, disruption, and maybe the potential for failure.

STOP FOOLING YOURSELF

Entrepreneurs, by their nature, are optimistic people. As I said earlier, they're also a bit irrational; otherwise the odds of failing would persuade them to abandon their ideas. So, there's a fine line between fact and fantasy, and it's not easy to tell when an owner may be fooling himself. An entrepreneur can be very persuasive in arguing convincingly that something will work out, and I know that I am at a disadvantage because the idea hasn't been on my mind twenty-four hours a day for the past eleven months. If things seem too pat, if I find myself having faith in the entrepreneur's faith, I get busy looking for the wormhole in the apple.

I worked with a young company that had grown so rapidly that it faced a serious liquidity crisis. Money was not available to pay accounts when due, and suppliers had put the company on a credit hold or a COD basis. The two owners were "firefighting"—jumping from one crisis to another. There is an established relationship between fantasy and stress, and under crisis circumstances it is easy to see salvation just around the corner if one can just hold on long enough. Don't fool yourself. It's a mirage.

I recommended three things to these two entrepreneurs: that we close an office in another city and terminate its staff; that certain equipment and vehicles be sold; and that product support should be subcontracted, thus eliminating that cost from the company's payroll. These changes would allow them to save the business, although with a reduced scope of operation. I also showed the owners a pro forma plan and its impact on cash. It was as if I hadn't said a word. One of the owners took off on a "save the company" scenario in which it was clear that fact and fantasy were interwoven. Nothing would be changed, and yet somehow things would be different. Collections would improve by "working harder," but they had been doing that already; customers would be asked to make advance deposits on orders, even though that was not a practice in that industry; and if advances were a condition of sale, the company would become less competitive. Unhappily, the company ended up in the hands of its creditors, who shut it down.

The refusal to cut losses in the belief that things will improve, without a shred of objective evidence to substantiate that belief, is like a Mickey Rooney marriage — hope outweighs experience. You're fooling yourself. Thinking that an employee will somehow perform differently in the future than he has in the past, when nothing has happened to compel a performance change or to suggest that the employee is capable of changing, is simply creative avoidance of a distasteful termination. Creative avoidance occurs with people, product lines, branch offices — every aspect of business — and trying harder is not the answer.

A trusted adviser, if one exists, may succeed in getting a business owner to face facts and cut losses. But this takes time, because the owner must "get used to it." Emotional investments in an unachievable outcome must be disengaged. The feelings of having failed must be dealt with. And sometimes there isn't enough time to get used to it before the final crisis occurs. But it's a problem requiring constant self-examination when things aren't working out. Are you fooling yourself? Because you want so much to believe things will work out, has fantasy begun to replace fact? Think about it.

TIME OUT FOR REFLECTION

John Steinbeck said the hardest thing he had to do was convince his wife that he was working when he had his feet on his desk and was looking out the window. Eastern cultures put a lot of stock in reflection and meditation; Westerners don't. We are too activity-oriented. Silence can't be tolerated—the first thing we do when getting in our cars is to turn on the radio; at home, it's to turn on the TV—even though we listen in neither case.

It is a common complaint among small business owners that they need to get away and think, but they don't have time. Sound familiar? Nevertheless, about a year ago, I created a getaway opportunity for fifteen business owners. We were to get away in a hotel meeting room for three hours once a month. I was to lead structured discussions on an agenda developed by them that addressed mutual problems and competitive issues facing small companies. At least that was the plan. One year later, the group had shrunk to three people. Little by little, everyone else had gotten too busy to attend the sessions.

Reflection isn't daydreaming. It is directed thinking, which is hard work! For example, I can't think with a client talking to me. So after gathering information, I must get away from all distractions (even to the point of inaccessibility at times) in order to reflect on a problem. You should do the same. You need to get away from your people, and they need for you to get away from them. Both of you will be better for it. Getting away at home is really not the answer, because there is another set of distractions and demands placed on you by your family. And since I think family time is as important to your well-being as work time is, there is only one answer: block out time you can take off from work. Take a day off, if possible, and go for a drive in the country. Or do something else that does not require you to concentrate on what you're doing and allows you to keep your mind free for thinking. A golf or tennis game requires attention and isn't what I'm talking about. If you can't take the whole day, take a half a day—perhaps an afternoon—off. Keep your cassette recorder near. And if you think these ideas are platitudes, read the first four books of the New Testament in the Bible. Look at how many times Jesus took time off, time to get away from people, time to get away from his disciples. He made the time available, and he had a bigger job to perform than you do.

SELF-RENEWAL

Twenty-five years ago, I read a book by John Gardner entitled *Self-Renewal* (Norton, 1981). It's a great book, and I believe it's still in print in paperback, so I highly recommend it. I read the book at an impressionable time of my life and feel that it has influenced my personal development over the years. Gardner noted that as we mature and as our careers develop, we narrow the scope and variety of our lives. Of all the interests we could pursue, we settle on only a few. And of all the people with whom we could associate, we select only a few. In other words, we intentionally limit the freedom that is available to us if we would only develop interests outside of our principal career—interests in reading, music, art. But we're caught in a web of fixed relationships.

Franz Kafka was a master at portraying what happens to people who don't use their potentialities. In *The Trial* and *The Castle*, the principal character has no name. He is referred to only by an initial—symbolic of someone who has lost his identity, his sense of self. In Kafka's short story *Metamorphosis*, the principal character is Gregor, a capable, young salesman who forfeits his potential by living a vacuous, routine life, returning to his home by the same route each day, eating the same dinner of roast beef each Sunday while watching his father fall asleep at the table. The sameness of his life is overwhelming. One morning he wakes up no longer a human being but a giant cockroach—a parasite that lives off the leavings of others. It is a frightening symbol of what happens when a human being abandons the fulfillment of his personhood.

A human being is a renewable resource. People are capable of being productive and learning throughout their entire lives. In fact, I read of a project in which 70- and 80-year-old Americans were taught the Russian language, which is not an easy language to learn. Think of it—a lifetime of learning new things—virtually anything you could want to know is available for you to know if you make the effort. The goal of the education system is to progressively shift the responsibility of learning from the teacher to the student. After college we are free to continue learning whatever interests us. But it doesn't happen. We seem to think that education is something that goes on only in school buildings and nowhere else, and that after college the focus is on doing. But a person's mind, said Oliver Wendell Holmes, "once stretched by a new idea never regains its original dimensions." That can happen at any age. And should.

Even though I hold four college degrees, I attribute almost everything I have learned of importance to self-education. I love to read. I would have a fun weekend if I were accidentally locked up in a library with enough food and water to make it until Monday morning. Like William Buckley, I'm afraid that I will be caught crossing a street between two opposing lanes of traffic and have nothing to read until there is a break in traffic to continue across. But I also enjoy music, art, drama. I recently relearned Latin, using the text that I had in high school. I taught myself classical Greek, developed an interest in baroque music, became an instrument-rated pilot, and have a consuming passion for eighteenth-century American history and culture. But that's me. It's not you.

Stretch yourself to pursue something new—even if you don't think you'll like it. Give it a chance to become likable. The compelling argument for a self-renewing pursuit is that it will make you a more flexible person and more durable in resisting most of the problems I've discussed in this chapter—something that being a couch potato can't promise.

BEFORE CLOSING . . .

As you can see, managing yourself is a big job. At the beginning of each college quarter, in the first class session, I always tell students, "I'll be the best 'me' I can be this quarter, so you can be the best 'you' you can be." In much the same way, managing yourself—being the best "you" you can be—has a positive effect on others.

But there's another sense in which managing yourself becomes important. I don't believe in luck, but I do believe in lucky opportunities. An opportunity can only be defined as "an opportunity" if you are prepared for it. How many people have said, "Why didn't I think of that?" A better question would be, "Why didn't I see that?" Because there was no preparation. One must be prepared in order to see. I think Winston Churchill said it best:

> To every man there comes in his lifetime, that special moment when he is figuratively tapped on the shoulder and offered the chance to do a very special thing, unique to him and fitted to his

talent; what a tragedy if that moment finds him unprepared or unqualified for the work which would be his finest hour.

It would be a tragedy. Manage yourself well. You're the most important asset your business has.

CHAPTER
FOUR

THE POWER OF YOUR PRESENCE

Leadership for Small Companies

Gustav Mahler, whom I consider to be one of the finest, late nineteenth-century composers, said, "There are no second-rate orchestras. There are only second-rate conductors." It's true. No organization can rise above its leadership. And the top person in an organization—both large and small—sets the limit on what the organization is capable of achieving.

In small businesses in particular, the influence of the top man or woman, usually the owner, is pervasive. And the truly successful ones don't manage from afar; they are deeply involved in daily activities—not because they are poor delegators, although some are—but because they realize the symbolic importance of their being visibly involved with "the troops," giving directions, cheerleading, providing feedback. In short, their thumbprints are on just about everything.

Let's face it. People must want to do business with your company. That is the inescapable responsibility of—you guessed it—you! You set the company's direction. You develop the company's flair—its personality. You create the sense of enthusiasm as if you were leading your team on a journey—because you are. The pervasive presence of a company's owner in its affairs is why I always refer to a competitor as a "him" or a "her"—not an "it." Especially when competing against other small businesses, you are up against a person, not an organization. And, as I have said on many occasions, you need to understand that person backwards and forwards.

Visible leadership is critically important to your firm's future. So, I want to describe for you both the phenomenon — the essence of leadership in small organizations — and some steps I feel are important in building a more creative company.

"ENCOURAGED BY HIS SPIRIT . . ."

In the Taoist *Book of Days*, I Ching states, "To unite men, one must first become collected within oneself." Think about what that statement really says. Your effectiveness as a business leader begins with self-examination, self-knowledge, insight. To be "collected within oneself" really says, "What are you trying to be?" As I've said, a small business is simply the extension of the personality and aspirations of its owner. Your business is the vehicle, the conduit, and the means through which your goals and interests will be achieved. And, if you don't have a clear vision of what you're trying to do, how can you direct others? Even though Western societies don't put much stock on reflection and meditation, having your act together by knowing precisely what you are attempting to accomplish in your life *through* the business is the beginning of the art and the science of leadership.

I Ching goes on to say, "Those who congregate around the leader are encouraged by his spirit." Therefore, leadership is spiritual, social, chemical in many respects. Today, most organizations, both large and small, are overmanaged and underled. There is an almost universal failure to recognize that the chemistry of success centers around the pervasive symbolism that the leader embodies in all that he does. Most small business owners vastly underestimate the power of their presence, the power of the examples they set. But they do embody the purpose of the business, and their visible presence provides guidance for the organization.

Look at an "also ran" organization. You find no power source, no heart. But look at an achieving organization, and you will see a business that has fire in its heart and future in its bones. And at its center is an individual who can inspire people to play over their heads. In other words, the leader enables people to be better than they are on their own. And how is that done? Well, I think I can demonstrate it best by using the following diagram.

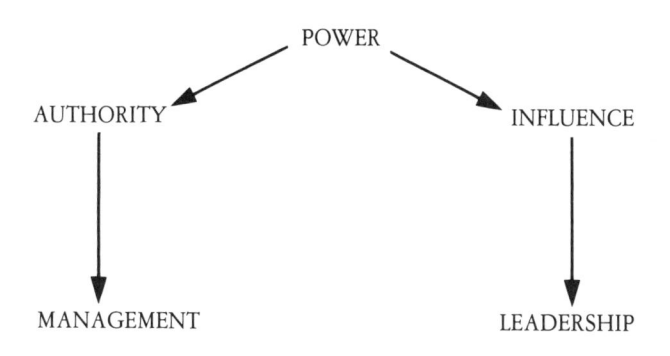

```
                    POWER
                  ↙       ↘
          AUTHORITY       INFLUENCE
              │               │
              ↓               ↓
          MANAGEMENT      LEADERSHIP
```

Notice, the diagram begins with *power*. When I ask people to define power, they will almost always define it in negative terms. But, power has a very positive sense. Power is the ability to make things happen. If you can't make things happen, you are of no use to yourself or your business. In Shakespeare's Henry IV, for example, there is a running dialog between two characters named Glendower and Hotspur. Glendower boasts, "Why, I can call spirits from the vasty deep!" To which Hotspur, after thinking about that statement, responds, "Why, so can I, and so can any man, but will they come when you call for them?" You see, anybody can call spirits, but power gets the response.

There are two ways by which power—the ability to make things happen—can be exercised in an organization. As the diagram shows, one way is through the mechanism of authority. Authority relates to rank. Some people wear rank on their collar, or their shoulder, or their arms, or as a title before or after their names. But however it is displayed, rank is something that is assigned to you, or more correctly, it is assigned to the position you hold. Therefore, when you're zipping down the expressway at eighty miles an hour, and you see the blue light flashing in your rear-view mirror, you pull over to the side of the road because you recognize the authority of the policeman. And if you don't pull over, and he succeeds in catching you, he will arrest you "in the name of the law," which is the basis of his authority. People who use authority to make things happen are called, what? Well, I call them managers, because they manage within a prescribed scope of responsibilities that is associated with the position they hold.

However, there is another way you can exercise power to make things happen. As the diagram shows, it is through the process of *influence*. Influence is a soft skill. Unlike authority, which allows someone to bring all the official sanctions of the organization to bear in order to make things happen, influence plays to the heart, or the head, or both. Influence occurs because there is a quality that is attractive to others, and in some cases, the influential person is charismatic. People who make things happen through influence primarily are people whom I call leaders.

If you look for historic examples of good managers, you would surely agree that Alfred Sloan, the architect of General Motors, would be among them. Dwight Eisenhower and his army boss, George Marshall, were also good managers. Their principal skills, as is true of all managers, have to do with their technical grasp of a situation. They are resource managers and have administrative personalities.

Historic examples of leaders, on the other hand, would certainly include Jesus Christ, perhaps George Patton, JFK, and a more modern example, Lee Iacocca (which stands for I Am Chairman of Chrysler Corporation of America). The leadership qualities of these people include their conspicuous visibility; they are articulate, and they are highly symbolic in the situations for which they provide leadership. Let's face it. The litmus test for leadership is *followership*. If you look back and there ain't none, you ain't one. So it's a little silly to say, "I appoint you to be the leader of this group," because the group determines who the leader will be. And leadership is fickle because followership is fickle. Look at the life of Winston Churchill, a charismatic, symbolic leader. He was in and out of office, depending on the whims of the British people.

Let me give you an example of how potent symbolism is in leadership. When Patton took over the command of the Third Army during World War II, the army was located at Fort Benning in Columbus, Georgia. Now, Patton knew that these troops would have to fight in North Africa, and if you have ever been to Columbus, Georgia, you know that there's nothing there that looks like North Africa. So, he moved his men out to the southwestern desert in the United States to train them in an environment that was more like the one they would fight in. There were 20,000 men under his command. When he would bed them down at night, they were arranged by companies alongside a thirty-mile strip of macadam in the desert. An infantry company at that time was about two hundred men, so there were one hundred companies, each of which had a bugler.

When it came time to hit the sack, Patton commanded the first bugler to blow taps. If you remember your high school physics, you'll recall that sound travels about eleven hundred feet per second, so it was several seconds before the bugler of the company next down the line could hear that taps had begun to be played, and when he heard it, he would play taps. Then the next bugler down the line would hear it, and he would play taps. So, what you would have heard was a roll of taps down through this valley in which the men were encamped. That roll of taps would start the night animals up in the hills to howling and give the men a sense of being joined with nature. In fact one of them, writing about the experience later on, said that it made them feel that they were part of an organization that had the power of all the armies of all the centuries. Was this planned by Patton? You bet! Patton had an uncanny sense for symbolism in everything he did, and it accomplished the precise results he wanted.

I knew a colonel at Fort Benning who was the commander of the new enlistee brigade, through which all new recruits in the infantry were trained. At the graduation ceremony, this colonel would wrap each man in the American flag and have him pledge allegiance to it. Symbolism. In business or in the military, management and leadership go hand-in-hand, but it is leadership that inspires greatness.

LEAD, FOLLOW, OR GET OUT OF THE WAY

An Atlanta entrepreneur, Ted Turner, is well known for his favorite expression, "Lead, follow, or get out of the way." Similarly, George Odiorne, a business author, says there are three kinds of people in organizations: those who *make* things happen, those who *watch* things happen, and those who have absolutely *no idea of what's* happening. Both statements recognize the need for visible leadership, which is a critical-to-success factor in small businesses. You see, a small business is not a miniature version of a big business. A small business is a totally different genre — something that people who write small business textbooks apparently don't understand. Big business abounds in staff, specialists, and layers and layers of management, which is referred to as a proper noun — The Management. It is conspicuous by its distance.

On the other hand, management in a small business is a uniquely personal process. No one typifies that better than Sam Walton, who is present in every Wal-Mart store at least once a year. That's a staggering achievement, when you realize there are currently seven hundred Wal-Marts in the United States. Wal-Mart is one of the largest small businesses in the country. Its founder is still at the helm. His values predominate. Unlike big business, leadership in a small business is conspicuous by its closeness to "the front-line troops."

Leadership in a small business stretches out in two directions. On one hand, it stretches out to the workers, whose energies must be unified and given direction. On the other hand, it stretches out to potential customers who must be persuaded to become zealous converts to the firm's superior way of doing things. It takes visible leadership to bridge this gap between the latent resourcefulness of people and the needs and problems of the customer following. How does Sam Walton do it? He leads employees in the company song before a new store is opened to the public. He checks merchandise. He works the cash registers. Leadership requires at the helm an individual with vision and a contagious enthusiasm for the purpose and the potential of the organization.

In your business, you are the living symbol of what the business stands for. And while you can't take the credit for everything it achieves, or the blame for everything it fails to achieve, whatever it does achieve is done in your name. And that is a responsibility that you cannot afford to take lightly. Your frequent presence in the workplace, where the profits are made (or lost), is required both to see and be seen. This is the symbol of your accessibility and your leadership. For example, in the dark days of the Chrysler Corporation, Iacocca was frequently seen on the shop floor, a visible and an accessible leader. Moreover, in tough times, comrades-in-arms can't be held at arm's length—the workers at Chrysler call Iacocca "Lee."

Similarly, you must give personal attention to all work done in your company, because in business you get not just what you expect, but what you also inspect. What you pay attention to is the most visible clue to the workforce as to what is really important in your company. To paraphrase a proverb, "The footprint of the owner is the best fertilizer."

Josiah Wedgwood was a sea captain who lost his leg in an accident and had to become a landlubber. He started a business to produce an exquisite form of china, which predictably came to be known as Wedgwood china. Frequently, he would go out on the shipping dock, or whatever they called it in the nineteenth century, and he would perform his own brand of quality assurance. Opening a crate, he would go through every piece of china looking for the slightest defect, and if he found one, he would destroy the entire contents of the crate and scrawl on its side, "Not good enough for Jos. Wedgwood." Workers were paid on the basis of pieces shipped, so a destroyed crate of finished product hit them in the pocketbook. The message got through. Give personal attention to all work? He gave it with a vengeance. Today, Wedgwood is a collector's item.

"AROUNDHEREISMS"

Every outstanding organization embodies what it stands for in its "aroundhereisms." Aroundhereisms are the obsessive values and norms in a business. They are the clues to what's important and what's not. They define the personality of the firm.

A business must have strong aroundhereisms to create cohesion; otherwise, it's a so-so business and certainly a lackluster group of people. In a small business, only the owner can define what's important and what's not, because he is both its hero and lawgiver. And these values are communicated through the owner as their role model.

Well-defined aroundhereisms create a "group mind." This is what will give your business its unique flair. When I go into the offices of a small company and see inspirational slogans, posters, statements of values, I know I'm in a great place. I know there's leadership there, and it uses these visual clues to paint a picture of what the organization is becoming.

But, the aroundhereisms must be consistent. Several years ago during my initial meeting with a new client, I asked him to spell out the one or two dominant aroundhereisms that characterize his business. His answer? Customer service—no doubt about it! Well, his employees had a different answer. They said, in effect, "What we really have around here is a 'theme of the month'—this month it's shipments, last month it was receivables, and next month? Who knows?" "And customer service?" I asked. Sure, they talked about it, but there was no consistent emphasis to make that part of the company's aroundhereisms.

It's critically important that aroundhereisms be transmitted to all new employees in whatever indoctrination process you use. (Many small companies, unfortunately, don't have a formal indoctrination process.) Because if you don't communicate those values in an overt way, the new employee stumbles around and finds them out by accident. And I can tell you both from my own experience and from research, that method invariably sets people up to fail. A clumsy initiation frequently ends in termination—for research also shows that most people are terminated from jobs more for reasons of chemistry than competence. In other words, it's not because they foul up, it's because they don't fit in. Obviously, the process of indoctrination begins before you ever hire the employee—you must make sure that you hire the right employee. But once on the job, the sooner that person understands the attitudes, the habits, the values—the aroundhereisms—that are embodied in your business, the sooner he can make a contribution to your firm's future.

CAN YOU HELP ME WITH THIS PROBLEM?

How would you feel if the President of the United States called you tonight and said to you, "I've been struggling with this problem for several days now, and I'd like to get your opinion on it"? Would you feel important? You sure would. And so would most people. You'd be saying to yourself, "My opinion? You want *my* opinion?" And what would you feel like? Well, you'd feel like a partner.

"Partnering" creates a sense of shoulder-to-shoulder. In my experience, people of good faith will help you if you ask for their help. They'll step up to a problem if they believe you value their input and will use it if it's worthwhile. Do you want to know the real secret of success in the Japanese style of management? Responsible participation by all employees. You see, the United States tradition of management is a form of organizational apartheid. There is a clear distinction between those who manage and those who are managed. There is no sense of power sharing.

In American companies, the hierarchy of the organization is the hierarchy of competence — all the smart people are in the top, and all the, well, not-so-smart people are in the bottom. But that's a distortion. I've found that most people demonstrate remarkable creativity — off the job. They figure out how to save enough money to send their kids to college. They balance their checkbooks. They fill out those pernicious tax forms that their government's "tax simplification act" has inflicted on them. They commit themselves to buying a house and paying for it over a thirty-year period of time without knowing if they'll have a job for thirty years — or be alive. They buy a car and commit themselves to forty-eight to sixty monthly payments, not having any assurance of what the future may hold for them. And we bring these same people into the workplace and treat them as if they didn't have good sense. Why, we'd never let an employee make a commitment with our capital that they make with their capital all the time. Would we?

The job of leading people is neither to tend nor to tame them, but rather to release the creative energy that resides in every one of them. IBM for years had a well-known motto, *"THINK."* In other words, good ideas can come from any place in the organization, and nowhere is it cast in concrete that only those in management think best. In fact, in my experience people are often quite perceptive and innovative outside their field of expertise. In other words, they don't have blind spots and vested interests. A secretary frequently knows why a procedure breaks down in another department. A delivery truck driver for a client of mine knew why the sales force productivity was down — they were calling on the wrong accounts, 'cause the folks he was making deliveries to were way off the beaten track.

Partnering is sharing the mental ability that exists in every organization. So, the next time you're stumped, why not stop somebody in the hall and ask him, "Can you help me with this problem?"

"FOUND A DAMNED GOOD SOLDIER TODAY!"

Patton, as I said earlier, trained his men in the southwestern desert of the United States during the early days of the war. Every day, he was on the lookout for some simple act of good soldiering. Didn't have to be great, just something that demonstrated good soldiering. And because he had a flair for the dramatic, he would often make the announcement of what he discovered in a very conspicuous way. For example, tanks might be involved in a training maneuver out in the desert, and he would get on the command set, call everyone to a halt, and announce over the command radio, "Found a damned good soldier today!" Then, he would tell what he had seen the soldier do, give the soldier's name, and give the name of the organization to which that soldier was attached. When a soldier knew that something he might do could be given special recognition by General Patton and 20,000 troopers, you better believe that every man gave his best effort every day!

The job of leading begins with teaching people what it is you want them to do. And then reinforcing it when they do it. I have a client who's a master at doing just that. He has on his desk a pad of forms that are about the size of a bank check. Each form has the company's logo at the top, a place to fill in a date, and the form says:

I like and appreciate _____
because _____.

Then there's a place for him to personally sign it. He sends these forms through the company's interoffice mail, but they are never inside an envelope. They go through naked. And, as his employees see these little blue forms drifting around within the company, they predictably sneak a peek to see who's been up to something that their boss likes and appreciates so much. Good leaders, you see, encourage small things in small ways, and they do it frequently.

Why don't we all do that naturally? How is it that people get to be managers or start their own companies? Because they have an affinity for solving problems, making things work right. They are "problem specialists," which is how they become so good at what they do. But unfortunately, this creates a "problem focus" about almost everything. Their attitude is, "If it ain't broke, don't fix it." In fact, pick up any management textbook, and as sure as I'm writing this, you'll find a principle called "Management by Exception." Which is just another way of saying "the only time you're going to see your manager is when you've fouled up!" You don't ever see the manager or the owner when things are going great.

I guess that's understandable in some respects. After all, what do you do when you put a quarter in the telephone, dial in your number, it rings, and the party on the other ends picks up and answers the phone? You don't say, "Well, ain't science great!" Or, what do you do when you put money in a vending machine, pull the lever, and your selection drops to the bottom, where you reach in and pick it up? You don't say, "Golly, this thing really works!"

But what do you do when you put your quarter in the telephone and you not only can't get the blasted thing to ring through, but also it refuses to give your quarter back? Or what do you do when you put your money in a vending machine and the product gets stuck? In both cases, you kick, you cuss, and you may leave nasty notes on the phone or vending machine — the machines didn't do what they're supposed to do. And that's precisely what many managers do with people. When they do what they're supposed to do, what does the manager do? Nothing. But when they do what they're not supposed to do, what does the manager do? Kick 'em, cuss 'em, and leave nasty notes on their desks.

People aren't like machines. And if you don't reinforce good results, pretty soon you won't get them. In fact, you need to particularly reinforce the little things in small ways, or sooner or later, you won't get the big things.

CHECKING HEADS

Robert E. Lee, that great general during the War of Northern Aggression, had a very interesting leadership practice. He would write out his field commands and give them to his orderly to read. And after the orderly had read the field command, Lee would take it away from him and ask him to repeat what the field order said. If the orderly couldn't get it straight, Lee would rewrite the field command, except this time in simpler terms. And again, he'd give it to the orderly, and again he would take it away and ask the orderly to tell him what the field command said. He'd keep this up until the orderly could read and recite the command correctly. Lee figured if his orderly could get it straight, his field commanders could too.

In a military operation, communicating the mission is everything. And good leaders in business constantly check the organization's understanding, its attitudes, and its heartbeat. Haroun al-Raschid, the caliph of Bagdad, would dress himself as a beggar and roam the streets. Since the people thought he was a beggar, when he would ask them how things were going, they would tell him—The Truth! He realized he was surrounded by people who had a vested interest to make sure he didn't know some of the truth. Or at least they would color it up a bit. So he'd get out in the streets and check for himself. You don't need to dress as a beggar, but you should check your organization's understandings and its heartbeat and independently verify what you're being told from time to time.

People can't solve problems that they don't understand exist. Nor can people solve problems when they only vaguely understand how the problem exists. People can't be led if they don't know where they're going. That's why checking heads is such an important part of leadership. Training often fails because there's too much emphasis on the hands, not the head. The head is where the problem is. And until the training focuses on the head, the employee can't really see himself doing the job the way you want it done.

Wars are lost in the mind before they're ever lost on the ground. Games are lost in the head before they are ever lost on the playing field. Thus, attitudes and understanding are inseparable from performance. And, as I've mentioned, as a soccer coach, I know the importance of my team's attitudes and their expectations before we play a game each Saturday. As their "leader," I never talk about losing, and I don't allow them to talk about it either. I don't want losing thoughts in their minds, because I want them to be thinking about what we want to happen rather than what we want to avoid.

Be a head checker. And do it often.

"YOU'RE BETTER THAN THIS!"

Want to lose some money on any given day? Then chew an employee out and make sure you do it in front of others. Then see how much work you get for the money you paid those people that day. They will probably spend their day grumbling about this sorry place where they work. Castigating an employee, or for that matter, any person, simply tightens them up with frustration which they usually pass on to others.

As an example, I heard a story about a boss who never fussed at an employee because the boss happened to like dogs. That's right. Because of his canine compassions, he never fussed at an employee. If he fussed at a man on the job, that man would go home that evening, and before he'd been in the house five minutes, he would cut loose on his wife about something she hadn't done right that day. Then, because Mom was uptight, she would blast the elder son about getting to work on his homework. On the way up the stairs to his room, the boy would drop one on his sister, telling her that if she came in his room, he'd make a war zone out of it. Now Sis had the mean spirit—so she would dump on Baby Brother. Since the little guy was low man on the family totem pole, he didn't have anyone to chew out, so he would go into the backyard and kick the dog. That's the reason the boss never chewed an employee out—it just gets passed along until finally some unsuspecting dog gets kicked!

So how do you change an employee's unacceptable performance without destroying him—and parts of the organization in the process? Clearly, you can't accept substandard work, but you don't build people up by tearing them down. People with bad self-images obviously don't produce good work. So, as a coach, a parent, a teacher, or a manager, when I encounter unacceptable performance, I say, "You're better than this . . . so I refuse to accept it." To change performance, you must separate the person from the problem. The person must see himself without the problem. In other words, he must have a self-image of a person who doesn't produce unacceptable work. It's your responsibility to help that person see himself differently.

Zig Ziglar, the nationally known motivational speaker, tells a story of Coach Vince Lombardi in a particular practice session where things weren't going well. One of the players, a hulking guard, wasn't playing up to Lombardi's standards, and finally the coach said to him, "You're not putting out! In fact, I doubt whether you're going to make this team. Go to the locker room!" About an hour and half later, Lombardi entered the locker room with the rest of the team, and the big guard was still there in his sweaty practice uniform with his head in his hands. Lombardi walked over to him, put his hand on the guard's shoulder, and said, "Son, you are a lousy football player. But inside of you is a great football player, and I'm going to stay by your side until *that* football player comes out." And with that, Jerry Kramer felt better, stripped his uniform off, and took a shower. Years later, he would be elected to the Football Hall of Fame.

All lasting change starts from the inside of a person and works its way out. It does not start on the outside and get forced in by the boss, a teacher, a coach, or a parent. You must admonish people without destroying them in the process, and you can do that by convincing them that you see something in them that they don't see in themselves. Why do people perform good work, win soccer games, produce "A" term papers? Is it because they are acting naturally or unnaturally? You know the answer as well as I. Top performers are simply themselves. They don't have to remember how to act. They act like themselves. They don't see themselves losing games, turning in shabby work, or getting nervous before speaking to an audience. That's the reason winners win. Unfortunately, it's also the reason losers lose. It's all in how a person sees himself. And, it begins by a believer telling an unbeliever, "You're better than this!"

Leaders must create a spirit in which people truly believe it makes a difference whether they do well or badly. Quality and service problems are one of the most critical competitive issues this country faces. So employees must care about the work they do. They must understand that their efforts as individuals mean something to the business and are appreciated by you and everyone else in the business. Beating people up impoverishes their self-image and often makes them more creative in not getting caught. But, building people up—by refusing to accept work which is not as good as they are—helps them to become the person they have the potential to be.

APPLAUSE, PLEASE

One of your most important acts as a leader is to be the spokesman for every individual in your business to every other individual in your business. In fact I have often said that if you wish to succeed, make sure that everyone around you is succeeding—first. All of us want to be somebody. We never outgrow that need. We just get more sophisticated in the way we want to be told.

The truly great business organizations are characterized by lots of applauding. When someone does something worth recognizing, he not only gets the congratulations of the boss but also the congratulations of all the other people in the organization. The word gets out, because the boss makes sure the word gets out.

I attended the quarterly business meeting of a client's firm in which he virtually shut the company down for a day in order to go over the past quarter's business performance — not only the things the company had done well, but also where it had stubbed its toe. Nothing was held back in these sessions. Revenue, expense, and profit figures were projected on a large screen so that every employee could see what had occurred in the business. Toward the end of the afternoon session, the owner began his ritual of recognizing outstanding performers throughout the company. Plaques and awards were given to individuals who were held up as the company's heroes. I sensed a great spirit of enthusiasm and not a modicum of jealousy.

Before the group broke up, the owner said he had one more story to tell and one more award to make. One evening about 6:30 P.M., a 22-year old secretary named Jennifer was headed out of the office, undoubtedly to go home and prepare dinner for her husband and small child. As she passed the empty reception desk, the telephone rang. Now if you want to really see how well-run a company is, why don't you call them at 5:01 P.M. — just see if anybody will answer that phone. A phone that rings at 6:30 P.M., well, that's probably trouble. Jennifer may have wavered two seconds as she thought about her awaiting family, but she picked the phone up and listened to a distraught customer tell about a problem he had. It wasn't in her area of responsibility, but she asked the customer, "Who was the salesman that serviced your account?" When she learned the salesman's name, she told the customer that the salesman had gone home for the evening but that she would call him at home, have him call the customer, and she would wait to call the customer back in order to assure that the problem had been resolved.

What she didn't know was that her boss, the owner of the company, was sitting in someone else's office about four doors down the hall and had watched the entire event unfold. Here was a 22-year-old who was already working after hours, and before she could get out of the building, she had become the owner of a problem that was not even in her area of responsibility. When he completed telling the story to his employees, he revealed to them who it was. It was apparent to me that Jennifer had totally forgotten the incident and was embarrassed by its retelling. But as she walked to the front of the room to receive her special award, the other employees rose to their feet and applauded her. As she and her boss stood together looking at the small crowd of employees, it was obviously an emotional moment. But the boss summed it up this way: "It's people like Jennifer that make all of us look good." And another hero was made.

THE DEATH OF THE TIGER

There is, unfortunately, a lot of talk these days in business books about a character type that is variously described as a sort of corporate tiger. I think it's sad when virtuous terms are used to describe a person who "wins through intimidation" or whose focus is "getting yours" or whose preoccupation is exercising abusive power over others. The corporate tiger is an individual who will step on anyone and everyone in order to climb to the top — wherever the heck that is.

Several years ago, I invited the founder of a company to speak to my entrepreneurship class, and at the end of his presentation, a student asked him to what did he attribute his success. He answered without hesitation, "As I was climbing up the ladder of success, if I saw anybody's hands on the rungs below me, I stomped on them and kicked them off!"

Earlier in his presentation, he had talked with delight about catching an employee who had stolen thousands of dollars from the company. Essentially the money had been stolen from him, since he was the company's major stockholder. His face was flushed, and I expect that he suffered from high blood pressure. An hour before arriving, he had flown in from Washington on his corporate jet, and in speaking with him before class, the smell of alcohol was on his breath. Whatever "success" he had achieved, he didn't seem to be having much fun with it.

The saddest thing about the corporate tiger is that his sole cause in life is personal career and ambition. But until he learns to detach himself from personal pursuit and define himself as a helper to the people around him, he won't be much use to himself or his organization.

Jesus said, "whoever would be greatest among you must first be a servant," and then he got down on his knees and washed his followers' feet. To understand the real significance of that act, you must understand a little about the Eastern culture of two thousand years ago. People traveled all over the known world on dusty roads. There were no traveling vehicles to speak of, so understandably people's feet were filthy. However, it was a breach of Eastern protocol to eat even the humblest of meals with dirty feet. So, just as today you would wash your hands before eating, guests' feet then had to be washed. It was the lowliest job that could be performed, and the host assigned it either to a household slave or his most insignificant servant. Guests were not allowed to wash their own feet. So there you have the picture. Jesus had been their leader and their teacher for about three years, and here he was, washing their feet. Then he left them with this message: "As I have done to you, so also should you do to others."

As I have said before, to succeed in life, commit yourself to the success of others rather than you own success. It never seems to work the other way around. "The best of all leaders," said Lao Tzu, "is the one who helps people, so that eventually they don't need him . . . and when his work is finished, the people will say, 'it happened naturally.' " In other words, the real leader is not a breast beater who says, "You couldn't have done it without me." Because, while that may be true, great leadership, like virtue, is its own reward.

Effective parents, teachers, coaches, and managers are enablers. They energize their followers and empower them. They don't make cripples or casualties of them. And in order to enable others, we must invest a lot of time in their lives. A friend told me a story that makes that point as well as it can be made. It seems a farmer in rural middle Tennessee would walk out of his house each morning, cross the dirt road in front of his house, and walk to the far corner of a hundred-acre tract of land on the other side of the road. Over his shoulder would be a hoe and some other hand tools, and beside him walked his eight-year-old boy. Back in a far corner of that hundred-acre field, the farmer and his boy had planted an acre of corn, and together they would hoe it, pull weeds, and tend it in whatever way was needed.

A neighbor down the road watched this go on for about as long as he could stand it, and finally one day, he told the farmer, "You know, I've been watching you two for a long time." Then he asked, "Why don't you grow corn on the entire one hundred acres instead of that little patch in the back corner?" The farmer beamed as he answered, "Oh, that's easy. Because I'm not growing corn, I'm growing a boy . . . and I don't need a hundred acres to do that."

In business, as in life, it is our investment of time in others that pays dividends that benefit us all. Invested time is the currency of real concern. But to do that, you must be able to see beyond yourself.

THE NEW CHRYSLER CORPORATION

Keeping faith in troubled times is one of the most difficult situations for leaders. Systems, norms, and traditions may begin to break down in the face of adversity. Fear, mistrust, and the inability to act with enlightened self-interest can put a company in a graveyard spiral. A siege mentality develops in which the company digs in for the duration. What company typifies this condition today better than Eastern Airlines?

In order to get things turned around, the leader must be a faith healer—not in the religious sense but by seeing that the problem confronting the business is its loss of faith in itself. In a crisis, the leader symbolizes the solution. The leader must see a new vision and create a new future for the company by making a clean break with the past. No one has done that better in recent times than Lee Iacocca. And in the early days of his turnaround, he constantly referred to the company as the New Chrysler Corporation, signifying a break with the legacy of past problems. In a similar spirit, Winston Churchill, in the darkest days of the Battle of Britain, rallied the British people to fight on so that in years to come, people would say, "This was their finest hour!" After a night raid by German bombers, Churchill would go to the scene of the worst destruction so that he could be seen by the people who were suffering and would often say, "We can take it." Roosevelt, on taking office, said we were in as much a mental depression as we were an economic depression, and that all we had to fear was fear itself.

In troubled times it is your devotion and your energy that allows the organization to retain faith in itself. And those leaders who do best in difficult situations are good communicators, but always they are among their people both to see and be seen. The leader symbolizes the solution.

In the Greek language, the words *agonia* and *pathemas* are translated into English as a struggle or a suffering. *Pathemas* is the word root for pathology, and it describes a struggle that is a destructive process and eventually leads to death. On the other hand, *agonia*, the word root for agony, is a constructive process in which a person is made stronger by virtue of the struggle. Thus, difficult times can either be hurtful or helpful. The leader makes the difference.

BEFORE CLOSING . . .

Of General George Marshall, his wartime military Chief of Staff, Harry Truman said, "I sincerely hope that when it comes my time to cross the great river, Marshall will place me on his staff, so that I may do for him what he did for me." Truman knew that Marshall's leadership had helped the country get through a difficult war. And in a similar way, we all admire people whose leadership enables them and others to achieve great things. It has been my distinct privilege to have a career that brings me into contact with some of the most interesting characters in American economic history: entrepreneurs. I suppose I've known a hundred of them personally. Most of them were successful, but all of them are interesting. They are at the same time alike and yet different. But of the ones that have achieved success on a grand scale, there is this common characteristic: there is a sense of adventure about them that inspires others to want to go where they go, knowing that somehow something significant will happen. I don't wish to overly romanticize entrepreneurs and small business leaders, but we would have a poorer world without the Steve Jobses, the Fred Smiths, the Mary Kay Ashes, and the millions of nameless small business founders. As the Robert Frost poem says:

> Two roads diverged in a wood, and I—
> I took the road less travelled by,
> And that has made all the difference.

It certainly has.

CHAPTER
FIVE

WHAT MAKES MARKETING WORK?

Products, Problems, and Possibilities

Marketing is about markets. And, markets? Well, markets are created every day at the intersection of Customers and Opportunity. It's an intersection that lots of folks have found — because there's a new millionaire in this country about every forty-five minutes.

While it's not well marked, I believe I can find that intersection twice in less than a minute if you'll answer two questions. How many television sets are in your house? Three? Four? Five? Next question. Excluding your children's cars, how many motor vehicles do you have for your family? One? Two? Three? Four? You see, when I ask these questions of an audience, I usually find most of the raised hands drop off around four TVs and around two vehicles. So there it is. A market opportunity exists for a fifth television set and a third motor vehicle.

To be sure, the fifth TV won't be like the four ahead of it. Perhaps it will be a pocket model. And the third vehicle won't be like the two ahead of it. Maybe an off-road vehicle? But these opportunities have already been recognized and in many cases filled. The point I'm trying to demonstrate is that most people own more than one television set and more than one motor vehicle, and that fact indicates there is a market for more of each — if you can create the market with a different version of a television or a vehicle.

Think about it. Your first television set was probably a large console for the living room or family room. Perhaps the second was a small black and white for the kitchen. Maybe the third was for a bedroom. And perhaps the fourth is for another bedroom or a basement shop. The fourth or the fifth TV will be determined by its need. Possibly it could be a small portable unit for vacations; a bathroom model, so you could watch the morning news while dressing; or one to set up in front of your exercise bike. But there *is* a market for a fifth TV. Why? Because most people don't have one.

Have you heard the story of the shoe salesman sent to the African bush who asked to be brought home because no one there wore shoes? And he was replaced by a salesman who telegraphed, "Send all the shoes you can spare, everyone here is barefoot." It all depends on how you look at things. Or how about this comment by Peter Drucker: "Only a fool would sell refrigerators to Eskimoes to keep food cold. But, a genius would sell them refrigerators to keep food from freezing." It all depends on how you look at things.

Who would have thought that you could stick a brand label on an apartment complex? Yet, that's what Post Properties in Atlanta has done. They've built tasteful architecture—not the stack of shacks you'll see in the commodity complexes—with beautiful landscaping and flower areas that are continually replaced throughout the year. And who would have thought that branding chickens would position them away from competitors' commodity chickens? Frank Perdue—that's who.

Sometimes it's easier to spot what it will take to succeed in the market if we instead identify the things that cause failure—and then eliminate those factors. Reverse thinking is what I call it. It works because I find folks understand failure better than they do success; they know what won't work, but they're still searching for what will work. I have no problem with that. Why things fail is just the other side of why they succeed—because everything in life comes in opposites. We can't have a plus without a minus. Otherwise, how would we define a plus? Where there's a top, there's a bottom—and where there's an up, there's a down. There's no way to make a front without a back. If we got rid of sadness, we would have to get rid of happiness. We couldn't eliminate death without taking away life. So, if we understand how we fail, we will have discovered how to succeed.

That's how I want to approach the topic, "What Makes Marketing Work?"—by discussing it in terms of "What Makes Marketing Fail?" Here we go.

PERVERSE PRICING

Pricing is usually ignored as a critical element in marketing. It's one of two determinants of profit, and it's a major influence in consumer choice. Ask most business owners how they determine their prices, and the answer will likely be "costs." A few will say, "competitors' prices." Pricing should mirror *demand*—which itself is a reflection of *perceived value*. Costs have nothing to do with demand. Costs are the consequences of *processes*—how something is created and distributed. The market doesn't care a flip if your processes are costly or niggardly.

Let me give you an example. In the mid-seventies, I visited an audio equipment store to buy a stereo system. I happened to look at an early version of a VCR, priced at $1,300. The conversation went like this:

He: "Why don't you buy one?"
Me: "I'll wait 'til the prices fall."
He: "Not likely."
Me: "We'll see."

I bought a stereo system as planned.

I also bought a VCR in 1981 (five years later) for $688. I wore it out and replaced it with two units which together cost less than the first unit. Pricing had to line up with my value perception (and that of lots of other buyers) before I was in the market. But cost-driven pricing prevented that until technology provided a way.

The pricing strategy in the early days of VCRs was perverse rather than greedy. RCA had introduced a video disc player at half the price of the VCRs then on the market. Had the video disc concept not been hopelessly flawed, the cost-driven, rather than demand-creating, pricing of VCRs could have been disastrous. Moral: If you can't get the price you need to cover costs because of the price/value perceptions of customers, either get control of processes at reduced costs—or get out of the market.

Value perceptions of industrial and commercial customers are exacerbated when that customer is in a low-profit industry. Everything they buy—from toilet paper to capital equipment—is relentlessly scrutinized because costs for these items generally can't be passed on in their pricing and, therefore, must be paid out of their low profits. When insurance premiums skyrocketed in the mid-eighties after years of foolish interest rate speculation by the major insurance underwriters, most consumers couldn't swallow premium increases of 300 percent to 400 percent. Besides that, insurance is perceived by the insured as adding costs but no tangible value to the insured's product. After all, if I buy a football helmet for my son, I'm not going to pay more for it because the manufacturer has been hit with higher product liability insurance. That's his problem. As a consequence, many businesses, particularly small businesses, "went naked" (self-insured), and others simply underinsured when premiums more than tripled.

Premiums fell about as fast as they rose, leaving the insurance industry Fat Cats in a confused retreat. "Pigs get fat, but hogs get slaughtered," so the adage goes. To further expose insurance pricing perversity, the CEOs of major companies were exposed by the New York State's Attorney General to have conspired to fix premium pricing in order to recover operational losses incurred after interest rates fell dramatically. On the news of their conspiracy, stock prices of insurance companies plummeted, stripping value out of executive stock options. What goes around, comes around.

Perverse pricing fails to recognize that high prices encourage substitution; high margins encourage competition. Both ways, the seller loses. But high margins created by cost controls (process improvements) can be protected because the low cost processes must be duplicated by the competition, assuming the competition understands them. The competition may not even know that a company's high margins exist if it is privately held and doesn't otherwise publicize its financial data—such as in credit reports.

The most perverse of all pricing practices is price cutting. For one thing, price cuts lower the value of your inventory. Price cuts beget further price cuts—so no one wins except the consumer. Moreover, price cutting is perverse because it rarely yields enough additional volume to offset the damage it causes. Rational price cutting is always accompanied by cost reductions. The spread between what you can charge your customers and what you are charged by your suppliers is your business's value added. All marketing and management practices should focus on driving that spread wider.

BROKEN PROMISES

Every marketing message carries with it an implied promise to perform. And marketing messages go forth even when you don't send them—in the form of unsolicited referrals or recommendations or put-downs.

> *Old Marketing Adage:* "Product must match the Promise"
> *New Marketing Adage:* "Product and its delivery system must match the Promise"

Stated differently, be sure you can handle the additional customers that successful marketing will produce.

Here's an example. A high-end restaurant in my home city opened its doors about five years ago. The decor was great, the service was outstanding, and the chef was renowned. I was one of its first customers. I gave it very favorable recommendations to my friends, and apparently other customers were doing the same, because the second time I visited the restaurant, the crowds were as large as Disney World's. Most people had lost their appetites by the time they were seated—up to an hour after their reservation times—and they were greeted with sorry service, hurried waiters, and marginal food quality.

Top-of-the-line restaurants don't advertise. They are promoted through referrals by their customers. Some of the best ones are so hard to find you have to have a map. When referrals end up as broken promises, the referrers look like fools. All the marketing that could be mustered couldn't put the restaurant I just mentioned back together again. A much smarter program for them would have been to say, "We're booked," turn the overflow crowds away, and then be patient. Curtailing supply might have even increased demand, and in this case people would probably have been willing to reschedule. Instead, this particular restaurant's early success blew its capacity—and its reputation.

Most companies start out conservatively: "What if we fail?" A better question is, "What if we succeed? Can we handle it?" If not, standby capacity must be available and readily engaged, albeit at a slightly slower rate than the growth in demand, which helps to keep customers interested.

Broken promises are also inevitable when messages create false expectations. Some firms have advertising messages crying, "We're great!" or "We treat you right!" or "We're number 1!"—then they have an organization and staff that removes all doubt that the expectations were ill-founded.

Recently, I was in a rush to get out of town on a business trip. I barely had enough time to get to the airport, but I realized I didn't have enough money for the length of time I would be away from home. Consequently, I stopped at an automatic teller machine (ATM) to make a withdrawal. When I arrived, there was a customer at the machine, so I stepped in line behind him. However, when my turn arrived, the device into which I insert my card was suddenly removed. You guessed it—it was money-changing time! I squatted down to speak through the newly formed hole and said, "Couldn't you wait one more minute; I have a plane to catch." Of course there was no answer. No doubt it was part of the bank's sophisticated security practices not to let the public know someone was inside the ATM cubicle—despite the fact that the bank's truck was parked beside it with the name of the bank painted all over the side panels and the card feed had mysteriously disappeared.

My wife, who was accompanying me on the trip, said, "Let's not wait; there's another one about three blocks from here." So, we jumped in the car and raced to the next ATM. And you guessed right again; someone had removed the card feed in that one also. At this point, I was desperate and ran inside the bank to make a withdrawal.

"I need to make a withdrawal on my card, and your ATM outside is currently inoperable," I said.

"That's fine, sir," the teller said, "all I need from you is a check."

"I don't have a check," I responded. "If I had my checkbook, I wouldn't be using the teller machine."

"Sorry, sir," she replied, "I can't do anything without a check."

"Then, use my card," I said, "play like you're the ATM."

"Can't do that, sir . . . the machine is currently out of service."

"Strange, I thought I had already said that!" I said, "Why don't you put the card feed back in for thirty seconds so I can make a withdrawal?"

"Can't do that either, sir—the bank has strict rules about closing out the teller machines between 2:00 P.M. and 2:30 P.M.," replied she.

"Well, spare me," said I, "I certainly wouldn't want to interfere with your 'strict rules,' after all, I'm only a customer."

Fortunately, my wife, who has more elasticity than I do when it comes to crummy service, had her checkbook with her, and we were able to make a withdrawal. We arrived at the airline gate with only five minutes to spare. Ironically, this bank had billboards all over town plastered with proclamations that they "treat customers with respect." Tell me about it.

Brainless behavior by a bank bureaucrat broke its promise. Obviously, the bank's marketing manager and its accounting manager don't talk to each other. "User friendly" is a computer term; "customer friendly" is a competitive term. Ford Motor Company discovered that a dissatisfied customer will tell twenty-two people about a bad experience, while a satisfied customer tells only eight. Examples of surly, insensitive employees are my favorite fodder for speeches and articles. In my own case, I've blown the Ford statistics with this bank incident.

You should make it easy for your customers to do business with you. Making it easy means the location of your place of business, product availability, high service levels, favorable payment terms, and a knowledgeable and courteous staff that is authorized to override bureaucratic rules when a customer is getting the short end of the stick. In a private enterprise economy, a purchase is always viewed as a favor conferred on the seller by the buyer. Customers will exercise their freedom of choice if you breach your promises.

FAULTY FOCUS

Niche market identification isn't a new idea. Treating each niche you serve as an independent business is. Research shows that more than two-thirds of all companies claiming to be multi-niche companies used:

- The same marketing approach for every niche.

- The same sales staff for every niche.
- The same service personnel for every niche.

In other words, the niche was simply a convenient way to classify customers— not a strategic way to run the business. The whole idea of identifying market niches is so you can focus company resources on them. Focus means *focus*. There's no focus when a company's internal structure and processes aren't specialized by market and customer.

Example. I have a client who recruits physicians for hospitals and group practices. The market consists of two principal niches, fee-for-service searches and contingency searches. The first type is a high-touch recruiting engagement in which a fixed fee is paid in advance. It involves advertising, screening candidates, interviewing, conducting community profiles for the benefit of the physician, licensure, malpractice insurance, and a number of other things that must be done to complete a successful search.

The second type is a low-touch recruitment. Essentially it is a brokering situation in which candidates are identified through broad-brush advertisements. A list of those candidates who apply are given to the client hospital or group practice, and the client takes it from there.

If the same organization serves both niches, it provides too little service to the first type and too much to the second type. Therefore, two separate organizations serve these niches—different staffs, different marketing organizations, different recruiting organizations, and different practices and methods. The two organizations aren't even in the same building. Their only shared resources are the physician database, the controller staff, and the owner's staff.

Faulty focus has botched more attempts at niche marketing than any other factor I know. And what happens if you serve only one niche? Answer: You probably don't—you just think you do. Markets aren't homogenous. There are niches within a niche, and there are niches within the niches within the niche. Why, taken to the limit, a customer is a niche. In fact, one of the cardinal rules of selling to key accounts—those customers who are most valuable to your business—is to treat a customer as a market niche.

Faulty focus can be prevented by looking for niches within niches. Example: I have a general lines insurance client who defined a niche within a niche and built a business around it within his broader business. Substandard automobile insurance is a niche within the motor vehicle insurance market. The niche within the niche was the high-end substandard market. In other words, we were interested in customers who drove expensive cars recklessly. One of this company's insured drives an $80,000 automobile, and his insurance premiums are higher than his annual loan payments. But, he doesn't care; he makes a bundle in income. It's a limited market, perhaps $25 million in annual premium volume, but this client dominates it. The result: a small but profitable business within a business serving a niche within a niche.

Think about your business this way: differentiate customers and assign them to niches. Design a special marketing program to each niche. You'll be surprised and pleased with the results.

NON SEQUITUR(S)

The plural of sequitur isn't sequiturs, because the word isn't supposed to be pluraled (just as plural isn't supposed to be used as a verb). Non sequitur is Latin for "it follows not." In southern King's English, it means, "That don't make sense." The plural means, "You do several things that don't make sense, boy." A non sequitur can't get you there from here.

I've seen lots of marketing programs that were non sequiturs. I asked someone, "What's your marketing program supposed to do?" His answer? "Why, make money, of course!" Hogwash. Marketing programs don't make money. Marketing focuses resources on improving business performance in an area that's critical to success. It's excelling in a critical-to-success factor that makes money in business.

Example. I own an apartment complex. What is its marketing program really supposed to do? Decrease vacancy rates, you say? That's close—but no cigar. Maintain vacancy rates under 6 percent? Ah, now the right marketing program will get me there from here—and it will make sense, because if vacancy rates are above 6 percent, the marketing program isn't working.

Marketing programs that are targeted on volume, revenues, or profits, rather than on strategic business objectives, are non sequiturs because they focus on the *consequences* of doing the right things, not on the right things themselves.

And how about marketing programs that have no target at all? Well—I can't mention the Latin words for that in print.

DAMMED DATA

The engine of business is information. Since marketing is about markets, market information enables marketing decisions to be informed decisions, that is, data-based decisions.

Let me give you an imaginary, but unfortunately all too typical, conversation:

> *Me:* "Let me see the kind of research data you use to make marketing plans and decisions."
>
> *He:* "Oh, I can't afford marketing research—it's too expensive!"
>
> *Me:* "I didn't say anything about paying for market research . . . use the information you already have . . . you've been in business for over a year . . . what competitive trends and opportunities do you see in your business numbers?"
>
> *He:* "What numbers?"
>
> *Me:* (We need some help here.)

Unless yours is a start-up business, there's a gold mine of information in your office—or there could be. For example, a retail client's principal focus was on the primary markets—the top fifty metropolitan areas in the United States. His is a small but rapidly growing company. Financial resources are always strained. A historic review of data over the past five years showed that the few secondary markets (population under 500,000) in which my client had developed a presence were less expensive to build out—the "red ink period" was less than a year as compared to two years in a major market; advertising was less expensive; and labor costs were two-thirds of what the retailer was paying in the major markets. In fact, every dimension indicated the client was focused on the wrong markets. So we changed.

Another client discovered through ZIP-code analysis that despite wide advertising on the radio and in the newspaper, the ad reach was only seven miles. Consequently, he used less expensive, highly targeted direct mail thereafter. Direct mail followed up by another direct mailing within two weeks doubled the response rate. Finally, another client, by studying historic data, discovered that costs to market and serve one particular group of customers were higher than any other customer group for that company. However, these customers were too valuable to kiss goodbye. Some simple records research revealed the cause of the higher costs, and we developed a novel distribution process that used intermediaries and brought down marketing and product support expenses, making a marginally profitable market quite profitable.

Customer surveys can be conducted more inexpensively than you might think. You should use them periodically to determine what your customers like and dislike about your company. And what they like and dislike about your competition. A San Francisco contractor who did this found that his competitors were disliked when their beat-up trucks were parked in the driveways of expensive client homes and when laborers tracked dirt on the clients' carpets. Using this information, the contractor became the top choice among high-end home remodeling customers within two years—a nice payoff for the intelligent use of data. Customers are valuable information sources for finding holes in your competitors' marketing programs—and you may find some in yours too.

I read of a manufacturer who produced a superior consumer product but it didn't enjoy the sales growth that was expected. The owner decided to visit department stores where his product was sold in order to watch customers make their purchasing decisions. Surprisingly, he noticed that customers would usually pick up his product and a competitive product, one in each hand, and it became clear that the competitive product often won out because it was heavier! In the customer's mind, heavier was apparently better. So, returning to his factory, the owner began to fasten weights to the baseplate of the product. Guess what? Sales increased.

This kind of data could not have been derived except by the "go and see" method. Unfortunately, important market data on ZIP codes, marketing costs by product line or customer, and customer trends is dammed up in storage files in most small businesses—unused. Smart marketing requires data in order to know who, what, and why customers buy from you. A company that has been in business several years has a wealth of information that can provide a competitive edge in learning what works and what doesn't. Profiles of successful stores or markets can be developed. Armed with these profiles, you should be able to predict how sales will ramp up in a new branch or store. The economics of your business can be precisely defined, thus providing performance data by store, or by customer, or by product line, or by salesperson, if necessary. When comparative store-to-store or customer-to-customer or product-to-product performances are different, why are they different? Go dig for more data. Just remember, customers aren't constants—they're variables. Watch the trends.

WRONGLY DEFINED

A line in the Gilbert and Sullivan operetta, H.M.S Pinafore, says: "Things are seldom what they seem/Skim milk masquerades as cream." When Ed Lowe joined his father's business after the end of World War II, the business sold sand and gravel, concrete blocks, sawdust that was distributed to meat packers to catch drippings, and clay granules that absorbed oil and grease on the floors of machine shops. One day, a neighbor asked Ed to bring home some sand for her cat's litter box. Instead, he gave her a bag of clay granules. She came back for more. So did other neighbors. Out of curiosity, Ed threw a few grocery bags of the stuff in the back of his car, handwrote the name "Kitty Litter" on the sides of the bag, and sold them to a local pet shop. Within a few years, the same product appeared in grocery stores under the name "Tidy Cat." Today that business has revenues of $250 million—a product originally intended for use on the floors of machine shops had been wrongly defined. Here was cream masquerading as skim milk.

"A Cinderella story," you may say. "That's luck." "Couldn't apply in my business." But, I have three clients who found they were selling the wrong product for the market, or the wrong market for the product. Put yourself through this mental exercise. If your market suddenly dried up, where else could you use your know-how and products? Next, if suddenly your product offering became obsolete, what else could you do for the market? Wrong definitions of products and markets can be a costly mistake and could keep you imprisoned in the worst of all classifications which is—going the wrong way.

TRAVERSING A TREND—IN THE WRONG DIRECTION

If you're caught going the wrong way in a trend, all the marketing you can muster won't help. Witness the Edsel. It was a fast, fat, gas guzzler that hit a market going the other way: the market emphasis in the late fifties was economy and safety. Today, you win an Edsel if you lose a contest.

I once was associated with a company that produced a product that substantially increased the productivity of real estate salespeople. It allowed potential home buyers to view the facades of prospective homes by inputting the homebuyer's preferred ZIP code and price range into a computer terminal tied to a VCR and video monitor. Previously, a prospective homebuyer might spend days in the back of a sales agent's car driving around the city. The sales agent was more of a chauffeur than real estate agent. However, the product hit the market in 1981. The country was in a deep recession, and the real estate market was headed down. Brokers had a bunker mentality—cut expenses to the bone and lay in until the siege breaks. Despite a successful test market outcome and sophisticated marketing and advertising, and although most brokers realized that the benefits far exceeded the cost of the system, the roll-out of this new product collapsed.

Marketing works poorly in stagnant, unstable, or declining markets. It also works poorly for products or services whose value-to-cost ratios are falling because of changes in customer needs. Management discipline, not marketing, is the answer when trends are against you. For example, if competitors are expanding capacity in an already oversupplied market, restrict your capacity to what can be utilized to earn a tolerable return on capital employed. You may lose customers in the short run, but you'll be in business in the long run. Maybe your competitors won't.

But, be watchful. As market trends shift, the ensuing market turbulence often creates new opportunities. American Airlines converted to jets early so they could sell their prop planes at premium prices. Because they saw the jet trend early and reacted quickly, they enjoyed the cheapest conversion to jets in the industry. The foot-draggers had to stand in line to get delivery on jets, and they sold their props in an oversupplied market—at bargain-basement prices.

The moral is clear. "Get out while the gettin's good." Don't buck a trend. And, look for opportunities in hard times. As a now forgotten poet put it:

> One ship drives east and another west
> While the self-same breezes blow:
> 'Tis the set of the sail and not the gale
> That bids them where to go.

BEFORE CLOSING . . .

Sometimes it helps to spot what works if you understand what won't work. Marketing is everything you do to create key customers—and keep them. However, marketing won't help pricing that is out of line with values, delivery systems that don't deliver what marketing promises, faulty focus, or the commodity curse.

Marketing does work when you use all of your available information markets to plan and make decisions. When you identify a niche within a niche and work hard to corner it. Marketing works when you have specific goals related to a critical-for-success factor in your firm, and when the market trends aren't against you. It's simple advice but often ignored. Good luck in making your marketing work!

CHAPTER
SIX

MANAGING INVENTORY

*Converting Inputs to Outputs —
With Less in Between*

What if no one carried inventory? Think about it. Orders would equal shipments, and shipments would equal demand. There would be no demand-driven order cancellations, no inventory cycles, no surplus or deficit production capacity.

Product quality would almost attain the 100 percent level because, without inventory, production defects would be discovered immediately. Lead times would approach zero, because capacity would match demand. Bottlenecks in the production, distribution, and retailing system would in time be detected and eliminated, because there would be no inventory to hide them. They'd have to be dealt with.

Return on invested capital would rise because none of it would be idled by inventory. And interest rates would fall, reflecting all of the capital freed from this country's inventory stocks. Real productivity would rise because people would be freed from producing goods for inventory — some of which spoils or becomes obsolete — not to mention the resources that would be freed from managing inventory.

The world according to GAAP (Generally Accepted Accounting Practices) says inventory is an asset. Is it? The conventional business wisdom says producers, distributors, and retailers should all carry inventory. Should they? (Incidentally, showroom inventory isn't inventory—it's capital stock—like a a sales tool.) Most businesspeople characterize inventory as a shock absorber or a spring. Is it really? Charles Revson, the cosmetic entrepreneur, said, "All management errors end up as inventories. They are the monuments to our failure to manage." Let's trace the role of inventory in business upturns and downturns to see if it is really a shock absorber or if it is an amplifier.

When a company purchases goods, those goods aren't delivered instantaneously—there's a delivery lead time. Depending on the lead time, the company keeps a certain amount of buffer stock as inventory, allowing the company not only to feed off this buffer or safety stock, but also to prevent stock-outs in the event that lead time is longer than expected. In other words, the company will carry slightly more than three weeks' of sales in inventory if the supplier's lead time is three weeks. Various inventory management systems have been developed to reflect these inventory requirements—for example reorder point purchasing, materials resource planning, and simply rules of thumb.

THE INVENTORY ROLLER COASTER

Assume that the Orion Manufacturing Company is operating at capacity (it makes no difference if it is operating below capacity—it just adds more time before the roller coaster begins). Orion's customer orders are processed and shipped in the normal lead time. Then one of Orion's customers orders more than it has been ordering in the past. Since the plant is operating at capacity, a longer lead time must be quoted for this order. But longer lead times must be quoted to all other customers too, even though their ordering rate is unchanged. In other words, all customers suffer when the Orion plant is pushed beyond capacity, forcing, in turn, every customer's buffer inventory (in terms of weeks of inventory on hand) to fall below levels based on Orion's historic lead time. This kicks off additional orders from Orion's customers to enable each of them to replenish their inventories to levels reflecting the new lead time. Orion must now quote an even longer lead time. Previously determined buffer stocks, based on the new lead times, are again inadequate, so more orders are kicked off. Lead times from Orion stretch longer, creating more orders from customers—and so on. Get the picture?

When the delivery date quoted for the initial order that started this mess rolls up on the calendar, Orion obviously can't satisfy all of the orders due to be shipped that week, because the plant is now well over capacity as it has been for some weeks now. Perhaps the customer whose order contains the greatest number of units due to be shipped will get its full allotment, but someone is going to be left out. Late deliveries encourage everyone to begin hedging—that is, increasing their safety stocks. Customers place extra orders in order to protect themselves.

This chain of events dupes the Orion Company management into thinking that the demand for its product is growing, when in fact virtually all sales have been inventory adjustments and replenishments. And as you would expect, a company that has been suffering because it has been operating over capacity for some time will inevitably expand capacity by adding space, or people, or subcontracting in the interim until additional permanent capacity can be brought on line. That's what Orion does. Then what happens? You guessed it. The added capacity enables lead times to fall. Since Orion's customers are now getting product faster than they anticipated, they no longer need the safety stock they had been forced to carry, so they reduce orders, forgo ordering for a while until their stock levels drop, or cancel previous back-up orders, since those orders are no longer needed. Fewer orders mean shorter lead times, shorter lead times mean less product is ordered—shortening lead times further—and so on, and so on.

Now Orion is really in a bind. Plant utilization is way below capacity, and something must be done. Employees are laid off, profits shrink and may turn negative, and the company thinks it's in a recession. Is it? No, the entire chain of events was caused by inventory adjustments, and real demand neither went up nor down throughout the period. When you add to this the problem of production bottlenecks on the upside of the cycle and the rumors and fears on the downside, Orion really gets a roller coaster ride.

AND THAT AIN'T ALL

Now, what happens to Orion's upstream suppliers while Orion is being jerked around on the inventory roller coaster? They really get whipsawed. The Orion customer who ordered more than expected not only forced the Orion plant over capacity, but also caused the company to make adjustments in its raw materials inventory, so Orion increased the orders from its suppliers. Undoubtedly, some of Orion's impatient customers shifted orders to Orion's competitors, eventually forcing the rest of the industry over capacity. That really jams it to the suppliers of Orion's industry. But the suppliers give their sales managers raises anyway and think that happy days are here again. The suppliers, of course, must increase their purchases from the next upstream producers—who now get it in the neck and magnify their upstream purchases, so the next group of suppliers are swamped with orders—and so on, and so on.

Now, step back and look what has happened. A very small increase in product ordered by an end customer—a retailer, a distributor, or even a warehouse—gets magnified as it moves up the distribution channel for several reasons: everyone carries inventory, everyone carries safety stock based on lead times, everyone has competitors who are undergoing similar illusions of increased demand, and everyone has capacity that is fixed in the short term. So, I'll ask the question again: Is inventory a shock absorber or an amplifier? If inventory was a buffer or shock absorber, inventory levels would have fallen until suppliers caught up. But the exact opposite happened—they rose. Suppliers think the phantom sales are up because demand is increasing when, in fact, only inventory adjustments have been occurring. In the long run, what goes up comes down, but in the short run shortages create shortages. Do you remember the Johnny Carson quip that cleared grocery store shelves of toilet paper when he jokingly announced he expected a shortage of it? Remember the 1974 gas crunch that was caused as much or more by people carrying more "inventory," that is, driving around with full tanks?

Because orders can't be filled instantaneously, backlogs of suppliers build up, and we all know that businesses love to see their backlogs increase. After all, backlogs are a good sign of future prosperity, aren't they? In fact, most business owners find security in the "number of months' sales" that are being carried as backlogged orders. But those backlogs can disappear in a flash if they represent phantom demand rather than real demand. In the last recession, a *Wall Street Journal* article on machinery sales made note of the fact that lead times for heavy equipment had shrunk from an average of fourteen months to an average of six months during the prior calendar quarter. That's an eight months' reduction in lead times, and it occurred in one calendar quarter. How does an industry build eight months' of product in three months? It doesn't. It builds three months' of products in three months and has five months' of product orders canceled.

TEN WAYS TO IMPROVE INVENTORY MANAGEMENT

What does all of this show? For one thing, order rates can be very misleading. Increased orders, as I've shown, may have nothing to do with increased demand, your sales and promotion efforts, the skill of that marketing director you just hired, or any of the other things to which we usually attribute increased orders. An order is not a sale. A sale occurs when a customer accepts a shipment and is obliged to pay you for it.

Ideally you should scale your operations to the demand of your market share, and then carry little or no inventory. Inventory consumes cash, requires space, and forces you to hire people to manage it. As Charles Revson's quote indicated, the fact that you must carry inventory shows that you don't have full control over your operations, your customers' order rates, and your sales mix. Even service firms, other than personal services, are affected by inventory mismanagement and problems.

Most of my clients carry inventory that, in some cases, amounts to millions of dollars that have been permanently removed from the company's operations. Some clients could be debt-free if they could eliminate or significantly reduce inventories, but when I start talking about lowering inventory, I usually get resistance from every level of the organization all the way up to the owner. And while there are practical reasons why inventory can't be altogether eliminated—that is, purchases can't be made to arrive "just in time"—the best inventory level is the least inventory level required to operate your company effectively. Here are ten ideas to help you keep inventory levels at a minimum.

• *Suspect rapid increases in orders.* Graph your order rate for the last year or two. If you haven't kept records on order rates, graph sales. Use your personal computer and software to project a trend line through your historic monthly (or even better, weekly) sales, and if recent sales have begun moving above the trend line, get suspicious. When it comes to dealing with the fickleness of a marketplace, expect nothing and suspect everything. And if your business is on the upstream end of the distribution channel—meaning that distributors, wholesalers, dealers, and even other manufacturers are between you and the ultimate customer—you should really get suspicious that a whiplash is headed your way if the order rate picks up quickly. Remember: destocking follows upstocking, and as I've said before, sales increases aren't necessarily demand increases. Find a way to determine if real demand has increased. Here's an example.

Several years ago, I was engaged by an industrial distributor who wanted to develop a competitive strategy for his company. He had branch offices throughout three states that sold primarily to producers of steel-fabricated products. These customers, in turn, sold to companies who used the steel-fabricated products as a subassembly in their own products, and their products were sold through sales representatives to the end user. So you can see that this distributor was three steps back from the end user (the sales reps didn't carry inventory).

Just before I was engaged on the project, my client had hired a new sales manager. Sales had begun to swing up, and the sales manager was patting himself on the back. Company procedures required the branch managers in the stores to send all purchase orders through the corporate office for approval. I encouraged my client to sit on these purchase orders until we could determine what was causing recent sales to move up dramatically. We called a random selection of one hundred customers to see if their sales had increased over the past 120 days, and there was clear indication they had. A real increase in demand? . . . Not yet. We called fifty of our customers' customers, and—you guessed it—those companies were gearing up for the "projected industry sales increase" that had appeared as a feature article in a trade magazine.

We got a copy of the article and called the editor to determine how he had arrived at several of his key conclusions. His "research" method was grossly flawed because he had used secondary sources rather than primary sources to develop data. I wasn't about to do his research for him, but I certainly wasn't convinced that anything substantiated such a rosy industry outlook. Over the howls of the branch managers and the new sales manager, purchase orders weren't allowed to go through other than to provide normal replacement inventory. Within two years, three of my client's major competitors— companies with sales exceeding $20 million each—were acquired by national firms. They had overexpanded, become unprofitable, and were purchased by companies who wanted their customer bases.

• *Manage throughput.* Throughput—the rate at which orders are processed through a company—has a significant impact on inventory. If it is smooth, purchases and inventory levels are predictable. If it is erratic, you'll be shortstocked in some periods and overstocked in others. Throughput problems are intensified when order rates and supplier lead times are erratic.

Match inputs to outputs—in other words, don't manage component items in inventory. Why have five hundred of one part and one hundred of another part when one each is required in your product? Many inventory software systems are based on purchase economics— purchases are made in "economic order quantities." Well, maybe so, but when does surplus inventory cease to be an economy? The software of most inventory control systems has nothing to do with product flow rates.

Switch suppliers may impose unreasonable requirements on your purchases from them, such as minimum order quantities or surcharges. With some exceptions, it's better to order a few units of an item frequently than many units of it infrequently. Ideally, products should be arriving from your suppliers at the same rate you are selling it to your customers. That is the essence of just-in-time inventory. It isn't always realizable because suppliers don't like dealing with small orders. But think creatively about matching order rates to your sales rates rather than accepting the order quantities you're offered. Can you place a blanket order that is progressively shipped? Can several different products be aggregated to make an order? Are surcharges less than the carrying costs of inventory—space, people, interest? What other inducements can be created to get suppliers to cooperate?

• *Manage purchases.* This is really a subset of the point just made. When your sales increase, purchases can increase faster than capacity.

For example, if incoming products received from suppliers exceed your labor capacity to use those products—to assemble them into your product or distribute them to your customer—that surplus product or material becomes inventory rather than product flow. If you can make twenty units a week and incoming material is sufficient for one hundred units, the material for eighty units is immediately surplus even if for only four weeks, but it's still inventory. If you're a distributor and sell twenty units a week but receive one hundred units from your supplier, the surplus becomes inventory. Inventory is what is left over after your product flow rate—throughput—is satisfied, and purchasing mistakes, as Charles Revson said, end up as inventory.

The industrial distributor client I mentioned earlier had over $2.7 million in inventory. Some of that inventory was warehoused in the building containing the corporate headquarters, but most of it was located in the branch stores. I did a category-by-category analysis of the inventory and discovered, much to my client's surprise, that we had over a year's inventory in some categories and two weeks' inventory in other categories. But, get this. We could supply any store in a three-state area from the headquarters' warehouse within two days! Therefore, there was almost no argument for having branch inventory. But, that's another story.

Once the owner saw the magnitude of his inventory problem, we set out to cut the company's inventory in half within a year. This required planning, particularly because theirs was a very seasonal business. So we worked out a sales projection on a category-by-category, store-by-store, and month-by-month basis. Although the company did a limited amount of manufacturing, it was essentially assembling purchased parts. The sales projections were translated into unit shipments, and those unit shipments were in turn backed into purchases. We determined the inventory we should have had on hand to support each month's projected unit sales in each category by branch, and we designated that as "budgeted" inventory. Of course, that figure wasn't what we actually had on hand, so our Inventory Management Report showed "budgeted," "actual," and "variance." Budgeted, actual, and variance columns were also provided in the Inventory Management Report for unit shipments, assembly labor, and purchases.

There are many interesting side stories that I could relate about what happened in the following twelve months, but they aren't relevant to the point I am making here. Suffice it to say that we lived off our inventory for most of the year over the objections of the branch managers (who thought we were playing with fire), and the company's purchasing manager was about as lonely as the Maytag repairman. But at the end of the twelve-month period, the inventory level was less than a $1 million! And by the end of the next twelve months, that figure was cut in half.

• *Manage capacity.* Space, labor, delivery vehicles, cash, and many other things determine the real capacity of a company. It is very important for you to know what your real capacity is, and I wish I could tell you how to determine it, but it is impossible to generalize. Real capacity varies from company to company—even companies in the same industry. But when market demand or order rates exceed your capacity, backlogs increase, inventory grows—particularly if your inventory management system allocates inventory to on-hand orders. Purchase orders are then triggered by your inventory management program, and lead times to your customers increase, which encourages them to place hedging orders. All of this is a part of the roller coaster effect I described earlier. But, as I mentioned, this chain reaction tempts you into expanding inventory in order to cope with these conditions.

Have a plan for expanding your capacity quickly to enable you to deal with what may be a temporary upsurge in orders. For example, cross-train personnel; subcontract work to outsiders, even if it means reducing profit margins; and work overtime, even though that clearly reduces productivity (you pay for ninety minutes but get sixty minutes). These things will probably impact profits negatively and create stress for your workforce. But do everything you can to delay adding permanent capacity, because permanent capacity can't be divested. Most people add physical capacity at the wrong time—at the top of the cycle.

I wrote my doctoral dissertation on production planning for the broiler industry—chickens, you know. Most of the costs of a broiler processing plant are fixed costs; consequently, the plant operates at capacity. The national breeder flock—all the hens that produce eggs from which broilers come—are comprised of "sets" of different ages—young chicks are added to the front end of the national breeder flock, and mature hens (whose egg production has dropped) are slaughtered on the back end of the flock. A breeder chick produces no eggs for six months. In order to recoup the cost of feeding that chick until she reaches egg-production age, a hen must stay in production through at least fifty-two weeks of her life, though hens can continue to produce eggs economically through the fifty-sixth week. Eggs produced by the national breeder flock are culled before being sent to incubators where they spend about thirty days before hatching as broiler chicks.

With a production system like this, there are few short-term adjustments that can be made to gear production up or down. If demand increases, the cull grading standards for broiler eggs is lowered, and the reverse happens if demand declines. If demand declines, breeder hens can be taken out of production early, but no earlier than their fifty-second week of life. Otherwise, the growers can't recoup their costs of feeding those hens during their first six months of life when they produced no eggs. If demand persists upward, the only solution is to set more breeder chicks, but that takes six months to become effective in terms of added egg production. And in anticipation of more broilers to process and market, the industry must build more processing plants. All of this hits, predictably, at the top of a cycle which tends to be about eighteen to thirty months from trough to trough. When I wrote my dissertation, the profit margin on a broiler was a tenth of a cent per pound! You can see why. Capacity, once added, couldn't be divested.

• *Sell what you have—buy what you sell.* Common sense, often violated. Salesmen hate to miss a sale, and may be able to convince you, "If only we carried Product X . . . " But salesmen shouldn't set product policy. You should. And you should do that after sensible market research. Here's why.

I worked with a client whose company sold products and supplies to hospitals and other health care organizations, such as health maintenance organizations and emergency medical centers. About half of the sales were initiated by a salesman calling on the health care organization, while the other half were initiated by the health care organization calling the company. In the latter case, it almost always was an emergency—a piece of equipment or supplies were needed quickly. For this reason, it was necessary to build stocking warehouses throughout the company's marketing area so that it could respond quickly to these emergency requests.

The company's sales force was no different than any other sales force. When a customer asked if they carried a certain product—and they didn't—the salesmen predictably saw the request as an unserved market opportunity and were often successful in persuading the boss to buy "one or two." The "one" got sold, because the salesman would go back to the health care organization requesting it; however, the "two" never seemed to get sold. As a result, the company had lots of "twos" in its inventory, and the sales force was, in effect, setting product policy.

What the sales force and the owner of the company didn't understand is, if they took into account all the costs associated with the special handling required for a product that was not in their catalog, that they probably lost money on every one of those sales. All of the company's routines and procedures were set up to purchase, receive, inspect, stock or reship, invoice, and pay for products in their catalog. But when special items were purchased, none of these procedures worked. The purchasing agent had to establish credit with a new supplier, the receiving clerk had to know who the special purchase was for, usually special handling was involved in the reshipping, and a salesman had to deliver the product (often to the health care organization's purchasing agent) because the delivery procedures for catalog products were handled differently. So, I'll say it again: Sell what you have, and buy what you sell.

• *Drive down purchase costs.* Purchase and acquisition costs consist of transportation costs, purchase paperwork, minimum order quantities imposed by the supplier, incoming inspection, payment authorization procedures, and the expense of cutting a check to pay the supplier. Most small businesses have no idea how much these costs mount up, but they are significant.

Carrying costs, on the other hand, consist of space costs, personnel costs, insurance to cover inventory, interest on money tied up in inventory, and the inevitable obsolescence or depreciation of inventory items that don't get sold.

Theoretically, the "economic order quantity" occurs when the carrying costs and the average purchase costs combine to produce a minimum total cost. Graphically, it looks like this:

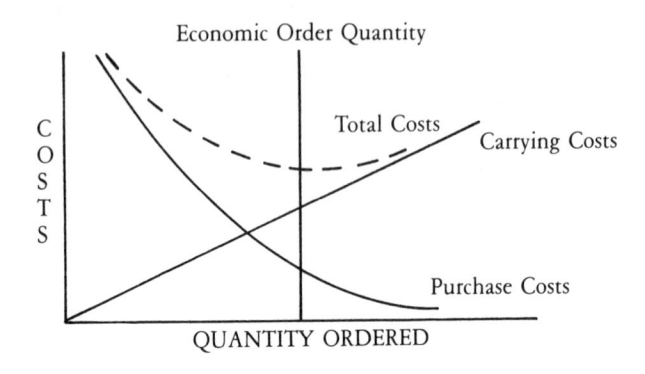

[Graph: Costs vs. Quantity Ordered, showing Total Costs (dashed) reaching a minimum at Economic Order Quantity, with Carrying Costs rising and Purchase Costs falling]

Usually, there is very little that can be done to reduce carrying costs. Interest expense, insurance, and technical obsolescence are controlled by outside influences. Unless the quantity of inventory carried is reduced, space costs and personnel costs associated with managing the inventory aren't controllable. But if you can drive down the purchase and acquisition cost factors, look what happens:

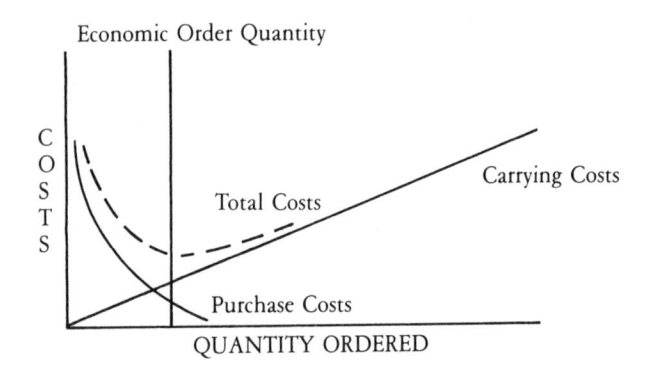

[Graph: Costs vs. Quantity Ordered, showing a lower Economic Order Quantity with reduced Purchase Costs and Total Costs curves]

Economic order quantity is reduced and, in fact, approaches one unit. Recognizing these relationships, you may find that the lowest-priced supplier may not be the lowest-cost supplier. For example, transportation costs probably favor suppliers who are close to your receiving point as opposed to far away. I have a client who uses a contract hauler to reduce transportation costs. Therefore, he selects suppliers less on the basis of their product prices and more on the fact that they are clustered so that the contract hauler can make a run out, pick up purchases from each supplier quickly, and return to the company's plant.

Purchase paperwork can be reduced by decreasing the number of purchase orders you must issue to the same supplier over some period—a year, for example. The supplier is given a blanket order for a year's anticipated purchases, and the release paperwork is simply notification to the supplier to ship a certain quantity on a certain date. So while the second graph shows how to economically minimize order quantities, it is necessary also to get the cooperation of suppliers, as I've said before. As much as possible, buy what the supplier offers as a standard product, even if it has features you don't need. Customizing a product costs you in two ways—the supplier must recover the modification costs, but also, if the supplier is to ship within reasonable lead times, special inventories of your version of the modified product must be carried on the supply end. Where possible, select suppliers who will allow you to buy as you need product rather than purchase minimum order quantities.

Incoming inspection costs can be reduced by weighing rather than counting incoming shipments. Also, incoming shipments can be packaged in a way that individual items can be counted in the shipping container without having to be removed and counted one at a time. The receiving clerk opens the top of the container and verifies that the container is full. If it is necessary for you to verify that the purchased products are in working condition, have the supplier's warranty extend beyond the period of time during which the product normally would be sold, rather than have your employee do this verification on the shipping dock. In that way, it can either be checked during assembly or before shipment, or checked upon receipt by your customer.

- *Know your inventory carrying costs.* As I said before, most small business owners do not know the true costs of inventory. They think it is the cost of the items they carry in inventory, but they do not take into account interest, space costs, people, insurance, and the risk of obsolescence. Do you know the true costs of your inventory?

- *Delay making inventory specific.* Which has the lowest "finished goods inventory"—a restaurant or a cafeteria? A cafeteria prepares a variety of product in advance so it may offer customers a diverse selection. As a consequence, it has high waste cost. A restaurant, on the other hand, prepares product on order. The component parts of a cafeteria's or a restaurant's product—foodstuffs—are the same but the restaurant combines them on short notice to make "finished goods." Restaurant menu items that are frequently ordered may be produced on an ongoing basis as a sort of "work-in-process" in order to reduce wait times. But restaurants can delay making their product specific. Cafeterias can't.

Apply these examples to your own business. If you produce a diverse offering of products, particularly if they employ common parts, don't invest the labor or commit the parts to producing finished goods. If you do, you will have the most expensive inventory possible. Like the restaurants, have an inventory that consists of components or subassemblies that can be finalized on reasonable notice when you receive an order.

- *Don't combat bottlenecks with inventory.* I was in a machine shop recently in which parts passed progressively from one machine to another as they received the various operations required to convert them into their final form. The machines employed were lathes, drill presses, horizontal and vertical milling machines, and finish grinders. The operations required at each machine station took from about one to three minutes to be performed. As the work at each machine station was completed, the part was placed in a container and three porters moved these containers to the next work station. What fascinated me most about this operation was that at no time did a container have more than three to five parts in it, though the machines produced thousands daily. Consequently, if a machine went down or a machine operator produced more than one or two defective parts, the entire machine shop operation would shut down within minutes. The boss wouldn't permit this to happen, so it was a very well-run machine shop. People make things right when they are required to.

Most machine shops, by way of contrast, allow four or five dozen parts to accumulate in a container on the input side of a machine station. That way, if an upstream machine goes down or defective parts are produced at one of the upstream work stations, it does not shut down the downstream work stations. To a casual observer, this method might seem to be a more sensible way to run a machine shop. But, in fact, what a shop like this does is use work-in-process inventory to cope with bottlenecks and breakdowns. Low inventory reveals bottlenecks, high inventory hides them.

This is true in almost any business. If the product flow through your business is made equal to the order rate, any breakdown or bottleneck will shut you down. So you have two easy choices. You can use inventory as a buffer and tolerate your crunch points. But, you will hide your inefficiencies in an expensive way—with inventory. On the other hand, you can combat the crunch points by not tolerating them. Then procedures would be revised to prevent breakdowns, people would be trained to do the work correctly, automation would be employed to do work that people can't consistently perform correctly, and many other things would be done that are both possible and preferable to throwing inventory at the problem.

The ideal inventory level is zero. When inventory must be carried, it is symptomatic of problems in your distribution chain—problems with your suppliers, with your company, with your distributors, and maybe with the end-customer. Businesses have used inventory too long to hide their failure to manage operations effectively, their failure to work out innovative arrangements with their suppliers, and their failure to be creative in the way they distribute their product through downstream distribution channels. It is an inexcusably wasteful practice.

• *Concentrate buying.* I was recently with a client who justified his practice of spreading purchases of identical products among three and four suppliers because he didn't want to be "single sourced." Most suppliers knew that they didn't have all of his business, so they were understandably indifferent whenever he made special requests of them. I persuaded him to concentrate his buying with one supplier, if only for a trial. By doing so, he was then able to wring concessions out of the supplier on price, delivery schedules, and many other things that were helpful to his business.

Concentrated buying provides obvious clout. If a supplier doesn't perform, the supplier knows it stands to lose a lot of business. In one case, a client concentrated several million dollars of annual purchases with one supplier on the condition that the supplier create a local stocking warehouse, eliminating the client's need to carry inventory. Both parties won. Concentrated buying encourages cooperation and loyalty and helps develop familiarity with each other's businesses. In many cases it reduces paperwork and even eliminates personnel.

BEFORE CLOSING . . .

When all is said and done, there is probably more said than done when it comes to managing inventory. I've known very few small businesses that had the amount of cash they believed they needed to do the job they were capable of doing in the marketplace. For that reason alone, small businesses must do a better job of managing inventory. Cash tied up in inventories and accounts receivable tends to be a permanent investment of working capital. Unfortunately, most small business owners have convinced themselves that they need more inventory than they really do need, and—as amazing as it may seem—it is difficult for me to convince them that the quickest source of funds is a reduction of inventory, not to mention the bottom-line improvements that come from the elimination of inventory carrying costs.

But sometimes, necessity *is* the mother of invention. I know a company that fought its way out of a Chapter 11 bankruptcy. It has no accounts receivable, because it can't afford them, and it has minimum inventory, because it can't afford that either. In order to buy something the company must sell something. It must put on a sales push to pay for the travel expenses associated with attending a trade show. Talk about a Spartan existence! But this company had no choice and proved it could be done.

Why not take a look at your own operations? I'll bet you could find at least a half-dozen ways to significantly reduce your inventories by redesigning procedures, developing creative alliances with your suppliers, getting estimates from your customers regarding their purchasing plans for the next six to twelve months, and looking for situations in which inventory is being used to hide management mistakes. You might be surprised at the number of opportunities you'll find. And new money too.

PART TWO
Improving Business Performance

CHAPTER SEVEN

WHO CARES?

How to Improve the Way Your Customers Are Treated

I had lunch in Baltimore recently with a friend who decided to take me to an upscale restaurant that specialized in seafood. I ordered a bowl of clam chowder—the house specialty I might add—and the waiter disappeared for what seemed an interminable absence. When he reappeared, he announced, "Sir, we've run out of clam chowder; I have brought you crab soup, and I won't charge you extra for it." I wanted to throttle him for assuming that economic motivations had determined my choice of soup. But my friend was embarrassed enough, so I assured him and the waiter that the substitute was acceptable.

Last fall, my wife and I flew to Boston with another couple for an extended weekend of sightseeing. We had planned to do a considerable amount of driving, and with four adults and lots of baggage, I had reserved a full-sized car from one of those major rental companies whose TV ads show smiling counter personnel promising "to take the worry out of travel." Unfortunately, the Boston crew hadn't seen the ad. They had my reservation, and they had my arrival time, but no full-sized car. I was given the choice of a compact car, or I could come back in an hour, when, perhaps, a full-sized car would have been turned in.

"Would you please tell me," I asked, "what was accomplished by my making a reservation for a full-sized car?" Her answer: "It assures you that you will get one if we have one"—a distinction I failed to grasp. As a parting shot, I said, "And your ads say you're number 1." "Tell me about it," she answered.

Recently, I was in a bookstore which is a part of a national retail book chain. I couldn't locate the book title I wanted, so I went to the "customer service" counter—at least that was what was printed on the sign hanging above the attendant's head. Scrolling through the computer catalog, he located the title. "We're out of it," the attendant said. After several seconds of ensuing silence, it became apparent to me that the attendant had concluded our brief encounter—in fact, he had left the counter to do something else. After all, I suppose, I was the one who wanted the book, not him.

As I was thumbing through the family mail recently, I came upon an important looking letter from a prestigious firm addressed to me—William H. Franklin. I opened and read the letter. It described a variety of financial services the firm could provide if I chose to become their client. Unfortunately, the letter began, "Dear Mr. *Williams*," evidence that the writer had signed the letter without reading it. I concluded that if the writer couldn't get my name right, he probably couldn't keep my account straight either. So the letter was routed to the trash can.

WHO'S RUNNING THE BUSINESS?

It should be a bit unsettling to business managers on hearing tales like these to realize that, as a practical matter, they don't run their businesses—their employees do; these examples prove it. When I buy a meal, or rent a car, or search for a book, I don't deal with the company's president, or its managers, or its stockholders; I deal with an employee. And the employee determines the service level I will receive. So, every workday when the doors are unlocked and the lights are turned on, employees take over the real control of this country's businesses.

But in a private enterprise economy, like ours, there are choices. And the customer, as the expression goes, is king. Customers ultimately determine which businesses will prosper and which will fail. A large part of that determination is the way they are treated. And when customers are treated badly, they usually don't get mad. They just don't come back. And their business goes to our competitor, probably permanently.

Think about this. About three-quarters of the people working in this country are involved in "service businesses." If we counted the number of people in manufacturing and other industries who don't actually make the product, that number would be higher. But very few of these people are involved in a personal service—like a doctor, a lawyer, an accountant, or a consultant. Most provide a service with a product. The service, in fact, is the intangible—usually the most valuable—part of the product. So the company that fertilizes and sprays my lawn four times a year provides a service with a product. The waiter who serves me a meal at a restaurant provides a service with a product. The mechanic who maintains my cars provides a service with a product. Now, notice that in each case, I begin with the service and follow with the product. However, that gospel never seems to get preached to the employees (assuming it's understood by the boss) in most small companies—companies that invariably define their existence as a product business. The service, then, becomes incidental.

What would happen if you went into a men's clothing store to buy a green sweater, and the clerk showed you a red shirt? You'd think the clerk was crazy, wouldn't you? You'd probably say, "That's not what I want!" Service is part of the product. In the case of a personal service, it *is* the product. And every time a customer doesn't get precisely what the customer wants—including good treatment—you or your employees have failed to deliver the right product. The right product is service first and the product second.

"Is this close enough?" Your tires aren't balanced *exactly* (so they'll probably wear out 4,000 miles earlier) or the door isn't hung square in the jamb exactly (so it won't close well either) or the insurance policy has the wrong jewelry description (guess who loses on that one?)—but, is this close enough? What's wrong with service in America? People aren't trying to get things right—they're trying to get them close. That was the problem with the waiter in Baltimore. Close was good enough. And that was the problem with the car rental agent and the bookstore customer service attendant. But, close doesn't count except in horseshoes and grenades.

Should we assume that employees who treat customers indifferently, if not badly, are perverse? I don't think so. The difference between Delta Air Lines and Eastern Airlines isn't the equipment or the personnel—it's the long legacy of leadership in both companies that goes back over four decades. Employees perform up to the level of their boss's expectations. They rarely exceed them. But expectations alone aren't enough. The performance you'll get is not only what you *expect*, but also what you *inspect*. The man whose letter incorrectly addressed me as "Mr. Williams" no doubt has high expectations of his typist, but he wasn't inspecting the letters produced to assure that his standards were met.

I have a friend who owns a specialty food gift shop in a shopping mall. He is one of about 350 franchisees operating in shopping malls around the country. No, that's not right—his is the number 1 franchise out of 350 franchises, because he sets records in almost everything he does. For example, he sells more jars of high-priced dill pickles than any other franchisee in the system. How? As you enter his store, the jars of dill pickles are stacked in a pyramid about five feet high. The display is impressive, but of course, the only jar that can be purchased is the one on the top because selecting any other one would pull the pyramid down. His employees hated the idea because "we're always having to straighten out the display because the customers mess it up when they buy dill pickles."

"Get rid of the display because customers 'mess it up' by purchasing our product?" he snorted. "What the heck do you think we're in business to do?" It obviously is not to keep displays straight. But somehow, that was the message that had gotten through to his employees. The customers were an interference to the work system. They were an abstraction, part of the flow of converting inventory to cash. As a practical matter, they were thought of with veiled contempt. Fortunately in this case, the owner spotted what motivational expert Zig Ziglar calls "stinkin' thinkin'" and gave his employees a thirty-minute lesson in how the private enterprise system works. But he is one of the few.

HOW TO SUCCEED IN BUSINESS

Success in business is built on paying attention to hundreds of little things every day and doing them better than the competition. Roger

Gilder, a Budget Rent-A-Car franchisee, invited me a while back to visit him so he could show me some new operations he had installed. We left the rental yard, and as Roger and I were mounting the bus that shuttles customers to and from the airport, Roger noticed that the outside of the van was muddy and said to the driver, "Elizabeth, this van is dirty—run it through the wash bay before going over to the airport."

"But, Mr. Gilder," she replied, "it's been misting rain all day, and with the construction around the airport, there's mud on the streets. If I wash it, it'll be dirty before I get back to the yard."

Replied Roger, "Then wash it on every trip—I don't want our customers riding in a dirty van." Now, that's a class act. If the shuttle van is dirty, subconsciously what would you expect the other services to be? That's right—marginal. Roger also poses as a traveler, riding back and forth to the airport, both to hear what his customers talk about and to talk to them about their reasons for selecting Budget Rent-A-Car.

Success is built on creative dissatisfaction—by setting high standards and challenging them every day. It is going all out for the customer. Like Roger Gilder. Like Federal Express which built its reputation on a 10:30 A.M. delivery time that they meet 99 percent of the time.

Recently, my middle child had a spend-the-night party for her friends, and they decided that for dinner they wanted something nutritious—a pizza. So, I called Domino's. You know, the people who guarantee a thirty-minute delivery. I was absorbed in watching the evening news when a young man appeared at the door. "Sir, I'm sorry that I was two minutes late . . . the pizza is free." I protested and tried to pay him, but he said he wasn't allowed to accept it." Another class act!

Customers aren't a pain in the rear, they're an opportunity to show off the best you've got. Regardless of how unreasonable or un-doable a customer request may be, it's still a chance to knock yourself out if you choose to. Last year, a friend decided to go to Europe with his wife, using his frequent flyer points. When he told his travel agent to book the reservations using his points, she told him that it took two weeks to get the necessary coupons. He was planning to leave in five days. So he called the frequent flyer redemption center, and the conversation went something like this:

"Hi, my name is Bill Gaston, and I have a problem."

"Well, Mr. Gaston, if you have a problem, then we have a problem . . . what is *our* problem?"

"I planned to use my frequent flyer points to visit Europe next week with my wife, and I just learned that it takes two weeks to get the coupons."

"Let me check your account to see how many points you have . . . Mr. Gaston, according to our records, you are five thousand points short."

"Really? I thought I had enough."

"Well, let me check to see if you have gotten credit for your sign-up bonus points."

"Yes, I know I already have those."

"Well, this is a special bonus you probably don't know about . . . ah, yes, you haven't received them, and when I credit those to your account, you're over the top!"

(This was an obvious ruse, because there was no "special bonus;" it was the service rep's way of overriding the system to help the customer.)

"Mr. Gaston, let me ask you a question . . . Would you be willing to pay the courier expense for me to get these coupons out to you right away?"

"Absolutely!"

"Great, then they will be on your desk tomorrow morning."

And they were.

Contrast this with an incident I observed at a hotel that is part of a national chain. I was checking out after speaking to a small business group. The guest ahead of me was a German gentleman who was reviewing his bill and noticed that he was charged for a pay-TV program. In this case, the conversation went like this:

"I watched that program less than five minutes . . . it was no good so I turned it off . . . why am I being charged for it?"

"I'm sorry, sir, when you turn on the pay-TV channel, you are automatically charged $5.50."

"But, I'm telling you that I didn't watch the program . . . I turned it off!"

"I'm sorry, sir, I've told the manager that these situations occur, but there's nothing I can do about it."

A mad customer—for $5.50! The average person knows 250 other people, and tells more of them about a bad experience with a product or company than he will tell of a good experience. Wherever that guy is today in the world, I bet he's told the story of that American hotel in North Carolina many, many times.

When you separate service from the product, what you have is a commodity. When the customer must take the lead, play twenty-questions, go over an employee's head to speak to the person in charge, and failing there, speak to that person's boss—which recently happened to me—then you're selling a commodity and deserve to be paid a commodity's price—which is very little. On the other hand, when employees combine their expertise with their appreciation for customers in a way that solves a customer's problem or complaint, then they are the customer's consultants and representatives. If you sell expertise, price documents its value as well as the benefits of doing business with your company—therefore, the price doesn't have to be apologized for.

GOOD CUSTOMER SERVICE IS . . .

Good customer service is getting everything right the first time—every time! Of course, that starts with leadership. As I've said before, employees usually perform in accordance with the boss's expectations rather than as the result of company standards or procedures. As a business owner, you must create a culture that holds customers in high regard, and that, in turn, determines how a customer is to be treated. Recently, the owner of a large chain of retail stores complained to me about an experience when he visited one of his largest stores. The store was empty at the time, and the boss waited for several minutes before the two store clerks in the rear of the store ended their conversation so one of them could wait on him. (I thought it strange that the clerks didn't even recognize the owner of their company, which may say something about his leadership practices.) At any rate, he proceeded to identify himself and then explained that the many hundreds of thousands of dollars he had spent on advertising that year, could have been wasted by this kind of insensitivity if he had been a customer.

Poor service doesn't "happen." It's caused. Stop poor service at its source—the employee. Obviously, that begins by being extremely selective in screening those people who come in contact with your customers in every capacity, such as sales, service, or delivery. Make certain that these employees are well-trained and adequately supervised to render good service. When your customers are subjected to indifference, or the wrong size, or a missed delivery date, these mistakes are caused by one of three things: lack of attention (an attitude problem); lack of knowledge (a training problem); or pressure (an organization or procedure problem). Because bad service is caused, it can be prevented. Prevention begins with your employees.

I read once of an office supervisor who took over the management of a typing pool. This was well before the advent of word processors, so typing mistakes were corrected with "white-out" or erasers. Frustrated that the typing quality in his department was not improving, the supervisor walked into the office one morning and announced, "Ladies, throw away your erasers." A new policy was instituted. Typing mistakes would not be corrected; the page would be thrown away and started over again. There was the expected grousing and complaints of unfairness, but within weeks the typing quality had risen to near perfect. As I've said, anything that's caused can be prevented.

Good customer service comes from asking customers to critique your service—especially when they're most inclined to tell you that it is bad. A good place to do this is a checkout counter or some other delivery point. Otherwise, customers cool off, forget, and never come back. And you won't know why. A sure sign of declining customer service is the absence of complaints. No one is that good. Think about it. When service is good, most customers won't say anything about it—they think it's their due, rightfully so. But, when service is bad, most customers won't say anything about it—to you. But they do tell their friends. Unhappy customers just don't come back. Neither do their friends. It's not easy to get customers to complain. A complaint takes time, and customers are always in a hurry. I'm sure you've seen forms that invite evaluations such as the "Will you let us know?" form used by many hotels and restaurants. I have no idea how many of these forms are completed and returned. But the form at least symbolizes an effort to convince customers that a firm really does want to know how customers feel about their service. And if it succeeds at that, it has accomplished its purpose.

Good customer service requires rotating employees out of high-pressure encounters with customers, such as busy phone lines and crowded counters. Working close to customers can be physically and emotionally draining—more than an employee can take for eight straight hours. The opportunity to relax for a few minutes can prevent a curt comment or an impatient exchange with an overbearing questioner. No question is stupid unless the employee has been asked it on hundred times already, and no complaint is unreasonable unless that's all the employee has heard all day long. So, if you'll give your employees some relief, you'll be giving your customers relief too.

Good customer service is positively reinforcing acts of good customer service in ways that lionize your stars. Preach examples of good service like a litany. Example. I was conducting a seminar for a client, and on entering the seminar room, I noticed that there was no overhead projector. The service representative said he had no order for an overhead projector but he would do what he could. That's the last I expected to see of him, but he showed up twenty minutes later with a projector he had rented on his own initiative from a nearby hotel. I was impressed and told him so, but that night I wrote a letter to the hotel general manager and recited the incident in detail.

The next week, as I entered the hotel to conduct another session of my seminar series, I ran into the service representative again. He thanked me for my letter and said that his boss had sent it to him along with the handwritten words "good work" at the top of the letter.

"Did he give you a bonus?" I asked.

"No," he said.

"Did he give you some time off?" I again asked.

"No, I had to work the entire weekend," he replied. What a bummer! But the service representative said again, "Thanks for your letter."

Good customer service is allowing employees to override the system when a customer inequity has occurred—like the airline service representative I mentioned earlier who helped my friend Bill Gaston get his tickets on time. "All Sales Are Final" may make sense to some, but it's little consolation to a customer who bought the wrong dress size. Regardless of who is "at fault," a business can't be conducted by standing on rules. As I've said before, the average person knows 250 people, and the retelling of a bad experience can cost more money than restocking a dress.

The willingness to lose money in order to be a class act was recently demonstrated to me by the owner of a successful hardware store. I was standing with my back to the front door chatting with him when a customer came in. Although I couldn't see him, the customer was apparently in a huff. As he approached the owner of the store, he broke into our conversation and began complaining that a drill motor he had recently purchased didn't perform as it was "supposed to perform." With each sentence, he spoke louder. The owner interrupted him and said, "Sir, I certainly wouldn't want you to have something that you don't need . . . give me a few minutes to work up the paperwork and I'll refund your money." The drill motor was a very specialized type used to drill through thick concrete walls, and as I looked at the motor and the drill bits, I said to the owner, "You were had."

"I know," he said.

I asked why he didn't put up a fuss. This guy obviously had purchased the drill motor with the intent of returning it after he had done a one-time job. Then the owner gave me a lesson in the private enterprise system. He said, "When I saw that guy come through the front door, I knew what was going to happen, and I had only a few seconds to decide whether or not I would take the purchase back . . . I decided that I would, and if I was going to take the drill motor back, why beat him up about it?" Now, the punch line—the owner said, "Look at our disgruntled customer now." I did. He was headed toward the cash register with an armload of merchandise, which he probably wouldn't have bought if he had been given a lot of grief.

Small business owners spend thousands of dollars to promote their businesses. Yet they sometimes haggle with their customers in a dispute that could save only a few hundred dollars. And if the owner "wins" the argument, he really loses. The Ford Motor Company estimates the value of a satisfied customer over the customer's lifetime is close to $200,000. What's your customer worth? I can tell you. It's years and years of purchases and repurchases. And, an unofficial member of your sales force.

EIGHT PRINCIPLES FOR DEALING WITH CUSTOMERS

PRINCIPLE 1: *Customers buy solutions—not products or services.*

Obviously, when someone has a problem, he wants it solved. I think too many selling situations overlook this fact.

Regardless of the way you promote your business, whether through advertising or direct selling, you raise the expectations of potential customers by what you say that you or your product will do for them. The customer buys the expectation of a solved problem and the benefits of the solution. For example, I don't really buy gas as much as I buy the right to continue to drive my car—and get to where I'm going. Gas is the solution that enables me to do both. I don't really buy a suit of clothes as much as I buy an image, nor do I buy a quarter-inch drill bit as much as I buy a quarter-inch hole. A fine meal in a five-star restaurant should be an experience. I can eat at home.

Better customer service will occur when employees understand that they are in the problem-solving business. If the employee follows all the rules and the customer's problem doesn't get solved, it's a "no sale," even though money changed hands. Employees mustn't forget that their expertise is on the line when they are in front of a customer—and that's the business you're really in.

PRINCIPLE 2: *Ask questions.*

If customers buy solutions, you must understand the problem to be solved. The difference between selling something and taking an order for it is who does the problem research.

Asking questions minimizes the chance of making a mistake that could later result in a frustrated customer, who may or may not come back to allow you to sort it out. Asking questions is clearly an important selling technique. It demonstrates interest and concern. From the standpoint of rendering customer service, it's important because it singles the customer out to be treated in a special way. A question as mundane as "Smoking or non-smoking?" at a restaurant indicates that there is some concern for a diner's comfort during a meal.

Several years ago I was shopping for a pair of binoculars. The clerk who was waiting on me began putting every model of the binoculars in the display case on the sales counter without a word. Apparently he thought I would make my choice based on weight and color. "Look," I said, "I don't know anything about these things, tell me something about them." Well, this guy had a sales IQ in the single digits because he said, "I really don't know binoculars, I usually work in cameras." I turned to leave, but another clerk, who happened to be waiting on a customer nearby and had overheard the conversation, interrupted and said, "Excuse me, sir, how were you planning to use the binoculars?" "To watch football games," I said. "Then this pair is what you need." The sale was made — but just barely.

PRINCIPLE 3: *Build relationships.*

Use the customer's name where it is appropriate, and give yours too. Recently, I took my wife to an upscale restaurant to celebrate our wedding anniversary. After being seated, our waiter approached the table and said, "Mr. Franklin, welcome to 103 West . . . my name is David, I will be in charge of your service tonight, and let me also introduce you to John and Marcos who will be assisting me." Each time he approached the table, he used my name again. I've dined at many five-star restaurants all over this country, and I'm used to first-class service. But somehow the waiter's tasteful use and reuse of my name when addressing me personalized the service in a way that made us feel that we weren't just one of several tables David was assigned to serve.

How do your employees look? How do they sound on the phone? Does your correspondence read like a canned speech? — or worse still, like stilted bureaucratese? How does your place look? All of these are important elements in developing lasting relationships with customers. People who are put off by the way your employees look or the way your place looks aren't coming back, because they're out of their comfort zone. I've seen this work in a curious way. A retailer had a store that was cramped, worn around the edges, and difficult to get to. Customer traffic was building, so he built a new store only two miles away. It was spacious, bright, on a main thoroughfare, and had plenty of parking spaces. Sales fell like a stone. What had happened? The surrounding customer base was lower-middle income. These people were used to being inconvenienced, to trading in cramped, frayed stores. When the new facility was opened, it got people out of their comfort zone — it was too uppity for them. So, many customers went elsewhere—where they felt comfortable. It was a hard-learned lesson. But people want to be treated as they want to be treated. Not as you want to treat them.

PRINCIPLE 4: *If you can't solve a customer's problem, at least say what you can do.*

Don't say, "I'm sorry, we're out of that book," (in other words, you have a problem, friend). Say, "We don't have a copy in stock, but I can check our other stores for you." At least the second approach indicates the clerk doesn't have the book, but he does have the problem to solve. So the customer can now let go of the problem. Nothing is more irritating than a mindless robot who in essence says, "I'm sorry, but I can't help you . . . period."

PRINCIPLE 5: *If a customer must be referred to someone else, at least have the courtesy to stay with the customer until the connection with the other party is made.*

This is true whether it is on the telephone or in person. Take the responsibility to run interference through your company's bureaucracy and make sure there is a clean handoff to the next person. Too many times, customers are told they must take the initiative to wander around without help to find the right department or the right person or the right telephone number they need to call.

For example, don't say, "I'm sorry that's not my department—you'll have to call . . . " Instead say, "Let me take you to Mrs. Harris to introduce you . . . " Then, before leaving the person with Mrs. Harris, ask them, "Is there anything else I can help you with before I leave you?" You have done your job, and by that last question, you demonstrated that to your customer.

PRINCIPLE 6: *If customers are angry, there's a reason. Deal with the reason, not their anger.*

Most customers prepare themselves to receive an insensitive, bureaucratic response to their problems. Anger can often be defused with sympathy. "I don't blame you for being angry that the dress doesn't fit. . . . Let's see what I can do about it for you." In other words, focus on discovering a solution *with* a customer. In the customer's mind, the two of you are on opposite sides of the problem.

You must convince that customer that you have come over to the "other side."

PRINCIPLE 7: *The resolution of a customer complaint begins with an agreement on a course of action—not an action itself.*

As I've just said, most problems arising out of botched customer treatment involve emotions. These must be dealt with first. Consider this: "Why don't you leave your car here and we'll look at it?" How much better it would be to say, "You may be right in suspecting that your front-end is out of alignment, but it could be caused by your tires. . . . Let's switch the tires to see if the car pulls in the opposite direction. . . . That won't take but a minute and is less expensive than putting the car on the alignment rack . . . Would that be agreeable to you, Mr. Clark?"

When a customer has gotten what he didn't want (the wrong suit, a compact car, no book, or an incorrectly addressed letter), it's also reasonable for him to expect he is not going to get his problem resolved either. After all, the person who has goofed it up can't be relied on to straighten it out. Moreover, a wronged customer feels powerless to bring about the necessary corrective action. Getting an agreement before acting is both symbolic and practical. It is symbolic because the customer is invited to participate in identifying corrective action. It is practical because it avoids doing something—even something that would work—that the customer isn't convinced will be satisfactory.

PRINCIPLE 8: *Do something more than the customer expects, then be sure that the customer knows it!*

Recently my wife took her car in for the third time to have the mechanic do something about its squealing brakes. Nothing could be found wrong. She refused to accept the car back. The service supervisor concluded the problem was the brake rotors. The conversation went something like this: "Mrs. Franklin, your brake rotors are thin; the manufacturer doesn't recommend turning them. We'd like to replace them and will do it for our parts cost only, if you are willing to leave your car with us tonight. Can someone pick you up and bring you back tomorrow?" They did more than expected, despite the return trips she had made to resolve the problem. And they were willing to lose money to make things right. After all, they were the brake experts, not she.

I've said on many occasions that customers have an internal accounting system. They view a purchase as a favor. After all, your customers can buy their products and services from anyone, but they chose to do business with you. Whether you conducted the business transaction correctly or incorrectly, customers now view the purchase as a favor, as a "credit," and they "debit" your side of the ledger so that you are always working your way out of a deficit condition with customers. This shop did a good job of breaking even in the only way it counts to a customer.

When you or one of your employees has fouled something up, you really owe the customer—big time. So it is essential that you not only correct a problem, but also you must be willing to lose money to set things straight. If Federal Express, for example, fails to deliver by 10:30 A.M., the service is free. They didn't do what they promised: "Absolutely, Positively, Overnight." I recently took my daughter to a very nice restaurant to celebrate her thirteenth birthday. The service was slow, and the waiter had reduced my bill before he handed it to me. And he told me why it was reduced. Just like the mechanic's approach—"We'll switch your front tires to see if the car pulls then in the opposite direction, and we'll do that at no charge to you. . . . How does that sound?" It sounds like a winner talking!

BEFORE CLOSING . . .

No discussion on how to treat customers would be complete without talking about the most abusively insensitive but most commonly used practice in mistreating customers. It's called telephone discourtesy. To wit: "Will you hold please?" (Click.) Is that some sort of question? If so, why am I given only half a nanosecond to answer? The fact is, it isn't a question—it's an order. Why not just go ahead and say it: "Look, Turkey, can't you see I'm busy? . . . Get in line and wait your turn." Let's not beat around the bush about it. I say give 'em both barrels.

I've given a lot of thought to the lack of telephone courtesy. Maybe I've watched Andy Rooney too much, but like him, I have often asked myself, "Why do you suppose they don't do something about that?" Then it hit me! Office life is sort of dull, but it can be livened up by the skillful use of the phone. Think of it as a game. Now the purpose of the game is to keep your caller "in play." In other words, if he hangs up in frustration, you lose. Here are six really good zingers that are guaranteed to incense your callers and push them right out to the edge of sanity. I wish I could claim they were original, but I learned them from businesses I call—maybe even yours.

• First, install more incoming lines than an octopus could handle. What fun you'll have watching all those lines lit up and blinking. Why, it'll look like the NORAD Command Center under a Soviet missile attack. And watch that receptionist scramble—Frank Tarkenton, eat your heart out. Make sure that you provide absolutely no backup for overflow calls—like calls that ring more than three times. That would be cheating. The purpose here is to see how quickly you can transform your receptionist into a ticking time bomb. Incidentally, as your business grows and requires more lines, don't make them outgoing lines only. That too would be cheating. Install a second receiver instead and make your receptionist use both hands and both ears. That's what they're for, aren't they?

• Never answer the phone before the twenty-first ring. Make the caller think "Did I call the right number?" That way he'll hang up and call again. Let it ring twenty-one more times. Now he'll think, "Does anyone work here?" Don't you wish you could see the puzzled expression on the caller's face? Maybe you will. He may get in his car, drive over to your place, and press his face against your office window to see if you've moved. Then you could jump out from hiding behind your desk and holler, "Surprise!"

• Make sure your receptionist speaks at a minimum rate of one thousand words per minute. Did you ever see that motor-mouth on TV who delivered the ad pitch at light speed? That's what I had in mind. What you want is someone who can blitz through your company's name at ninety miles per hour. Like, "Hello, this is X!#? + @0." If your receptionist can't talk that fast, insist that your company name be mumbled. The trick is to get the caller to say, "Huh?" You see, most callers are too embarrassed to ask for the company's name again, and if they're returning a call originated by someone in your company, they won't have the foggiest idea who the heck they're talking to. And if the caller got your number by mistake, you may be able to keep that sucker in the dark for fifteen minutes before he finds out he's talking to the wrong company.

• Set new world records by seeing how long you can keep people on hold before they hang up. You could have contests with this idea. I have a friend who was kept on hold so long, he forgot why he had called. The longest known hold in telephone history is twenty-three minutes. I know because I set it. I even had time to eat a sandwich and write a letter to my mom. When the receptionist finally got back to me, she said, "Who have you been holding for?" and I said, "I have been holding for . . . ever."

• Never volunteer information or provide help to your callers. Let 'em dangle. Here's one I like: "I'd like to speak to Mr. Jones, please," says the caller. "He's out to lunch." (Long silence.) Is that a statement of his mental condition? Will he ever return? If your receptionist remains really quiet, the caller may begin to wonder if there's still someone on the line. Keep the caller in suspense. Force him to break the silence by asking your receptionist if she has any interest at all in taking a message. But nothing should be written down until the caller's message has been stated fully. Then have your receptionist say, "Wait, I'd better write this down. What was the message again?" It's really fun when the message is a long one. And, oh, I almost forgot the most important part. What the receptionist really writes on those little pink pads isn't the message but simply, "Call Mr. Smith: 934-1047." That way, when Mr. Jones calls back, Mr. Smith gets to repeat his message a third time.

• One I recently heard is what I call the "Polite Caller Jerk-Around." The polite caller is one who volunteers his name without being asked. "Hello, this is Willis Cook, may I please . . . " Have your receptionist shout, "Who?" "Willis Cook . . . " "Who? . . . " "W-I-L-L-I-S C-O-O-K . . . " "Could you spell that name?" The purpose here is to make your callers think they must be speaking in a foreign language. This trick works best with simple last names like Smith or Jones or Cook. The receptionists that are really good at this can spend up to two or three minutes just getting a caller's name. Maybe his sanity will go next.

Of course, there are many variations of these basic telephone techniques that will insult and frustrate your callers. Like disconnecting them from time-to-time. A disconnect after a long hold is really a nice combination. Once I called a company at 10:00 A.M. and a recorded message said, "The office is closed for lunch . . . we will return at 1:00 P.M." I thought that was a nice touch. With a little creative thinking, I think telephone rudeness can be raised to a new art form.

Recently I called a company whose receptionist was the grand champion of rudeness. But this time there was a new voice. "Good morning, this is the ABC Company. I'm handling other calls, so may I put you on hold please?" What is this? No cattle prod? No opening insult? I was in shock. She only lasted a week. Not a team player, I guess.

Excuse me. I've got to make a call.

CHAPTER
EIGHT

COMPETING IN THE SERVICE ECONOMY

How to Position a Firm Whose Product Is Service

In 49 B.C. Julius Caesar crossed the Rubicon, a river dividing Cisalpine Gaul and Italy, to begin his march upon Rome. It was an act that would change his country forever. Suetonius reports that upon crossing the Rubicon, Caesar said, *"Alea inacta est"* ("The die is cast"). There could be no turning back. Once over the river, Caesar had violated the orders of the Roman Senate and was committed to fight Pompey in open civil war.

The U.S. economy crossed its Rubicon in the mid-fifties as it entered a new economic era from which there would also be no turning back. Before the mid-fifties, the production of goods created more jobs and represented a greater share of the gross national product than the service sector. After that, the reverse was true, and the service sector has continued to grow every year since. There are now more people employed by McDonald's than are employed by U.S. Steel, a phenomenon that caused George F. Will to write in a *Newsweek* column, "Golden arches, not blast furnaces, symbolize the American economy."

Here are some service industry facts that will put the importance of our new economy into perspective. Fifteen million new service jobs were created between 1975 and 1985 — about nine out of every ten jobs created in that period. And contrary to the claims made by the liberal press, more than half of the people employed in service industries earned wages above the national average income. Moreover, it's the high-pay, high-skill service jobs that are increasing fastest—not the low-pay, low-skill service jobs. So we aren't becoming, as some claim, a nation of janitors, sales clerks, and warehouse attendants. Even capital is more efficient in service jobs. A 1983 article in *Business Week* reported that technology investments in service workers were twice as productive as the same money invested in industrial workers.

When local and regional economies serve up lemons, the service sector makes lemonade. The Houston economy, for example, while undergoing severe restructuring because of the collapse of oil prices, has nevertheless enjoyed a significant increase in new business starts. Their owners? Laid-off managers and executives. And what kinds of businesses are they starting? Mostly service businesses. The Houston economy is expected to be a booming economy of service entrepreneurs within five years.

Young people often begin their work careers in part-time service jobs. An impressive 7 percent of American workers—one out of fifteen—got their first job under the golden arches of McDonald's. Service jobs are less disrupted by a part-time workforce and are better suited, therefore, to the available work times of high school and college students. While many of these jobs are hardly an enriching work experience, they fulfill an important function, indoctrinating first-time workers to the workforce. Most of these young people will move on to hold more responsible work roles.

But for all that the service sector has contributed to the American economy in the past four decades, it continues to take it on the chin from critics who view the post-industrial economy with alarm. A major oil company recently published a full-page ad in *The Wall Street Journal* headlined, "Oxymoron: a post-industrial economy." None other than Chrysler's Lee Iacocca was reported by *The Washington Post* as saying: "We can't afford to become a nation of video arcades, drive-in banks, and McDonald's hamburger stands." The prophets of an economic doomsday attribute declining U.S. productivity to the rise of its service economy.

Well, partner, those dogs won't hunt. The revenue generated per employee in the service and manufacturing sectors is virtually identi-

cal at around $130,000. But the value added per employee is higher in service sector jobs than in manufacturing sector jobs, primarily because service industry material purchases are less than manufacturing industries. And even though the service economy has some giant firms—phone companies, major banks and brokerage houses, insurance firms, and publishing houses—these giants have produced about as many original ideas in the past seven decades as the U.S. government. The really exciting service innovations have started in small firms:
- Federal Express (reliable, overnight package delivery)
- McDonald's (fast meals of consistent quality)
- Domino's Pizza (home delivery in 30 minutes, or it's free)
- Temporary Employees (pay for what you use)
- Jiffy Lube (10-minute oil change)
- Century 21 (a national realty firm operated by local real estate entrepreneurs)

Unlike manufacturing jobs, which can be lost to cheap foreign competition, it's pretty hard to export a service job. The production, delivery, and consumption of a service almost always occurs in the same place and at the same time, so the revenue stays with the producer rather than with an intermediary or an end-distributor. And service companies, while not recession proof, don't suffer severe downturns as much as their counterparts in manufacturing. Why? Because services can't be inventoried for a later sale. And service oriented products, like a lawn service, can't be stockpiled by customers, allowing the demand for them to be jerked up and down like the yo-yo demand that occurs because products can be stockpiled. (If you've read Chapter 6, "Managing Inventory," you saw how volatile these swings can be.) Consumption of many services also can't be suspended in economic hard times. Product consumption can. For example, the consumption of health care services, maintenance service on durables, and certain personal expenditures continue on an as-needed basis without regard to the economic climate.

These examples demonstrate that service industries aren't the bane of industrial society that they have been portrayed to be. But nevertheless, there's plenty of room to improve their effectiveness. Here are twelve critical issues that must be addressed by any firm which hopes to compete profitably in the service economy of the future.

PERCEIVED VALUE

Services, like tangible products, experience differing value perceptions based on what the service does for its consumer. A product, whether tangible or intangible, is a commodity surrounding know-how. When there's little or no know-how associated with a service, you have an empty shell—a service commodity. Examples of service commodities are:
- Babysitting
- Lawn mowing service
- Letter couriers
- Dry cleaners
- Fast-food counter service

Service commodities don't command high market prices unless there are temporary shortages. Long-term shortages are automated out of existence. Know-how adds value to services and increases its prices. Examples of high value-added services are:
- Landscape architecture
- Legal defense
- Software development
- Specialized consulting
- Creative businesses (like advertising)

Know-how is brandable knowledge that is unique and is delivered by a professional or a group of experts.

Since a service product is either totally or largely intangible, the consumer is exposed to a potential risk in its use. For example, in many cases the consumer must pay or commit to pay in advance of the delivery of a service. If the service is unsatisfactory, it can't be returned for a refund like a product. The perceived risk is reduced when a firm or individual has acquired a reputation for results. For example, Federal Express built its impenetrable service-level reputation on 99 percent on-time deliveries. No other competitor can boast or warrant that service level. If a consumer of a service is concerned with its risk-in-use, that concern can reduce or eliminate the perception of the service's value. Therefore, one of the most important challenges to service providers is to find ways to reduce risk perceptions. This can be done in many ways, but the most common is to create a way to allow the customer to sample the service, to require payment only after the service has been delivered and deemed satisfactory, or to warrant "satisfaction guaranteed"or the service is free.

SERVICE FORMAT

Service format is the way a service is delivered and the expectations that the format creates in the consumer's mind. Wendy's changed the service format for the fast-food industry with the development of the drive-through window. As a consequence of this format change, 40 percent of Wendy's sales went "out the window," which allowed them to use a smaller building and a smaller parking lot. Competitors who have many outlets in the field lose big time when there is a an important format change, and the drive-through window was a competitive master stroke against the industry leader, McDonald's. Restaurants that had not been designed for drive-through windows required major modification to relocate their kitchens. Domino's Pizza also introduced a changed format in the form of home delivery, and some hamburger fast-food restaurants as well as gourmet grocery stores and soft goods retailers are now experimenting with a similar home delivery service. IBM and Sears are joint venturing the PRODIGYinteractive PC home marketing service as the result of research that shows leisure time in America has dropped from twenty-six hours to seventeen hours per week in the last fifteen years. Home delivery formats are booming because, among other things, there's less time to shop.

A service format creates the basis for the "rules of competition." If it's the right format in the eye of the consumer, every other competitor must comply. Sometimes failure to recognize the importance of a format change can have devastating consequences. For example, Wendy's didn't make its breakfast program work. Extending a fast-food restaurant hours into breakfast time was a format change. Over time, consumer buying patterns changed, so that many of the prepackaged salads are now purchased by breakfast customers. They take them to the office to be eaten as lunch to avoid the inconvenience of going out for lunch. Because Wendy's failed to make their breakfast program work, their lunch business has also suffered. On the other hand, McDonald's, Burger King, and Hardees, all of which have successful breakfast programs and sell prepackaged salads, have not suffered the loss of luncheon revenues even though fewer customers may be coming to their stores at lunch time.

Service format is what the customer is buying. The automatic teller machine is a format that provides bank customers with twenty-four-hour access to their money. An air shuttle is a continuous flight service between cities—a different format than scheduled flights. Fast-food is a format. Self-service is a format. A credit card is a format. A 1–800 telephone number is a format. Choosing the correct service format is critical to the success of a service firm because it is inseparable from the customer's perception of value.

TANGIBILITY

The problem with services is their lack of tangibility. Services often can't be sampled, tested in advance, returned if unsatisfactory, or consistently reproduced by substitute providers. So, as I've said before, the customer must often bear all of the risk of use. Service providers should attempt to reduce the perception of intangibility (and, consequently, risk) by packaging the service within a tangible "wrapper."

For example, Spectrometrics, Inc. is an international service firm providing spectographic analysis of engine oil samples—a sophisticated intangible service that spots trace elements in engine oil and predicts when an engine will fail. The user purchases an oil sample bottle and a return mailer for it, both of which are tangible representations of an otherwise difficult to comprehend service. A law firm uses its office decor as a subtle clue to the quality of the legal services a client will be provided, reducing the perception of risk. Pest and lawn services insist that their service providers wear clean uniforms, while NTW, an Atlanta tire retailer, has a "white glove lady" who inspects customer restrooms and waiting areas. These wrappers demonstrate that the companies are fastidious about incidentals, and indicate they will be even more so about fundamentals. They are symbols that provide a tangible wrapper to an otherwise invisible service, enabling the consumer to understand the service and feel more comfortable in its use.

When designing a service format, you must "tangibilize" its intangibles as much as possible. For example, Domino's Pizza guarantees delivery (a tangible) or the product is free. Delivery people are told to *run* to the customer's house—an additional tangible symbol of their fast turnaround time.

PRODUCTIVITY

As mentioned before, service firms are often castigated for poor productivity. What's overlooked by these critics is that even in a manufacturing firm, many employees provide service to the producers; they do not produce the product itself—for example:
- Managers and supervisors
- Order takers
- Clerks and secretaries
- Delivery people
- Customer service personnel

I'm not saying these functions aren't important, but the functions don't directly produce revenue like selling something, making something, or distributing something. But try operating without them. What would happen to the productivity of the producers? So a service business must create a service that's needed by its consumers or else there won't be a market for it. Services are sold to *producers* who become more productive as a result. As an example, I don't paint my house, care for my lawn, or apply pest extermination chemicals. I buy these services from others, freeing me to produce revenue from my business activities. In fact, the revenue I'd lose by performing these services myself is more than the services cost me. This economic fact is the only rationale that gives rise to service markets—a point that has been totally missed by those who say our national productivity is being depressed by the rise of service industries.

Managers and supervisors and support people don't create revenue, but some do add value in other ways. However, if their value-added is low, the revenue per employee or revenue per payroll dollar falls. This is a good indication that productivity has decreased rather than improved with the addition of management and support staffs. For example, I worked with a service firm that had a serious productivity problem. Revenue per employee was low because there were too many managers and clerks who created too little synergy as a group. I wasn't convinced that there were too many people, but I was convinced that the mix of people was wrong—a classic example of more chiefs than Indians. Moreover, the owner, alarmed at the low group productivity, had put a freeze on hiring, so that a lot of work was done in overtime. As I've said before, overtime is a productivity killer—you pay for ninety minutes of work per hour but you get only sixty minutes of work—theoretically.

This company eventually improved its productivity by:
- Using up-to-date technology—in particular, computerizing routine activities.
- Training employees—higher skills required less management.
- Implementing systems and procedures—systems and procedures reduced the need for judgment, discretion, and variability on the part of management, which in turn reduced the need for management.
- Providing a system for feedback—unlike a product company where output can be counted, service output is harder to quantify and requires the development of output "proxies"; several were used by this firm to monitor its performance.
- Maximizing throughput—where automation wasn't feasible, methods were were developed to produce labor-intensive work as quickly as possible without sacrificing quality where automation wasn't feasible.

QUALITY

Quality is probably the most difficult variable to control in a service business. Often quality is a by-product of the skills of the performer. For example, quality is defined in terms of the skills of a hairstylist, a waiter, a retail sales attendant, and an auto mechanic. Service companies invite quality problems if they don't have well-designed and equally well-enforced service delivery systems or service protocols that the service providers are required to follow. In the absence of systems and procedures, a service provider's skills, attitude, and time pressures determine the service quality level.

Breaking service tasks into components often improves their quality as well as the productivity of the provider. Most personnel recruiting firms assign the task of marketing and recruiting to the same individual. A client separated the recruiting and marketing functions and assigned them to different groups of people. In his company the number of candidates recruited annually per recruiter are the highest in the industry because the recruitment and marketing functions are specialized.

MARKETING

Services, particularly high-touch personal services, are hard to market becasue of their:
- Intangibility
- Potential quality problems
- Perception of risk by the consumer
- Format, which has perceived low value
- Marketing and production which often are in conflict when each function can't be separated.

Each of these reasons has been mentioned before. The marketing of a service requires much more focus than the marketing of a product. The service provider must concentrate on identifying "markets within markets" because service products and formats often don't have broad appeal. For example, first class air travel, document delivery, rent-to-own furniture and appliances, and ten-minute oil change are services with limited appeal.

Sometimes a service is marketed to the wrong party. For example, a personnel search service has a higher value for an employer than for the candidate seeking a job. Think about it. Who has the biggest problem? In the case of physician recruitment, most hospitals are faced with problems of declining bed census. Despite the fact that there is a national surplus of physicians, bed census problems have put hospitals into head-on competition, forcing hospitals to recruit physicians into their service areas who will refer patients to fill the hospital beds. The hospital bed census problem is more economically severe than the physician surplus problem. Consequently the recruitment service is marketed to hospitals, and the hospital pays the recruitment fee.

Similarly, services should be marketed, when possible, to the provider of affiliated services. A home loan requires a closing attorney, a termite inspection, title and mortgage insurance, and various other services. The providers of these services should market them to the home loan provider.

Service providers, particularly in small firms, often find themselves with a time conflict. If the service can't be separated from the service provider, which is frequently the case, then the service provider is in a jam. If he's *providing* a service, there's no time to market it; if he's *marketing* the service, there's no time to provide it. Since marketing and production can't be done simultaneously by a single provider, the provider is essentially out of business, or at least out of half of the business, all of the time. Marketing generates business that must then be produced; production takes time away from marketing. It's a thorny problem unless the service company can discover a way to separate service marketing and service production, as my recruiting client has successfully done.

One final important point—the development of a reputation reduces marketing expense. Experts are sought out—they don't have to sell. Reputation brands expertise—find a way to brand yours, and your firm can spend more time producing than marketing.

ORGANIZATION AND OPERATIONS

A service is often transaction-intensive. For this reason, services are virgin territory for improvement through automation and technology. The automatic teller machines significantly improved the organizational efficiency of banking, eliminating the necessity for adding tellers as the number of transactions grow. Unfortunately, bank executives have failed to recognize that the automatic tellers benefit the bank as much as or more than they benefit their customers, so they have begun to levy a charge on the use of ATMs. Explain that to me. Predictably, growth in the use and the installation of ATMs has slowed in the face of these surcharges.

The prompt generation of management information in a service business is critical in spotting problems with quality and productivity. Management information has present value just as money has present value. But the present value of information in a service business is higher than it is in a product business because of the intangibility of services—the provider does not get visual clues that things are going haywire. For this reason, measurements of output, overtime, quality or rework problems, time spent in nonrevenue-producing activities, and the ratio of revenue producers to managers and staff support personnel, are all figures that service-producing firms should monitor closely. When I say closely, I mean week-to-week, maybe day-to-day—not month-to-month. In fact, the best-managed service firms have created a culture in which these critical service parameters are a matter of pride.

To operate a service business efficiently may require putting the customer *in the loop*. For example, copying machine manufacturers now provide extensive instructions that allow customers to troubleshoot routine breakdowns. If that fails, a 1–800 number allows customers to be talked through the correction of a problem in order to get the machine back into operation. Putting customers in the loop allows them to do many activities for themselves that otherwise would have to be performed by the service provider. Improved productivity is the payoff.

LEVERAGING KNOW-HOW

As I've said before, one of the most difficult features of a service product is its inseparability from the service producer. This is particularly true in the performance of a personal service. However, interesting strides have been made in leveraging personal know-how by using junior associates to provide the more routine aspects of the personal service. For example, doctors have always used nurses to provide routine services, but they are now using physician's assistants to perform certain examinations that do not require the extensive knowledge of a doctor. An anesthesiologist leverages know-how through certified registered nurse anesthetists whom they supervise during operations. Allergists, after an initial diagnosis and the prescription of an injection protocol, have the injections performed by nurses. Law firm and accounting firm seniors provide oversight and know-how to junior associates, who perform routine tasks associated with a client's needs. Insurance companies and financial service companies use junior staff to perform the due diligence necessary to evaluate a client's risks and needs.

STANDARDIZE THE TANGIBLE— CUSTOMIZE THE INTANGIBLE

Service efficiency improves when routine elements of the service are standardized allowing the intangible elements to be customized to individual needs. For example, a will (a tangible) is modified to your need (an intangible). A lawn treatment service (a tangible) carries with it customized handwritten service notes describing particular lawn needs and problems that the customer may be experiencing (an intangible).

Once a service format is determined, the systems, procedures, and organization must be designed to maximize productivity, deliver the expected quality level, and manage the capacity of the service system so that it will respond to demand swings without deterioration in productivity and quality. Remember the problem experienced by the restaurant when it was overwhelmed by its own success? Standardize the routine tasks; customize the nonroutine.

As has been mentioned previously, a company will often serve two or more niches in the market, each requiring different service levels. For example, a securities firm may provide to one set of clients a full range of advisory services—a customized service. To another set of clients, it might provide a low-touch, brokerage service—a more routine service. If the same organization provides both levels of service, the tendency is to overserve one client group and underserve the other. Therefore, the organizations should be entirely separate.

PRICING

Pricing is a reflection of the amount of know-how required to provide or perform the service, in other words, it documents perceived value. Pricing is also symbolic. One noted national motivation speaker receives a fee of $10,000 per speaking engagement. He could charge a lower fee, but the symbolism of the lower fee would put him in a category with many other speakers. Positioning himself through pricing is one motive for the fee charged. After all, how can he be one of the best and also be the cheapest? Pricing also aligns demand with capacity. When a service provider has more business than can be handled, prices should be raised to remove those customers from the market who are most price sensitive. In the speaker's case, the price is also keyed to the speaker's capacity,—mainly, a desire to spend no more than one hundred nights per year on the road.

Several ratios indicate service pricing effectiveness. A measure of productivity in a service system, as mentioned before, is revenue dollars generated per employee. I don't mean revenue per revenue-producing employee; I mean all employees—every warm body in the company. As an organization grows, the number of nonrevenue-producing employees often increases faster than the revenue-producing employees. If that happens, the revenue-per-person would fall, alerting service company managers that potential productivity problems exist.

A second ratio that should be watched is the service contribution margin—the revenue dollars produced per payroll dollar. Service pricing obviously must cover the cost of payroll, but pricing must also cover corporate overhead expense, sales expense, materials expense, and a reasonable profit. What is the optimum spread in revenue dollars per payroll dollar? It varies from company to company. I have seen ratios of 1.8 to 1 in a general lines insurance company—which means the service contribution margin is less than 50 percent—and I have seen ratios of 5 to 1 in an equipment rental company. An equipment rental service achieves significant leverage from its capital assets, driving up the service contribution margin. But low revenues per payroll dollar may also signal a poor use of support staff. Highly paid people are presumably the most valuable to the company. They should devote themselves strictly to duties that they are uniquely qualified to do, using lower paid staff to perform tasks requiring lower qualifications. An accounting firm principal, for example, might initially meet with a new client to whom he would introduce an associate who is assigned to the client. The associate performs research, calculations, and routine tax preparations for the principal's review. While the accounting firm may have a low revenue-per-person ratio (because it employs more staff associates), it could still have a high revenue-per-payroll ratio (because the principals achieve considerable leverage through their junior associates).

EMPLOYEES

Employees determine the service level in all businesses. But that fact is most critical in a service business. As many times as I have stayed at a Marriott hotel, Bill Marriott never waited on me. As many miles as I have flown on Delta Air Lines, its president has never served me a meal. As often as I am in my local bookstore, the owner has never searched for a title for me. But in all three cases, their employees did. A culture must be created in which the desire to provide unparalleled good service is obsessive. Jan Carlzon, president of Scandinavian Airlines System, turned his company around from an $20 million loss to a $54 million profit in one year. How? He did it by preaching a litany of customer service sermons centered on the theme that his company was confronted with 50,000 "moments of truth" each day. Research had shown that the average passenger came into contact with five airline employees, each contact being a "moment of truth"—an opportunity for SAS to show its stuff. When pilots arrived late at their destinations, they could expect either a personal telephone call from Carlzon asking for an explanation or a message for the pilot to call Carlzon.*

Not long ago, I was to speak to a trade convention on Long Island. Everything went wrong. My plane arrived late, so I didn't reach my hotel until after midnight. My luggage didn't arrive when I did and was delivered to the hotel in the wee hours of the morning while I was asleep. When the attendant delivered my clothes bag to the room the next morning, the suit and shirt I was to wear looked like they had been slept in. And I was scheduled to speak at 10:00 A.M.

I called the desk to see if I could get my suit and shirt pressed and was told the normal pickup was 10:00 A.M. and clothes were returned at 5:00 P.M. When I explained the dilemma to the desk clerk, there was a pause—then she said she'd send someone up. To make a long story short, the hotel manager sent my suit and shirt to a local dry cleaner, had the attendant wait for it, and returned it to my room by 9:00 A.M. And the charge was the usual fee for pressing a suit and shirt. Needless to say, I was effusive with my praise, and though the service was priceless, I gave each person a big gratuity for going beyond what could be reasonably expected even in my desperate situation, and I've used it as an example in many speeches.

The following lesson can be learned from such experiences. Employees perform to the level of their boss's expectation. They don't provide outstanding service because of systems and procedures. Remember: in business, you get—not what you expect—but what you expect *and* inspect. When the boss doesn't follow up by auditing service levels, and when he doesn't come down hard on lapses in customer service, the message comes through loud and clear to the

---

*Carlzon has now published a book entitled, *Moments of Truth* (Ballinger, 1987).

employees: service isn't that important. The rules are there; the enforcement isn't. But look at all the excellent service companies in this country. Delta Air Lines, for example. It's all in the leadership.

CUSTOMER RELATIONSHIPS

The worst thing you can do in any business is to lose touch with customers after the delivery of a product or service. "Bugs" Burger has service audits performed by his daughter to assure that the quality level of his pest extermination company is what it's advertised to be. He's that interesting character I've mentioned before who dropped out of the National Pest Control Association because they wouldn't change their name to the National Pest Elimination Association. ("Bugs" claimed their job wasn't to control pests, it was to eliminate them.) Customer relationship is jealously guarded in his business. As I pointed out earlier, if a step is accidently omitted when the pest elimination service is provided, the service person is to call back to the office and alert his supervisor of the oversight. If "Bugs" 's daughter finds out that the service step was not provided when she conducts her service audit, woe be unto that service rep. This is the company whose motto every service rep knows by heart: "Mistakes are forgiven, liars aren't."

Many companies conduct customer satisfaction surveys. I have a client whose company conducts them by telephone continuously. Hotel checkout counters and rooms contain a satisfaction card asking customers to rate their service. Doug Davis owns White Oak Landscape Company, a fast-growing commercial and residential landscape contractor in a large southern city. Immediately after the installation of a landscape, Doug calls the customer and asks, "Did you get what you paid for?" He calls again one month later to see that the landscape is still satisfactory to the customer.

Home Depot, one of the fastest growing do-it-yourself retailers in the United States, employs do-it-yourselfers as salespeople. Bernie Marcus and his senior executives personally train the salesforce in ways to help customers. If you buy a kitchen sink from Home Depot, the salesperson can tell you how to install it — and usually will volunteer the information. The salespeople are enthusiastic about what they do because they are being paid to pursue their hobbies — fixing things. NTW, a large tire retailer, provides brake and alignment services to customers. It's an industry that's been sullied by fast-buck artists and incompetent mechanics. But NTW has built a reputation for dealing squarely with customers and cultivating long-term customer relationships. Customers are given choices and advice when a potential repair is "on the line," meaning it could be delayed if the customer chooses. But the customer is helped to understand the consequences of delaying a repair so an informed decision can be made. Customers also are encouraged to return their cars two thousand miles after a repair for a free inspection, allowing a mechanic to reinspect work for latent defects. More importantly, this free service demonstrates to customers that the company is interested in the quality of its work, unlike the "take the money and run" *modus operandi* that typifies many brake and alignment repair shops.

Obviously, the most effective advertising is an unsolicited referral by someone whom a potential customer trusts. Developing relationships with customers initially, then maintaining those relationships to insure repeat sales, is simply good business. Unfortunately, most businesses end the relationship when they have your money.

COMPETITIVE BARRIERS

The bane of the service industry is its ease of entry—usually. Because many service industries have low initial capital requirements and easily learned know-how, the industry becomes overpopulated with mom-and-pop businesses, resulting in marginal industry profits. Moreover, most service businesses have no economies of scale, so getting bigger doesn't produce a competitive benefit and may, in fact, produce diseconomies of scale. The challenge in a service business is to find ways to erect entry barriers that discourage potential "me too" competitors from jumping into the business.

For example, Spectrometrics, Inc., the oil analysis company that I referred to earlier, has created an enormous database from the millions of oil samples it has tested since the business began operation. This database consists of trace element histories on thousands of different types of engines, allowing computers to compare an incoming sample with samples from engines of similar age and type to predict when the engine will fail or wear out.

A competitor spectroscopist, could equip and staff a lab and compete against Spectrometrics—except for the fact that the most important resource, the database, would have to be created. This would keep a potential competitor from being truly competitive for years. Similarly, Jiffy Lube, because it has over a thousand units in operation, possesses an invaluable database that relates store revenues to the demographics of surrounding communities. This is a distinct competitive advantage when locating future units. Clearly, when data developed over years of operating history can be used to the disadvantage of new firms entering the industry, older service firms can have a competitive barrier for some time.

Capital assets and economies of scale provide a distinct entry barrier. For example, Federal Express and MCI each had to build an entire system before any part of it was viable. In other words, piecemeal development wasn't possible—customers aren't interested in sending packages or making calls to a few cities. The capital required to create the system was staggering. Similarly, cash requirements create a competitive barrier that keeps many temporary staffing businesses small. Why? Because the temporary employee expects to be paid weekly, or at the end of an assignment if it's less than a week, whereas the service business owner often invoices a client monthly and usually will not be paid for yet another month. Consequently, the temporary business service owner is financing forty-five to sixty days of payroll costs for each client. And the larger the business grows, the more cash it consumes to finance the cash gap between paying out and getting paid.

Competitive barriers can also be created in more subtle ways. Loan brokers, for example, rely heavily on contacts and the "good old boy" network to quickly place unconventional loans for clients. It's a relationship business, and new entrants must create a similar network of clients—which is not an easy task. Insurance carriers sometimes place computer terminals in the offices of their larger general agents, enabling the agents to gain instant access to policy information on insureds. This creates a virtually paperless office, faster processing of claims, and the general agents are able to operate with lower expenses than competitors. Until those competitors increase their premium volume, they can't qualify for the terminals. This may mean years of working at a competitive disadvantage.

SERVICE PERFORMANCE INCENTIVES

As previously mentioned, service quality and service productivity are often hard to control. Assuming you have designed a service system format that delivers the advertised service level, the people who work in that system are its principal variables. Incentives for improved service quality and productivity are a key element in assuring that the people deliver the service level you are promoting. The design of service incentives is a subject itself, and incentive design is unique to each job situation. But in all cases, a baseline of historic company or employee performance must be determined so that company or employee performance going forward can be judged in terms of this baseline. This is the basis of an incentive payment program. (See Chapter 10, "Winning Together," for a fuller discussion of this process.) The examples that follow demonstrate how service incentives work.

When customers have their tires rotated and balanced or have new tires mounted, vehicles are sometimes damaged by mechanics who don't pay attention while maneuvering cars in a confined space. Dents, scratches, outside mirrors that are broken off, hub caps that aren't replaced tightly and later come off—these are common occurrences in a tire-mounting shop. Damage results in customer claims that must be paid, but worse still, an irritated and inconvenienced customer will likely be lost forever—that's the real cost. NTW, the tire retailer I mentioned earlier, has made impressive inroads in reducing these damages and their consequent customer claims. How? The company calculated its historic claims for each store and budgeted them as a line-item store expense. If damage claims for any month are less than the budgeted amount, the remainder is paid out to the tire mechanics as a bonus. If claims exceed the budget, the overbudget amount is carried forward to the next month, potentially reducing the amount that could be paid out to mechanics in that month. You may wonder how the company wins if it pays out the entire claim expense savings to its mechanics. Goodwill. Preventing customer hassles is more important than the monetary expense. Also, tire mechanics perform a very routine service and their wage levels aren't high, so the bonus helps them. Peer pressure to protect the bonus encourages extra care when moving cars around in the shop.

The second example involves a company that sells a proprietary software package that it will customize to its customer's requirements. There were both productivity and quality problems—too many overtime hours, too much time on the phone talking with customers, too many meetings, and too many errors that irritated customers who requested software changes. A baseline of historic work output per hour was established. Then a service incentive was created that would pay off when there was a drop in overtime, errors, and wasted time. Improvements were converted into salary bonuses paid monthly. Predictably, productivity began to improve, errors fell to less than 1 percent, and overtime was virtually eliminated.

BEFORE CLOSING . . .

Like it or not, our economy is restructuring itself around the transfer of know-how—services founded on selling or using information. Because services don't usually require a complex distribution system, the intermediaries required in the distribution of a product-based economy will be conspicuously absent in the future. Knowledge workers are replacing muscle workers.

The use and sale of information has been virgin territory for service entrepreneurs, and I think that will even be more so in the future. It will certainly be a very different economy than the one in which our parents worked. And the one in which our children work will be even less recognizable. The naysayers and service industry critics can wring their hands and roll their eyes, but I think Dorothy had it right when she fell into the Land of Oz: "Toto, I don't think we're in Kansas anymore."

CHAPTER
NINE

WHAT CAUSES UNDERPERFORMANCE?

Is the System Working Against Your People?

Martin Luther King, Jr. has said:

> If a man is called to be a street sweeper, he should sweep streets even as Michelangelo painted, or Beethoven composed music, or Shakespeare wrote poetry. He should sweep streets so well that all the hosts of heaven and earth will pause to say, here lived a great street sweeper who did his job well.

Most don't. Many can't, because even the best-intentioned people can be set up to fail if they work in a system that works against them.

Underperformance is almost always blamed on the employee. In fact, a cynic said, "No employee is totally worthless . . . he can always be used as a horrible example." But, the bottleneck is at the top of the bottle—and in business, that means management is often at fault. So, when things go haywire, I look first to see if failure is built into the system.

For example, I once read of a U.S. Army officer stationed in Aachen, Germany, a city that had been recently occupied as World War II drew to a close. He was ordered to London immediately, and, therefore, went to the U.S. Army headquarters to get his traveling papers. The sergeant in the adjutant's office said that the only plane leaving for London for the next several days would be leaving in thirty minutes and the airfield was twenty-five minutes away. The officer knew he couldn't travel without orders, and that process normally took anywhere from several hours to several days in a well-established headquarters. This headquarters had been opened only one day and was totally disorganized. But the officer persisted in explaining his need to travel. The sergeant laughed, and in a few minutes produced the travel orders. The officer was shocked. What efficiency! But the sergeant said, "Sir, you're just lucky that we weren't organized." In other words, had they been, the headquarters would have underperformed.

The majority of eight thousand seventeen-year-olds who were surveyed in a recent cultural literacy test

- Thought that the Alamo was an epic poem by the Greek poet Homer.
- Identified Socrates as a great American Indian chief.
- Believed Leningrad was a city in Jamaica.
- Couldn't place the American Civil War in the correct century.
- Didn't know which national document contained the phrase, "We hold these truths to be self evident. . . . "
- Thought the Great Gatsby was a magician.

But the problem isn't with the student—it's with the teachers and the education system. Both the military headquarters and cultural literacy examples are clues telling us to cast our nets broadly when looking for answers to underperformance. And when I've done that, I've found that there are ten major reasons for underperformance in business.

POOR TRAINING AND PLACEMENT

I recently went to a fast-food restaurant with my son and his friend. I wanted them to eat a light lunch, so I ordered a "one trip" salad bar for each of the boys, a regular salad bar for me, and three small drinks. As you know, the cash register in a fast-food restaurant is not really a cash register, it is a computer terminal, and the keyboard is laid out with various product names. Therefore, the operator only had to find "one-trip salad," "salad bar," and "small drink" in order to ring up my purchase. This guy passed his finger over every button on the keyboard for *each order entry*! He was in mental meltdown. I believe I even saw wisps of smoke come out of each ear! And the order? I got one regular salad bar and two prepackaged shrimp salads. Apparently he had confused a "one-trip" salad with a "one shrimp" salad. Instead of three cups, I got only two.

This wasn't the first time I've gotten bad service in a fast-food restaurant. It's a typical example of poor training, poor selection, and a general indifference by the store manager regarding who works the counter. Now, make no mistake, fast-food dining is not expected to be a gourmet experience, but the inability to get adequate personnel is shutting down the industry's competitiveness. So the industry is responding by experimenting with ways to automate people out of the system, since they are its biggest bottleneck. From what I hear, the fast-food restaurants of the future will have very few people, and the product will be prepared, packaged, and delivered to the consumer automatically.

A recent General Accounting Office study discovered that IRS "service representatives" (I believe that term is an oxymoron) gave wrong answers to routine tax questions 40 percent of the time during the prior tax season. Again, poor training.

Training is often abbreviated because workers aren't productive while they're being trained. In other words, they aren't generating revenue. And the effects of poor training are usually detectable only over long periods of time. Why? Because no one writes a check to someone called "Poor Training." Therefore the impact of poor training is not as dramatically demonstrated as, for example, a decline in sales or profits.

Nevertheless, the economic argument for improving worker and manager training is compelling. Consider this: I was engaged by a small company to train graduate engineers who had worked up through the ranks to become project managers and senior program managers. I sketched out a design for the training program, estimated the cost of it, and presented it to the owner of the company. He nearly fainted. He said, "That's a lot of money!" I agreed that it was, but I also said that everything is relative. There were thirty engineers to be trained in this program, and they were paid approximately $30,000 each on average. So I said to the owner of the company, "Let's assume that whatever value there will be in the training course will be fully realized and depreciated, and that its effects will not exist after two years. Is two years a fair period within which all training benefits will be realized?" The owner agreed that it was. So I pointed out to him that during those two years he would pay these thirty people about $1.8 million, and I again asked him, "How much money would you spend to maintain a $1.8 million computer? A $1.8 million building? A $1.8 million product line?" The cost of the training program paled into insignificance. Everything is indeed relative.

Training is needed at every level of your company from the rank and file to management—including you!. In most cases, however, whatever training does exist is devoted to management and supervisory personnel, so that rank-and-file training is woefully neglected. But it is a fact that there is a right way and a wrong way to answer the phone, make a bed, close a sale, or write a letter. And there are more wrong ways than there are right ways. Left to their own experiences, rank-and-file workers invariably learn to do their jobs the wrong way.

I was in Savannah, Georgia, to speak to a convention several years ago, and I had messed up both of the beds in my room. The maid asked permission to clean up the room as I was preparing the final touches on my speech, and I watched her make up both beds in less than three minutes. She stood between the two beds, stripped the sheets and covers, replaced the sheets and covers and tucked the coverlet under the pillow on one side, turned around repeated those steps on the second bed, then went to the far side of one bed to complete it, returning to the far side of the other bed to complete it. As I said, in less than three minutes! I said to her, "That's impressive!" But as we talked, it was apparent that she had been well-trained, and most importantly, she was paid by the room.

Training is not a one-shot affair. Training must be ongoing if it is to be effective. As a person does a job over and over again, it knocks all of the "sharp edges" off his abilities, making periodic retraining necessary. But even knowing this, small businesses neglect training at all levels of their companies because they believe in four myths. The first myth is, "The work is 'obvious'." That's never true. There is no job that is so obvious that it can't be studied and found to have a "best" way to do it. This best way can then be taught to the person doing the job. Furthermore, people must understand why the job should be done in a particular way, or they will employ their own methods.

The second myth is, "I can't afford training." Nonsense! You pay for it anyway. You pay for it in sloppy work practices; in customers who become irritated, leave, and never come back; in co-workers who must do their own jobs as well as the untrained person's job. There are many ways that training is paid for. Why not turn these wasted dollars into training dollars and produce good performance rather than underperformance?

The third myth is, "Let the fellow employees teach them." They will. Their way. The worse thing you can do is lose touch with a new employee by turning him over to co-workers to "teach him the ropes"—probably not the ropes you want taught.

The fourth myth is "On-the-job training is the best way to learn." Again, nonsense! On-the-job training is irritating to customers and unbearable to co-workers. I don't think employees in training should be put on the front line where they interact with customers, but that's especially true if the employee is wearing a "Trainee" badge. The symbolism of a trainee badge is awful. It says to the customer, "Don't expect as much from me as you should . . . I'm in training . . . at your expense." Trainees who are completing their learning on the job should first be trained off the job. Only then should they assist someone who knows how to do the job. In time a trainee may do the job under close supervision. After that, the person is no longer a trainee and may be allowed to work with normal supervision.

Training isn't a program—it's a process. Programs have beginnings and endings. Processes are ongoing. And as I've said, if there isn't an ongoing commitment to training all people in your business, eventually whatever training they have been exposed to will depreciate. People are assets—renewable resources. But like any other asset, the tendency is to wear out with use. Through training, that tendency can be reversed; and indeed, training makes people more valuable both to themselves and to you.

But training processes must be correctly designed. As just mentioned, training should start "out of context." In other words, the basics of the job are taught to the employee off the job. After this, training continues "in context;" having learned the basics of the job, the trainee learns the relevance of what has been taught out of context. Then the training continues out of context again to review and understand the basics in the light of having done the job. Finally, the trainee returns to further training, in context, with improved understanding and, hopefully, improved performance.

I have a client who trains all new salesmen for two weeks before they are allowed to work at the sales counter, where the training continues under the supervision of the store manager. Thereafter, the new salesmen, along with all other salesmen, attend weekly sales meetings that have a strong training focus. Even the most mundane tasks performed by mechanics in this particular company are trained into new employees, because the company wants the new mechanics, despite the fact that they have done similar work for other employers, to learn it "our way." The training objective for both sales and mechanical personnel is to maximize service. This translates into minimum waiting times for their customers—a distinct competitive advantage and a benefit to the customer. Employees are monitored by district managers and store managers, and when training gaps are spotted, the individual is sent back for retraining, or if that fails to improve performance, the individual is terminated.

So much for training. Placement has to do with putting the right person in the right job. Mark Twain said, "You can't put a round man in a square hole . . . You've got to give him time to change his shape." I say, you don't have such time—your customers simply won't put up with misplaced, inept employees. But don't give up quickly on an ineffective employee. I have a client with an employee who performed miserably in one role but did well in another. Sometimes people are simply misplaced, rather than incompetent. Poor placement isn't the employee's responsibility—it's yours. A chance in another position is an opportunity to salvage your investment in a new employee's orientation and indoctrination time.

I continually preach to clients and audiences: service, service, service! More business is lost through poor service than through poor products. But the ability to deliver good service begins with good training and correct placement.

DEFECTIVE WORK METHODS

As I've said before, there's a right way and a wrong way to do a job. Workers and managers left to their own experience will invariably find the wrong ways to do their jobs. A consulting associate of mine was engaged to study the way maids clean rooms in a hotel, develop the correct method for the cleanup practices, then teach the correct methods to the maids. For example, if there are six rooms side by side, should the maid make up the beds in every one of those rooms, return to clean the bathrooms, and finally return to vacuum and dust the rooms? Or should a maid clean an entire room before moving on to the next room? I don't know the answer to those questions, but that was the job my friend was assigned to discover—correct work methods.

While in a client's retail store several years ago, I observed an employee dialing a phone (which had a rotary dial) with his left hand, despite the fact that he was clearly a right-handed person. His job was to call customers every week to remind them to come in and make payments on their purchases, and he had to do this eight hundred times every week! A few seconds saved in dialing could amount to a significant weekly time savings. When I asked him why he was dialing the phone with his left hand, which took several seconds longer, he said because the phone was on the left side of the desk he was using. The phone could have been easily moved to the right side of the desk, but he never thought to do it. Because he was inadequately supervised, this man was unthinkingly using a defective work method.

Frederick W. Taylor is well-known in management literature as an early pioneer in work methods design. His classic experiment was with a German immigrant named Schmidt, whose job was to load pig iron onto a railroad flat car. Schmidt's output was loading about twelve and one-half tons of pig iron each day. By studying the job and then programming rest periods between each trip to the flat car so that Schmidt would not work himself into exhaustion by day's end, Taylor was able to increase Schmidt's production to forty-seven and one-half tons of pig iron loaded every day—a 400 percent increase! Taylor was a magnanimous man; he believed in rewarding laborers for increased output, but not too much. For Schmidt's 400 percent increase in output, he received a 60 percent pay raise to $1.85 per day. Taylor defended criticism of this disparity by saying Schmidt was not working harder, just smarter—through improved job design. Schmidt's comments were not recorded.

Taylor's work methods would be considered offensive today. He believed that work divided into small pieces required no thought and, therefore, could be performed more quickly. A curious mix of paternalism and arrogance, and a Quaker by faith, Taylor possessed a strong work ethic and a no-nonsense outlook on life. No doubt he genuinely believed that fitting the man to the job was good for everyone: the laborer's wages increased, company profits increased, and society enjoyed cheaper goods that were produced more efficiently. He also preached an early brand of human relations: "the employer who talks to his men in a condescending or patronizing way, or else not at all, has no chance whatsoever of ascertaining their real thoughts or feelings." But Taylor also characterized the average worker as "so stupid and so phlegmatic that he more resembles the ox in his mental makeup than any other type." And of his experiments with Schmidt he wrote, "The workman who is best suited for handling pig iron is unable to understand this class of work.... He is so stupid that the word 'percentage' has no meaning for him, and he must consequently be trained by a man more intelligent than himself." Undoubtedly, by Taylor himself. Nice guy.

Obviously, I'm not talking about taking work design to Taylor's extremes. But in every office, warehouse, shop floor, and retail store I have had contact with as a consultant, I have seen patterns of ineffective work—paper-handling routines, trucks loaded in the wrong order, route sales and delivery patterns that require wasteful backtracking, and many instances of unnecessary work. Many Burger King restaurants, for example, let customers fill their own drink order, because a cost/benefit analysis determined that it saved both time and cost to allow customers to serve themselves, even if customers go back for free refills.

I was in a client's plant recently in which product is pushed from work station to work station on a roller conveyor. The plant had been in operation for years, but the shop manager had apparently never noticed that the roller conveyor sloped slightly upward. As work was progressively performed at each work station, the product became heavier and harder to push uphill to its final assembly, thus slowing the work process. On another occasion, I was in the office of a client and observed a file clerk going through her refiling routine. She would take a folder from a large table, walk to the appropriate file cabinet, file the folder, return to the table, and repeat the process, one folder at a time. In some cases, her round trip was more than fifty feet. It would have been better to sort the files in alphabetic order, then take all of the "A's" to the "A" file and file them, returning to get the "B's," and so on. She not only would have reduced the refiling time but also would have been a lot less tired at the end of the day.

These two examples show that even the most mundane tasks can be done incorrectly. Poorly designed jobs make people work hard unnecessarily. They also make jobs harder to fill. For example, I worked with a rapidly growing company that relied heavily on its sales force. But it took two years to get a new salesman up to speed—an intolerable problem for a fast-growing firm. After the owner and I studied the activities performed by a salesman, we decided to break the sales job into two jobs—a sales job and a service and support job. By assigning the tasks to two people, where one had done them before, we were able to reduce training time for each job to ninety days. And both tasks were performed as well by two people after ninety days of training as they were by one person with two years' of training and experience. Similarly, I consult with a recruiting firm that, unlike most of its competitors, subdivides the marketing of the firm's services and the recruiting of candidates. Competitors assign the job of marketing and recruiting to the same person. People who can both market and recruit not only are hard to find but also often leave to start their own firms.

The moral of these examples is that almost any job can be broken into tasks that can be learned quickly, and the redesigned jobs can also be filled quicker than would have been possible in the past. Many people fear that job simplification will lead to duller jobs, pointing to the assembly line as an example, but it does not. (An auto assembly line job, for instance, is the epitome of a job that has been pulled into too many pieces. I'm certainly not advocating that.) But simpler jobs make more sense than do complex jobs.

Incidentally, workers don't have a monopoly on working incorrectly. I've seen managers employ defective work methods also. I traveled with the district manager of a client in order to observe how he did his job. He had eight stores in his district, and he was in every one of them each day. Consequently, he was unable to spend much time in any one store, but he was spending a tremendous amount of "windshield time" driving from store to store. I recommended to his boss—my client—that it would be far better if the district managers would go to one store, and stay there a half or a third of a day, thus reducing the number of stores visited daily to two or three. By spending more time in each store, each district manager would be much more effective.

INADEQUATE SYSTEMS AND PROCEDURES

Prior to the Civil War, the basic army fighting unit was a brigade, and it was commanded by an officer whose rank was brigadier. The attacking unit was formed in a square consisting of row after row of riflemen. In those days, the maximum effective range of a musket was about two hundred yards, so the attacking brigade would advance to the defenders and the first row would fire. Then half of the first row would pass around the right side of the square and the other half around the left side, proceeding to the rear as they reloaded their muskets. Following the same procedure, the second row would fire, then the third row, the fourth row, and so on.

However, rifling, developed in the second year of the Civil War, allowed a projectile to be spun in the gun barrel as it was fired, increasing the maximum effective range to a thousand yards. Obviously, the pre-Civil War brigade unit was slaughtered when it continued to fight the old way, so a skirmish line was developed in which the attackers were stretched out in long single rows, requiring the defenders to shoot at a man rather than shoot into a group. But this created another problem—the general officer could no longer easily call commands to his troops because they were so spread out. Consequently, he had to ride up and down behind the skirmish line to give orders. Predictably, many officers were killed. In fact, there were more general officers killed during the American Civil War than in any other war this country has fought—sixty-five in the battle of Gettysburg alone.

Given this new problem, the basic fighting unit was reorganized into squads led by sergeants who were officered by captains. But the lesson to be learned is this: Good people in bad organizations get killed. In the case of the Civil War, technology forced progressive changes in organization and tactics. Similarly, in business, successful companies are often those that have adapted and discovered new work procedures that give them a competitive advantage through cost reductions, more efficiency, better quality control, or some other competitive benefit. The system, not the person, gets the work out correctly.

A correct system converts *unprogrammed* decisions into *programmed* decisions as much as possible. An unprogrammed decision is one in which a person must think; whereas, a programmed decision is one in which the person simply acts. For example, in soccer, I have developed play patterns that allow ordinary, even weak, players to win games. If a forward is unable to shoot on goal, he turns and passes the ball back to a midfielder, and immediately breaks to the center of the field. The midfielder passes the ball to the center of the field where all three of the forwards will be converging. The forwards react to every pass-back situation in the same way. An unprogrammed decision — "what do I do now?" — has been converted into a programmed decision. Business, like soccer, confronts employees with shifting situations that require prompt decisions. Procedures — "if this happens then I do that" — help convert many of those decisions into programmed responses.

A *high-touch* job is one that requires lots of personal involvement. A *low-touch* job is one in which the system produces the work rather than the worker. Good systems and procedures also lower the *mental touch* by converting unprogrammed decisions to programmed decisions and reducing the amount of worker discretion that is required — something that a supervisor must constantly monitor. Furthermore good systems and procedures increase both the capacity of your company and its productivity. Why have more incoming telephone lines than a receptionist can answer? After two or three rings, have a first backup, and if that person is busy, have a second backup. It is infuriating to a caller for a telephone to ring eight or ten times, causing him to wonder, "Does anyone work there?" As the company grows, install lines that are outgoing only. If the added phone lines work both ways, it overworks your receptionist, and the quality of telephone answering and dispatching declines.

I have a client whose company sells tires and performs alignment and brake work. Many cars need only one of those services, but about half of the customers need both tires and alignment service. In an effort to improve shop throughput, I suggested that service people mount the tires when the car is put on an alignment rack. The idea was initially met with resistance—"That would tie up an expensive alignment mechanic who would have to wait for the tire change for five to eight minutes." But, when the times required to bring a car in from the parking lot to a tire rack, return it to the parking lot, then retrieve it from the parking lot and drive it on an alignment rack were added up, the time wasted driving a car back and forth to the parking lot exceeded the expense of having a mechanic stand aside for five minutes.

You should subcontract work, such as payroll, that can be done more efficiently by outsiders. Or, pool work in one place so that it can be done more efficiently by creating a critical mass with some economies of scale. A client with branch offices throughout the country performs all invoicing in Atlanta rather than in the branches because he can create efficiencies that couldn't be afforded in each branch. Similarly, a client in the insurance business processes all claims in one place rather than through his offices over the state because he can handle claims more efficiently if they are pooled and processed.

Don't build in unnecessary constraints—they restrict the flexibility and the capacity of your system. A large auto repair service company at one time encouraged customers to have work done on their vehicles by appointment. That practice built a constraint into the system because work on a particular vehicle had to be done in the appointment time period. Now, customers are encouraged to leave their vehicles; this way work can be queued and requeued as a problem arises—usually parts requirements that stop work until a parts runner returns. If a customer insists on an appointment, one will be given, but the emphasis on appointments versus leaving a car has been reversed because of the unnecessary constraint that appointments impose on flexibility.

If work arrives in bunches, it will temporarily overload the capacity of your work systems. Therefore, have emergency reserve capacity, such as the telephone backup system previously mentioned. As emergency reserves, use people who have jobs that can be temporarily abandoned if more work arrives than can be handled by the routine system.

SYSTEM SHORT CIRCUITS

Inevitably, systems and procedures will be outgrown. In my experience, companies hold on to systems and procedures far too long and often change them only when a total breakdown occurs. So, as systems and procedures age, employees find ways to make do, patch around the inadequacies of the system, and generally make an outgrown system work in spite of itself until a breakdown occurs, precipitating a system overhaul.

But even a correctly designed system is sometimes short-circuited by employees who don't understand the system design or refuse to follow it altogether. In times past, system updates routinely occurred by sending, for example, a white copy to Department A, a blue copy to Department B, a yellow copy to Department C, and so forth. Today, updates are done by computer programs. Screens are sequenced in a particular order, and that order provides the necessary updates. This was not known to one supervisor, who became so annoyed at having to scroll through a succession of computer screens he never used that he wrote a line of code to by-pass them. The result? His company had $200,000 in inventory that it didn't know about, because reorder programs kicked in automatically when other programs were blocked out by the short-circuiting of the "unneeded" screens. This man didn't bother to understand the effect his shunt would have on other parts of the business—but he had time to think about it while he was out looking for a new job.

In another case, a client was being defrauded by his controller despite three consecutive annual certified audits. The controller was caught when the company changed accounting firms. How? The previous auditor skipped verification steps he thought were duplicates of other verifications he had performed. The controller knew this and consequently was able to beat the system, stealing almost $50,000 over the three-year period. It's been said that no system is foolproof because fools are ingenious. Maybe so, but that's why there are checks and balances.

FAILURE TO USE UP-TO-DATE TECHNOLOGY

I worked with a client several years ago whose business was paperwork intensive, involving lots of manual reporting. The company should have automated its operations at least two years before I began working with them, but because they had not, employees were overly stressed and the company was experiencing 240 percent turnover rates. In another instance, a client had computerized some of his operations, but after five years—despite the woeful limitations of his aged system—he was reluctant to junk it and endure the year of debugging that new, custom software typically requires. His business had grown by 300 percent in those five years, and the inadequacies of his hardware and software resulted in management reports that were out of date by the time they were generated; data that were needed to run the business well couldn't be compiled by the antiquated hardware/software; and as a practical matter, his people worked for the computer rather than having it work for them. Failure to use up-to-date technology has many costs. But in most cases, the costs are never known—because no one writes a check for waste, delay, or impossible-to-retrieve data.

By contrast, I have a client—a large medical practice—whose business office consisted of three people in 1983. The computer they were using at that time was primitive by any standard. It was replaced with a used but adequate system that was periodically upgraded. That system has recently been replaced with new hardware and custom software that cost less than the system it replaced, yet it has three times the memory. Throughout the five-year period that I have worked with this client, the number of patients more than doubled, the number of doctors grew from six to fourteen, yet we still have the same three women working in the business office!

Office automation is routinely eliminating jobs human beings once performed, including the supervisors who would be needed to manage these people. But automation is not just limited to offices. For example, in warehouses products are being picked from the shelves by robots that run on rails, go to the correct row, and proceed down the row, raising or lowering their pickers to the correct bin. Delivery truck routing, once determined with "Kentucky windage" (subjective rules of thumb), is being replaced with computer-driven routing that minimizes drive time or maximizes revenue per delivery stop. Timekeeping systems and inventory or asset-tracking systems now employ modern bar-code readers—like those used at your grocery store checkout—to replace manual recordkeeping.

Using up-to-date technology doesn't always mean high technology. It can mean using a forklift to carry something where a person now carries it; contracting out work that can be done better—and usually cheaper—by specialists in areas such as payroll, inventory counting, building maintenance, and janitorial work (Each week American Airlines flies over twelve-hundred pounds of documents to Barbados, where they are transferred to magnetic tape by low-cost labor, then beamed to the central computer in Tulsa via satellite.); or putting phones in cars—where customers can contact the salesmen—or radios in trucks, so that trucks can be diverted to an unplanned pickup.

SUPERVISION

How does supervision cause underperformance? Well, think what a supervisor does—he *manages* work. If a supervisor is *doing* work, he is neglecting supervision. Poor supervisory training often is the cause of "doers" rather than "supervisors." Candidates for supervisors often come up through the ranks, consequently, they know better how to do than to supervise.

Supervisory work is:
- Determining what needs to be done.
- Establishing priorities.
- Assigning work to others.
- Following up periodically to evaluate the status and quality of the work being done.
- Getting incorrect work redone.
- Dealing with the unexpected—breakdowns, bottlenecks, problem employees, and problem customers.

But supervisors need a program to follow in order to supervise effectively. I rode with an area manager as he visited various stores under his supervision. When we arrived at the first store, he checked the customer waiting room, the bathrooms, watched the sales counter in operation, walked through the shop, and went to the warehouse. Because I have worked with the company for a number of years, I knew what he was doing in every case except the last one—the warehouse check. When I asked him what he was looking for, he said he was "checking the stock." "What does that mean?" I asked. He really didn't know. He was simply looking at the stock but didn't know what he was looking for. The fact was, there were many things he could do to make sure that the correct inventory was at the store, in the correct quantities, and located in the correct places, but he had no program that enabled him to do that. The company didn't furnish him sales information that would have allowed him to stock the right inventory items; he had no procedures for moving material from store to store; and there was no system to track where inventory was located throughout the company.

Supervisors must have a program to follow or their supervision will, in many cases, simply consist of watching people work. Systems and procedures can reduce the amount of supervision required but never eliminate it. For example, systems and procedures minimize the number of unprogrammed decisions, which — as I've said before, — often require a supervisor's intervention. Procedures also eliminate the need for workers to use discretion and judgment. Worker discretion often requires constant monitoring by a supervisor. A correctly designed system accomplishes the work, rather than having the people accomplish the work. The supervisor's role is to make sure people are following the procedures. When there is a breakdown, and the procedures have been followed, the supervisor should determine how the procedures can be changed so that the breakdown will never occur again.

Obviously an inadequate supervisor is a drag on the business. The supervisor interferes rather than helps get work accomplished, causing the organization to underperform. Therefore, selecting supervisors is as important as the selection, training, and placement of workers. The really good supervisors are people with "other" orientations. In other words, they are "teaching pros" rather than "playing pros." A playing pro, such as a good salesman or a good mechanic, is really interested in developing his own skills and success. Sure, he can show someone else a few tricks of the trade, but his real preoccupation is with his own performance. Whereas a "teaching pro" may very well be a good salesman or mechanic, but his real forte is spotting and developing talent in other people.

HIGH-VALUE PEOPLE DOING LOW-VALUE WORK

I work with a retail company whose counter salesman in the past would take an order, go into the warehouse area and pull the purchased items, then return to the sales counter to generate an invoice and accept payment. The time the salesman was off the counter pulling stock was about fifteen minutes, and at any point in time throughout the day, about half of the counter salesmen were in the warehouse. Although they were paid by commission, the average salesman's earnings were about $12 an hour. A stock puller could be hired for $6 an hour. When the stock-puller idea was suggested, the initial response was that it couldn't be afforded. Sure it could. The company was already paying for stock-pulling—$12 per hour. Eventually, stock pullers were hired and assigned to each store. Counter salesmen were well-trained, experienced people but their knowledge and experience added absolutely no value to pulling stock. And the company needed fewer salesmen when it got them out of the stock-pulling business.

In another example, a client who owns a steel fabrication company is an outstanding salesman. But he is only an average manager and hates having to return to the office from time to time to straighten things out so that orders can be delivered on time. A business manager, however, could be paid from the margins on $145,000 additional sales, eliminating the necessity for the owner to ever come back into the office from the field unless he chose to. When asked if he could sell an additional $145,000 in product if all of his time was devoted to selling, he said he could do ten times that amount—another instance of a high-value person doing work for which his skills and instincts added no value.

One more example. The salesmen in a company were required to make up their own catalogs, which were loose product sheets placed in the pocket of a folder. They had to type their own correspondence and the customer's order. It was a terribly wasteful use of their time. One salesman's annual sales are $2,000,000, and recognizing the value of his own time, he personally paid his children to make up a week's worth of catalogs on Sundays. But his manager doesn't provide clerical help for the salesmen—they are required to perform the routine clerical work and do many other mundane things that could be done better and more cheaply by someone else. When I asked why clerical help couldn't be provided, the sales manager defended the practice of catalog makeup and letter writing because, as he said, "it's good for them."

All people in small businesses must do work for which they are uniquely qualified, not work they're overqualified to do. When people repeatedly perform tasks—even short-term tasks—for which they're overqualified, the company loses money—something a small business can't afford. When supervisors engage in "doing" work rather than supervising work, the supervisory skills they possess add no value to the work they "do," and supervisory tasks are probably being neglected. All people are high-value people when they do what they are qualified to do.

As a business grows, the owner should be especially careful about adding managers because layers of management are killers. Managers don't produce revenue; consequently, they must add value in other ways. As one example, I worked with a small company whose revenues were about $30 million. There were six levels of management from president to the workforce! I said, "Even the Dana Corporation [a $2 billion company] has only five levels of management!" In one department this small company had several operating groups consisting of workers, their supervisor, a manager of the supervisor, and a manager of the manager! The supervisor provided a valuable function—scheduling, dispatching, and generally controlling the work. That supervisor's boss was partially needed, but primarily he was a supervisory backup when workloads became excessive. However, the next manager was totally useless. He engaged in busywork and, for all intents, simply watched other people work. It's human nature for people to refuse to be insignificant, so his "watching" was accomplished through endless meetings and trivial memos.

In a similar instance, I helped reorganize a company's operations so that the branch production manager and the branch sales manager reported directly to the region manager. There was no branch manager, and each region manager was responsible for four to six branches. The recommendation to operate with no branch managers was initially met with significant resistance by many people in the company. "What is he going to do? . . . There's no job there," I said. "Well," I was told "there just ought to be one there."

There is only one justification for having intermediate management: work will not be accomplished if the management of the work isn't there. The work to be done by a manager must be unique to that manager's job, and the information that he uses to manage should be unique with regard to the information his boss uses or his subordinate supervisor uses. But what often happens is that the intermediate manager looks at data that is merely the compilation of all of the data or information being looked at by his boss or subordinate supervisor. That adds no value whatsoever. So the task that the so-called manager accomplishes is as I've said before, simply to watch other people work.

INSUFFICIENT FEEDBACK

I was engaged by a manufacturer whose business required him to produce thirteen-hundred units each day, and work continued until the thirteen hundred were produced, whether that occurred in eight hours or ten hours. On one occasion, after working ten and one-half hours, it was obvious that the daily production quota would not be met. The next day I was on the production line with the foreman, and I asked him if he was going to make production that day. He looked at his watch. It was ten o'clock in the morning, and his answer was "yes." "How do you know?" I asked. "Because," he said, "if we have run all of the 'double-mold orders' by this time, we will be able to meet today's quota." I asked, "Do these [the production] people know that?" His answer: "No."

Here was a situation in which the foreman knew that the workers would or would not make production because he understood certain mental milestones that were clues to him, but the workers knew nothing. How can people achieve quotas if they don't know what's going on? In this particular case, the foreman responded to my further questions by saying he did go out on the line and praise people for meeting the production quota, but praise is a long way from hard, frequent, data-based feedback.

People love being measured. Why else do people weigh themselves? How satisfying would it be to go bowling if a curtain across the alley blocked your view? You could hear the pins go down, but you wouldn't know which pins, and it would be impossible to score the game.

Feedback changes performance. In one case, the output from three lathe operators in a manufacturing firm was inadequate. Three production graphs were created, one for each lathe, and the lathe operators were told to mark that day's production on their output graph at the end of the day. The company's owner would go into the shop at the end of the day and conspicuously study the graphs so his operators could see him. Predictably, production increased. And I remember in one notable case a lathe operator's output was less than he had produced the previous day, so he quickly pointed out to the owner, as his output graphs were being studied, that his lathe was down with technical problems part of that day. Before graphs were kept, the operator didn't care whether his boss knew why output was off.

Similarly, a mechanical contractor had no idea whether he would make a profit or a loss on a project until the project was complete. Although he personally reviewed and approved payment of every invoice for purchases, he failed to communicate invoice charges to his project managers, who had no idea what had been charged to the project for which they were responsible. Since each project manager supervised several projects at any one time, keeping track of project profit budgets wasn't always easy. Procedures were revised so that the project manager was responsible for using the bid budget as a standard, and once a week he would update a form that showed project cost expended to date. He would also make a projection of an estimated cost to complete the job. All invoices were diverted to the project managers for approval, so they could know which project costs had or had not yet been incurred to complete the job.

Before implementing this procedure, which was essentially a method for providing self-administered feedback, the company had suffered a $300,000 quarterly loss. The first quarter after the program was fully in effect, the company broke even, and in the four quarters following implementation, the company made almost $1 million before interest and taxes. At one weekly company meeting, one of the project managers got into an argument with the owner of the company because a $5 package of sheet metal screws had been charged to one of the manager's projects! Before the self-administered feedback program was installed, he wouldn't have cared.

When quantifiable goals exist, I like to use a graph to demonstrate employees' short-term progress toward their goals. That way everyone who affects the performance can see progress on the graph. Graphs have a positive impact on performance. I saw a cartoon once in which two cavemen were looking at an upward sloping graph on the wall of their cave. One said to the other, "I have no idea what it means, but every time I look at it it makes me feel good." If you're digging a ditch or painting a wall, why do you stop frequently to look at your progress? It's a way of rewarding yourself. And it spurs you on to finish the task.

For a retail client, I had store employees place monthly sales-to-date and gross margin month-to-date graphs in the office area used by the retail sales personnel. For an equipment rental store, I had the office personnel graph credit memos issued, because credit memos were a good indication that someone had made a mistake. In the collection department of another client, I had the collection clerks graph the number of days' sales that were outstanding. Obviously, in this case, I wanted to see a down-sloping graph, indicating good collection results. Feedback should be as prompt and as personal as possible. Graphs are a great way of accomplishing that.

NEGATIVE INCENTIVES

I had my first experience with negative incentives in a summer job at a unionized Western Electric plant while I was a college student. I was told in no uncertain terms to stop working so hard because it made my full-time fellow workers look bad. Although I was not a union member, my co-workers were, and I witnessed several instances where union members physically roughed up a worker to enforce their wishes. Aroundhereisms are, as was mentioned in an earlier chapter, "the way we do things around here," and this plant was filled with negative aroundhereisms.

Positive incentives reinforce people when they perform as they should—they are given bonuses and praise, and they see their good work on graphs or receive other forms of feedback. But the absence of a positive incentive is a negative incentive. "What difference does it make?" the employees think, so they underperform. People do what *they* want to do, and if that isn't what *you* want them to do, look for negative incentives.

Examples. Training conducted in two companies was ineffective because it was performed on the employees' time. In another company, while the employees were paid for time in training, they were trained after a long day's work. They were tired and understandably disinterested in training.

More examples. Reports sent to the corporate office from fifteen retail stores each day were filled with errors. The store managers had to stay late after closing the store in order to complete these reports. Erroneous reports were returned to the errant store manager by accounting personnel (who could have fixed the errors easily) as a penalty for sending in reports with errors in them. When this happened, the store manager would then have a current report to complete plus corrections to the reports that had been returned. Predictably, the store reporting continued to be a mess.

Useless work is also a negative incentive. If people don't understand why something needs to be done, it is perceived as unnecessary and won't be done well. For example, paperwork that's rarely used is a negative incentive. Having to stay late to do something and then being caught in the homeward bound traffic is a negative incentive. Pay raises that are not based on performance are a negative incentive.

Employees who are loyal, hard-working people often have additional work dumped on them because they are dependable. In other words, when other employees don't get their work done on time, the remaining uncompleted work is given to the guy that can always be counted on to get it out. Consequently, an employee who performs well gets more work to do. As the old adage goes—when you want something done assign it to a busy person. Negative incentives.

THE BOSS'S EXPECTATIONS

The final reason for underperformance is the boss's expectations. Pygmalion was a mythical figure who could never find the perfect woman. Therefore, he carved a statue of what he considered to be the perfect woman, treated the statue as if it were real—bringing it gifts and fine clothes—and even making love to it. Venus felt sorry for Pygmalion and sent Cupid to turn the statue into a real woman. Hence, the term "the Pygmalion effect"—your expectations (and hence your treatment) of someone affects what he or she becomes. It is a self-fulfilling prophesy.

Professor Henry Higgins in *My Fair Lady* believed he could convert Eliza Doolittle from a "squashed cabbage leaf" into a duchess. And he did. His expectations of her became a self-fulfilling prophesy.

I've seen expectations at work among youth sports coaches. Teams are formed through a draft process that assures an equal distribution of good players, average players, and weak players. Many coaches neglect the weak players, believing that they have no potential, and these coaches spend their time and attention on the good players — which is the reverse of what they ought to do. But I can tell you from experience that weak players become good players when they're given the same coaching that everyone else receives and when they are *expected* to play on a par with the better players.

Underperformance often results from expectations by a boss that people or things will go wrong. The boss will seldom be disappointed. How much better it would be if the boss showed data indicating the poor performance and said something to the effect, "Come on folks — we're better than this!" In other words, turn those negative expectations into positive expectations.

BEFORE CLOSING . . .

There are a lot of similarities between the performance of a business and the performance of an athletic team. In fact, Robert Keidel has written a book, *Game Plans* (Dutton, 1985), drawing on their similarities. When an athletic team wins the game, the coach may share the credit, but he can't take the credit. Players win games, coaches don't. When teams underperform, that is, when they lose, the coach may share the loss with the team, but he can't place the blame on team members. Placing the blame on individual players in effect says that it is the players' responsibility to generate the collective effort necessary to win the game. In fact, that is the job description for a coach — not the players. When a team underperforms, it is traceable to poor training, poor play patterns, coaching inadequacies, insufficient feedback to the team, criticism (negative incentives), and the coach's negative expectations of certain individual players. And those are the reasons a business underperforms too.

CHAPTER
TEN

WINNING TOGETHER

*Sharing the Gains of
Improved Business Performance*

When you were a kid, did you ever try to pull the "heads I win, tails you lose" stunt? I did. If I could blurt it out fast enough, I could take my chums who were slow on the uptake. Back then it was for small stakes, and as much a prank as it was a con. But some people never outgrow the "I win, you lose" game. I think American business is afflicted with it. The business game is more sophisticated, because adults designed it. But the outcome is the same. Let the owners win, the stockholders win, the managers win, the bankers win, but the employees? Sorry, Charley—you lose. I know an owner of a retailing chain who bets money with his store managers that they won't meet their weekly sales quotas. It's all done in jest, of course. But when he wins, he loses. Think about it.

Too many opportunities to gain a competitive edge in business are missed because too few people have a stake in spotting them in most companies. It's sad. Failure to make employees stakeholders has a particularly high price in small companies. Who currently has the greatest stake in your company's future? You do. And what do your employees have at stake? Typically, their jobs. Now, there will always be other jobs for your employees if things "go south," but there may not be resources for you to start another company. Usually it's the owner who loses big time when the company fails to be competitive and then fails altogether.

How people are managed is an important part of a company's ability to be competitive. And finding a way by which the owner and the employees in a small company can win together is an essential element in creating the environment in which the employees have a stake in whether a company does well or poorly in the marketplace. For example, I can't recall talking with a small business owner who didn't have some complaint about the quality level, service levels, and productivity of his workforce. Well, why shouldn't there be problems? The boss can't do everything, and there's no incentive for the employees to think like owners. "That's a pretty jaundiced view," you may be thinking. But I happen to believe that people in a healthy, competitive organization really see themselves as being in business for themselves. I also happen to believe that people who do jobs day in and day out see all kinds of opportunities to improve the effectiveness of those jobs, and I'd like to give them an incentive to step up to those improvements. After all, we keep reading about how awesome the Japanese workforce is, but we refuse to recognize that the Japanese worker is paid for productivity, while the American worker is paid by the hour.

In the chapter on leadership, "The Power of Your Presence," I talked about partnering, that is, creating a sense of being shoulder-to-shoulder in the business. In that spirit, I believe a company can make strides in improving its productivity and its quality if those gains are shared between the owners and the employees. The alternative is to get no gain at all. So what is to be shared is something that doesn't previously exist, and the only way it can be made to exist is through creative teamwork among employees and the owners and managers of a company.

WHAT MAKES GAINSHARING WORK?

I've designed and installed over two-dozen gainsharing programs in small companies and can tell you from experience that companies using some form of gainsharing will outperform those that don't. Let me give you an example. After giving a speech on gainsharing about three years ago, the owner of a small manufacturing company chatted with me about the possibility of installing some type of plan in his company. In our initial meeting, I determined that the company had operated at essentially its break-even point for the past four years; some years were marginally profitable, and others were marginally unprofitable. The manufacturing margins were pretty stable at about 44 percent of sales. Even though the owner thought the margins should have been better, the fact was they weren't, and he hadn't fired anyone. So we established a baseline for improvements at 44 percent of sales. In other words, if employees could improve their performance, the manufacturing margins should rise above 44 percent. And there were many things employees could do to effect improvements—minimize overtime and waste, cut out contract labor, stop losing tools, produce more in less time, not make mistakes, and be there—that is, avoid injuries and absences. I proposed that we split all gains above 44 percent, fifty-fifty—half to the employees and half to the company.

The owner's reaction to the fifty-fifty split was to cough and pull at his shirt collar. "Fifty-fifty! That's kinda' steep, isn't it?" He suggested formulas like seventy-thirty or sixty-forty. But I replied, "How about zero-zero? Because, that's what you'll have to share if margins don't improve . . . the fact is, you're not giving them 50 percent of anything. They're giving you back 50 percent of the gains they produce!"

To make a long story short, he paid out $55,000 in productivity bonuses to employees during the first year, which means the company had manufacturing profits of $55,000 that it otherwise would not have had. The second year, gainsharing bonuses of $171,000 were paid out. The employees were ecstatic and so was the owner. But, the competitors weren't. They were getting creamed in the marketplace by this company whose product quality had grown superior. Its delivery time was now half of the competition's, and the sales force was motivated to take orders it knew the company could deliver on.

It's not unusual to pay gainsharing bonuses that are 20 to 30 percent of a person's base salary. In fact, the legendary Lincoln Electric Company pays an average salary of $17,000 per person and an average gainsharing bonus of another $17,000—and they have a two-year waiting list of people who want to go to work for them.

QUALITY, PRODUCTIVITY, AND COMMUNICATIONS IMPROVE WITH GAINSHARING

Quality improves in a gainsharing program because poor quality work is offset against productivity gains. Obviously, a company does not get ahead by making something wrong and then doing it over again to get it right. When it's made wrong, the quality is already created at that point; quality control inspectors don't create quality, they simply sort out bad product from good product. Quality is created by the people who do the work. And gainsharing provides the incentive to produce the work right the first time.

Obviously, productivity improvements lower your operating costs. This allows you to either reduce your prices or give more value to the customers than your competition gives, either of which makes you a more competitive company. But, the elimination of unnecessary work can't eliminate jobs. People aren't going to propose clever cost savings that put them out of work. So the assurance of employment security is critical in making a gainsharing program work. How then does your company improve if unnecessary jobs are not eliminated? By doing this: you eliminate the unnecessary work but keep the worker on the payroll. Consider it a postponement of savings that will accrue to the benefit of your company over time through normal turnover or terminations for cause. You simply don't replace people who leave, and you assign people displaced by newfound efficiencies to jobs that might otherwise have required you to hire outsiders to do them. Let's face it, the last people you should want to terminate are people who can figure out ways to eliminate unnecessary work. I'd hope they would find other ways to eliminate unnecessary work. Wouldn't you?

Perhaps the most important benefit in a gainsharing program is the improved communications that result between your company's management and its employees. You should never hand employees an incentive bonus payment without showing them what made the bonus possible. Similarly, you never withhold a bonus without showing them what they failed to accomplish that would have enabled you to pay a bonus. In addition, I always recommend that bonus payments in a gainsharing program be paid at a different time and with a different check than the employee's paycheck. This keeps employees from confusing bonus payments with paychecks; otherwise paychecks and bonuses become merged in employees' minds, and the impact of bonuses on employee performance decreases.

PROFIT SHARING ISN'T AN INCENTIVE

A shocking statement? Maybe. But profit sharing as it exists in most companies today is a failure. Profit sharing originated in the early nineteenth century in France, where shared profits were paid out to the workers. However, as it has evolved in this country, the profits are not paid out. They are paid in — to a retirement program. The last thing a twenty-five-year-old has on his mind is something that he is going to get when he is sixty-five years old — forty years from now! In fact, the last thing that a fifty-five-year-old has on his mind is something that he will get ten years from now. Profit sharing, in my judgment, is a waste of money. It is a retirement benefit, not an incentive, not a reward for productivity improvements or quality improvements or service level improvements. And, since most profit-sharing plans are managed very conservatively, the gains in a plan's value frequently don't come from the plan's investment yields, but rather from redistribution of the shares earned by employees who leave before their vesting period in the plan activates.

Moreover, the symbolism of profit sharing is awful. It's a form of private sector social security. In essence, what you are saying is, "If I pay this money out to you, you would squander it, so I am going to put it in a savings account on your behalf and give it back to you when you retire." In other words, profit sharing suggests that employees are incapable of making decisions for themselves regarding preparation for retirement. You know as well as I do that the savings needs and abilities of a twenty-nine-year-old, a forty-nine-year-old, and a fifty-nine-year-old are all different. Young people need as much money as they can get to create a household. Employees with college-aged kids need money for college expenses. Only after their kids are out of college can most people begin thinking about and making preparations for their own retirement. And generally, people will have twenty to twenty-five years in which to do that. As far as I'm concerned, profit-sharing plans are like giving a blood transfusion from one arm to the other arm with a leaky tube in between — the value received at retirement is a lot less than the value given up today. I encourage clients to collapse profit-sharing plans, pay the plan contributions out to employees, and let them make their own decisions regarding preparation for retirement.

The traditional profit-sharing plan is also a bad business decision in another sense. Gainsharing provides bonuses to people according to their performance. Whereas, the tax law, in its eminent wisdom, requires that qualified profit sharing shall be done on an equal percentage basis—regardless of performance. Moreover, those laws change every year, requiring endless and costly, though meaningless, revisions of a plan by the plan manager. It is becoming evident that a by-product of the so-called tax reform legislation of 1986 is an increasingly militant IRS, determined that, in a capitalist society governed by democratic principles, we shall nevertheless share employment benefits equally without regard to performance or the importance of one's contribution to the success of the business. In any other environment, we would call such a bias communism.

PREPARING FOR A GAINSHARING PROGRAM

The commitment to improve the performance of your business must be companywide. In other words, gainsharing is not a patch job that focuses on one department in your company. A company is like a machine, and all of the parts must work together effectively. Trying to improve the performance of one department through incentives without creating a reward system for other departments is a sure way to disrupt cooperation. And it would suggest that various departments are not really part of the team but rather a loose federation of individual work groups.

You must create and sustain a company climate that encourages innovative thinking. Change is often resisted by employees because they suspect the proposed change will make their jobs harder. However, in a company that hopes to benefit by gainsharing, change is not only necessary, it is desirable. Employees must be adaptable and willing to experiment. They must be on the lookout for opportunities to eliminate unnecessary work or tasks. But, as I've said before, the elimination of work cannot eliminate jobs.

There must also be a recognition of the difference between quality gains and quantity gains. It's in vogue to say that we don't want people to work harder—we want them to work smarter. Well, I want them to work harder and smarter—and get paid for both. Improved performance occurs because the quantity and the quality of work improves. And you get ahead both ways. Bad quality work is wasteful because the work has to be repeated or thrown away, but in either case, it generates no revenues.

You also must employ the latest technology in order to get the work done productively. Many small businesses are service businesses, such as retail, distribution, wholesaling, and personal services. Productivity is characteristically low in these service businesses because labor isn't leveraged off of capital assets as it is in manufacturing. Consequently, process improvements and technology must be employed to improve performance. The use of computers is one way, but it isn't the only way. The most common error people make when they acquire a computer is to use it almost exclusively for accounting transactions. What should be done is to automate the business, which means the computer should take over every function a computer can do better than a human being. Process improvements also include subcontracting work that can be more cheaply performed by companies that do it as a business, such as payroll check preparers, maintenance services, inventory counters, and employee benefits management.

In many cases, the organization of a company and the design of its jobs prevents any real improvements from being made in the work the company does. The reason for this is that most organization forms and procedures evolve more than they are designed. And what an outsider, like me, sees when coming into a business for the first time is often a hodgepodge of procedures and tasks that were created to accomplish some now-forgotten purpose. The organization must be restructured, if necessary, so it is possible for work groups to keep control of their work output and quality, and jobs must be designed to foster motivation and cooperation.

Improvements in productivity, service levels, and quality must be measured and monitored continuously, and fed back to employees graphically, so they can see how they are doing. Employees should be encouraged to participate in quality and productivity. There should be a wide degree of shared information regarding where problems exist and what progress the company has made in resolving them. Remember the cartoon I mentioned earlier in which two cavemen were looking at an upsloping graph and one said to the other: "It makes me feel good every time I look at it"? It's true. Provide ways for employees to see that progress is being made. Graphic feedback is essential in improving performance.

The bottom line is this: regardless of the type of business you are in, a small group that consists of the owner and several supervisors can't possibly come up with all of the good ideas or spot all of the opportunities for improvement as well as a group that includes all of the people who do the company's work everyday. I'll bet your employees could give you twelve money-making ideas before the day is out. So, why don't they? Because there's nothing in it for them. Moreover, ignored suggestions are belittling. Sharing the gains that come from improved company performance solves these problems.

MEASURING IMPROVEMENTS

It should be apparent that every gainsharing program is unique to a specific company—it must be designed for the company's needs and its style of work. Performance outputs can be measured in many ways—sales revenue per employee, sales revenue per square foot, units per labor hour, sales dollars per labor dollar—but all have a common input/output relationship. The things that convert inputs to outputs are the company's work systems, its organization, and its procedures. Most companies pay little attention to this input/output ratio and focus on inputs only, such as costs. Or attention is paid to outputs only, such as units produced. But what really matters is the number of units produced per unit of cost. That will tell you how efficiently the company work systems are operating. An example will demonstrate this point.

I was engaged by a client to develop a gainsharing program that would give the employees an incentive to improve both their productivity and their quality. The business was a high-touch, people-intensive service business, and as is true of all service businesses, there were few economies of scale. Managerial leverage was low. In other words the business could not improve its efficiency by adding more layers of management. Therefore, the critical-to-success factor in this, as in most service businesses, was to maintain a high ratio of revenue producers to nonrevenue producers. This company had not. As I began to review the organization, its systems, and its work procedures, it became apparent that there were too many managers and supervisors who added no value in getting the work out.

In addition to the managerial deadweight (some of which was also deadwood), there were too many mistakes being made, too much overtime being spent, and too many nonrevenue-producing activities being performed by the revenue producers. Understand that a revenue producer is not only someone who sells something; it can also be someone who makes something that can be sold. Or who assists a revenue producer by keeping him totally involved in producing revenue—not in performing support functions. Obviously, a work group can improve its productivity in four ways: eliminate errors, eliminate overtime, eliminate or minimize nonrevenue-producing activities within the workforce, and minimize or eliminate management.

I developed a recordkeeping system for the company and implemented it for a nine-week period of time in order to get some basis for evaluating the productivity of the work group. Employees were required to keep track of their time by charging it off to a customer's order, the correction of an error, or so-called "other" activities. Managers and supervisors charged their time to overhead. Overtime hours were also collected and recorded. The company had historically judged its "productivity" in terms of only one variable, the number of work orders processed—an output. A work order, however, could consume ten minutes or ten hours. But even worse, a work order was an output variable rather than an input/output relationship. This prevented its use as a productivity measure.

After reviewing the data for the nine-week period, I redefined productivity, that is, the ratio of output to input, in this way: output was now defined as the total number of hours spent on performing work orders less the hours spent on correcting errors. Input was now defined as the sum of the time spent on work orders, *including* error correction, time spent on "other" activities, supervision and management time, and an inflation factor for overtime hours. In short, output was the sum of the revenue production time of all employees; input was that figure plus other time-consuming activities that produced no revenue. Since overtime hours produced sixty minutes of work but overtime is paid out as ninety minutes, the overtime hour inflation factor was 150 percent.

Using these factors, I calculated the average productivity for the nine-week period to be 53 percent. That figure became the baseline by which all future periods would be judged in terms of improved company performance. If we could find ways to increase output without increasing input, then an improvement in productivity would have occurred. This could be translated into dollars saved and became the basis for a performance-based bonus system.

Predictably, productivity began to improve, largely as a result of reductions in "other" activities and reductions in overtime. Training improved employees' ability to produce work without errors. Greater reliance on systems and procedures reduced the dependence on managerial judgments, allowing the company to grow without adding managers in the process. It was a classic win-win situation for both the company and its employees.

QUESTIONS I'M OFTEN ASKED ABOUT GAINSHARING

How often should bonus payments be made? — weekly? monthly? quarterly? Well, I'm against anything longer than quarterly. Gainsharing works because it's positively reinforcing. When employees do something that improves the performance of the business, a bonus should be paid as soon after that action as is possible. In some cases, weekly or monthly payments are not possible because the business varies too much on a week-to-week or month-to-month basis. In that case, an average over a quarter is a better measure of improved results. But paying bonuses every six months or once a year is not immediate enough.

Are bonus payments ever capped? Heck no! If you cap employee gains, you'll cap your own gains. As I just said, the ideal is to pay out a bonus immediately, but if external conditions cause fluctuations, you may want to create a temporary escrow account, pay some percentage of the bonus into this account, and make a partial bonus payment to employees. For example, suppose an employee's earned bonus is $100; you may choose to pay $60 and escrow $40. In this way, if business fluctuations or an employee's performance drops, there is an escrow reserve to prevent the employees from going so far into a performance deficit that they feel there's no way to work out of it. If that ever happens, the incentive system may actually become a disincentive.

Furthermore, the gainsharing system should be designed so employees can't go "all out" one month or quarter in order to win a bonus, then slack off in the following period. If this occurs, the company loses because it can't take a bonus away once it's been paid in order to make up deficit performance. The escrow payment is a way to encourage consistent performance. In one instance, I designed a plan in which 50 percent of the earned bonus was paid out for the first three quarters of the fiscal year using an estimated cost of goods sold, and the payout in the fourth quarter was determined after a physical inventory count established actual cost of goods sold for the year. The final bonus included everything earned in the fourth quarter plus everything that had been held in the reserve throughout the year.

I have seen incentive commission systems that actually worked as disincentives. A salesperson, for example, might be paid 10 percent on the first $100,000 in sales, 7 percent on the next $100,000, 5 percent on the next $100,000, 2 percent on the next $100,000, and I suppose after that the salesperson is expected to work for free! Dumb! The incentive is the exact reverse of what it ought to be. A salesperson should be paid 2 percent on the first $100,000 in sales, increasing perhaps to 10 percent on the fourth $100,000 in sales, but then should be allowed big commissions on anything over a certain amount. What do you want to happen? You want the salesperson to push out—way out on the commission curve—where their effort creates the greatest return. Commission systems that shrink the commission rate as sales increase are self-defeating.

Are sharing formulas created for all time? Nope. Except changes are never made in bad faith. To increase the baseline or performance standard when employees do what you wanted them to do, and attempt to excuse the increase by saying the standard was bad, or that the employees cheated, or make up some other lame excuse is a sure way of destroying any motivation to repeat the rewarded performance. However, here's an important point: what was an equitable division of gains at one time may not be equitable at another time due to technological or equipment changes, new product additions or deletions, and pricing or marketing changes that obsolete the old output/input ratios. Gainsharing plans must have flexibility and good faith on both sides. If it isn't a good deal for the company, it's not a good deal for the employees. If it isn't a good deal for the employees, it isn't a good deal for the company. Both sides must win together.

Now, I have some questions for you.

Is gainsharing right for your company? Before installing a gainsharing program, you should assure yourself that the basic concept of sharing is consistent with your values—and the values that exist in the company. Both you and the environment must be right in order for gainsharing to work.

Are the accounting and other information-gathering systems able to support gainsharing? Information feedback is absolutely critical for gainsharing to work well. And the feedback must be prompt and must be essentially accurate. I know companies that have trouble getting accurate financial statements within thirty days after accounts for the month have been closed out. By that time, the information is almost useless in changing employee behavior. Imagine how frustrating it would be if you engaged in an athletic contest but could not learn the score for several weeks. Likewise, employees want to know the score, so that they can alter it to their favor in the future.

What is the ideal gainsharing group? I can't conceive of a case where a business owner wouldn't want the entire company to work together as a team. However, in some situations a company has gotten so large that its various parts may have become semi-autonomous—meaning that there is no way for those parts to help each other. When that is the case, each part of the company would be an independent gainsharer. Work groups must be able to help each other and control the outcomes in order to be a gainsharing group. But if a gainsharing group is defined too narrowly, its output can't be determined; its product is an interim product. Work groups or procedures may need reorganizing so that each group has an identifiable product and its people can be measured. The rule is, if they can't measure it, they can't manage it.

How could you introduce the program so as to get maximum employee involvement? Success, as has often been said, has many fathers, whereas failure is an orphan. Involvement is critical in implementing any new program in a company. I have experienced situations where the idea of gainsharing was initially greeted by the employees with skepticism because they thought it would defraud them of future salary increases. Haste makes waste in anything that involves a person's income. Therefore, employees must know from the outset that a gainsharing program is being planned, and they must also have an input into its design. I accomplish this with lots of interviews in which I ask questions, but I also try to get employees to suggest ways in which they could be compensated by their efficiency improvements.

Finally, how will the program be monitored? Yogi Berra said you can observe a lot just by watching. Circumstances change. Gainsharing plans must, therefore, be flexible if gainsharing is to be good for both the company and the employee. Communication, as I have said earlier, is absolutely the make-or-break factor in a gainsharing program, especially in the early periods after its introduction.

I *always* tell employees that we have come up with what we believe is the best plan for both the company and the employees, but that the plan is subject to modification and adjustment as we—both employees and management—learn more about the plan's effectiveness. However, employees should be assured that changes in the plan will never demonstrate bad faith. In fact, experience indicates that employees nearly always will be in agreement with the rationale that a change is necessary. In one case, I have modified a gainsharing plan five times over a six-year period, and the employees are as delighted with its equity today as they were the day that it was introduced. They were involved in its changes—and agreed with all of them.

BEFORE CLOSING . . .

In no way do I want to represent gainsharing as the beginning of a new millennium. It is not a panacea or a cure-all for every organizational ill. Gainsharing will not make dull jobs exciting, it will not make incompetent supervisors competent, it will not motivate the unmotivatable. Gainsharing, like vitamins, makes a reasonably healthy organizational body healthier.

Effective small companies are rooted in their leadership practices, namely their commitment to work together as a team, to win together, and to share the rewards of winning. If you (or anyone) attempt to install any incentive or performance improvement and sharing program as "the new fad on the block," without understanding both its practical and symbolic impact on your company, you may be setting yourself up to fail.

The best example I can give of that is not one I learned in business. As a freshman in college, I read Charles Lamb's classic essay, "Dissertation on a Roast Pig," which was written in 1822. Lamb's essay is about an ancient and poor Chinese village in which the families lived in fragile houses. They took their farm animals into their houses each evening to avoid losing them. One night one of these wood and paper houses caught fire and burned to the ground. The family escaped alive, but the family's favorite pig didn't.

The next day, the family's elderly grandfather was searching through the ashes to see if anything could be recovered from the destruction of the fire. As he placed his hand in the ashes, he touched the pig's carcass which was still hot, and it burned his fingers. Instinctively, he put his fingers in his mouth to cool them, and the burned fingers tasted good! He invited family and friends to touch the pig, and their fingers also were burned, but also tasted good when they put them in their mouths. After that, there was a rash of house fires in the village in which many family pigs predictably perished.

Obviously, if the villagers didn't know how to roast a pig, there were destined to be lots of fires in the village. And if you don't know what causes gainsharing to work, you may be destined to throw lots of money away without reaping the benefits gainsharing is designed to produce.

CHAPTER ELEVEN

WHAT'S THE COMPETITION UP TO?

How to Collect and Use Competitor Intelligence

Whenever one of your competitors makes a move in the marketplace, you should instinctively ask, "What are those guys up to?" and, "How will that affect me?" If you don't know the answer to the first question, you can't answer the second one. And how do you get answers to the first question? — by establishing a program within your company to systematically collect and analyze the activities of each of your key competitors — in other words, a competitor intelligence program.

Unfortunately, the words *competitor intelligence* evoke images of cloak-and-dagger behavior — sneaking around, stealing information, and inducing people to act inappropriately — which it is not. The Russians gather most of their intelligence on the United States not from spies but from published information sources: newspapers, trade journals, and speeches. During World War II, the United States and its Allies gathered most of their intelligence in the same way — from newspaper accounts of plant closings, from railroad schedule revisions, and by monitoring radio programs. The collective analysis of this information helped the Allies determine the impact of the war effort on Germany.

THE NEED FOR COMPETITOR INTELLIGENCE

Although business competitor intelligence has its origins in military intelligence, it doesn't employ spies. Legitimate intelligence gathering doesn't engage in unethical, immoral, or illegal activities. In short, business intelligence is an organized attempt to know what anyone else could know about competitors if the effort is made.

In the absence of comprehensive competitor intelligence, business decisions must be made in a vacuum. There is no way to even attempt an understanding of the reasoning and decision making that may have gone into the planning of a competitor's moves. Thus, if you compete "in the dark" against other companies, there is always a risk that an advantage will pass to a competitor either through luck (assuming the competitor was not gathering intelligence about your company) or because you failed to use all the information that could be available to you to help run your business well.

CLUES COME IN FRAGMENTS

Putting together an intelligence profile on each of your competitors is a lot like putting together a puzzle when you're not quite sure what its completed form looks like and some of the puzzle pieces are permanently missing. But gathering competitor intelligence on small, privately held companies is easier than you might think.

In small businesses, the competitor is a him or a her. In many cases you will (or can) know the owner of a competitor business personally, and decisions and plans in that business are totally or strongly influenced by this person. Personal knowledge of the individual, for example, provides insight into his thought processes, business aspirations, inclination toward risk, and other personal attributes that allow you to interpret what the person is doing with the business and will likely do in the future. However, some types of information on private companies are difficult to obtain because the business affairs of the company are not published as they are in a publicly held company. Therefore, this kind of information has to be pieced together indirectly from fragmented clues you obtain in the marketplace.

Competitor intelligence about public companies is more accessible information, but offsetting the availability of information is the fact that management decisions are an amalgam of the management team's thinking rather than that of a single person, making it more difficult to pick up a clear direction.

Competitor intelligence gathering consists of three steps:
1. Profiling your competitor's personality—what is he like?
2. Studying the competitor's historic moves in the marketplace to determine the significance of these moves in light of his (or their) personality.
3. Interpreting current intelligence against Steps 1 and 2.

It's not a perfect process, but it's essential to your being an effective competitor.

PROFILING A COMPETITOR

Profiles should be created on the owners or key managers of the top three or four companies you are up against in the marketplace. To do this, you should keep a file on each of them and add to the file from time-to-time any new insights or information you gain.

Mao Tse-tung said, "Know your enemy." While a competitor may not be an enemy, take time to understand his style, motives, and especially analyze his market moves as if you were in a chess game. Done well, you should be able to characterize every key competitor in considerable detail.

When I work with a company in an engagement where knowledge of competitors is important, I usually will ask the client to help me profile each competitor in the following way. (Hereafter, I will refer to "the competitor," but what I say applies to *each* competitor.)

General Information. How long has the competitor been in this business? Every business has a learning curve. In order to predict or understand a competitor's moves in the marketplace, it would make a difference to me if the competitor had been in business twenty years as opposed to two years.

What previous business experiences has the competitor been exposed to? An individual with a history of successful business experiences—perhaps having started and sold several businesses or having had the opportunity to understudy a successful entrepreneur—would likely be a formidable competitor. I have had clients in their fifties who are involved in their third or fourth business; their prior business experiences or relationships were both diverse and cumulative, positioning them for greater success with each succeeding business.

Did the competitor create the company, purchase it, or inherit it? People who start companies are typically pursuing a technical skill— the ability to make something, to sell something, or to solve some type of problem. On the other hand, people who inherit or purchase companies may not have the technical know-how necessary to be an effective competitor. For example, a man with a successful *Fortune* 500 career that had made him modestly wealthy purchased a company in Florida from the family that founded it. The terms of the purchase required the previous owners to remain under a management contract for one year. That period has now expired, the founding management is moving out, and the new owner has obviously underestimated the technical skills and know-how required to manage the business effectively. It is unlikely that he can learn enough to survive the industry outlook that is forecast for the next three years.

An age and education estimate are important for several reasons. A young, well-educated competitor may be more ambitious than a man in his sixties, or more capable than one less educated. As an example of this, I know a thirty-two-year-old, second-generation business owner with a master's degree in a specialized field. His father had never developed the business much beyond the family's livelihood, but the son is out to make a name for himself. In less than seven years he has acquired five companies in his industry. In another example, a young, single woman with the personality of a street fighter took over the family equipment repair business and built it into a successful equipment sales and rental business in which the original repair service is insignificant. As a single person, she works constantly— unlike her competitors.

Ambitions and Goals. What is the competitor trying *to be* through the business? Small businesses in particular are extensions of the personalities of their owners. Egos, personal values, and aspirations are all wrapped up in the way these people operate a business.

The founder of Jiffy Lube, Jim Hindman, was raised in an orphanage after his parents divorced. That experience influenced his adult life immeasurably, making him an intensely ambitious and competitive person. At thirty-three, he "retired," as a millionaire after selling a chain of nursing homes he owned, and became head football coach of Western Maryland State College, a voluntary pastime too tame to hold him. Returning to the business world to start Jiffy Lube, he now predictably views business as a struggle, an athletic contest: a team must be assembled, plays must be developed and executed well, and the word *winning* peppers his conversation. His athletic intensity has enabled him and his company to survive situations that would have taken lesser men down because he is out to create another McDonald's—not to make himself richer.

I also know an individual who was raised in public housing, didn't know his father, had an alcoholic for a mother, and lived through six foster home assignments when his mother could no longer care for him. By the age of thirty he was worth several million dollars for several reasons: he was out to prove his self-worth, he had developed a controlled, aggressive personality, and he suffered from a chronic sense of time urgency that forced him to be impatient with the pace at which things moved and that pressured him to overachieve.

Mary Kay Ash and Xavier Roberts both came from desperately poor backgrounds. Each was driven to succeed—she through her cosmetic products and he through the creation of Cabbage Patch Kids—successes enjoyed in flamboyant style. Their businesses were vehicles to achieve the wealth and fame that they had only daydreamed of as youngsters.

Risk Attitudes. What kind of risk taker is the competitor? Some competitors are calculated, measured, even cautious in their approach to business opportunities, while others are "hard chargers" or "gunslingers" in the belief that they can handle almost any situation that comes their way. While it is difficult to generalize out of context, a conservative risk taker may be slow to act in introducing a new product line, opening a branch office, or increasing the sales force. A high risk taker, on the other hand, may be vulnerable through his impulsiveness, his willingness to take unreasonable risks, or his over-estimation of personal ability. In fact, I know such a person. He repurchased his company from a group to whom he had originally sold it and who had virtually run it into the ground. He believed that he could turn the failing company around. I had advised him to start up a competitive company rather than repurchase the sick one, but his ego and risk attitudes wouldn't permit it. Within two years, he had lost everything.

Assumptions and Blind Spots. What assumptions does the competitor hold about himself, the business, and the future of the industry? Do any of these suggest evidence of blind spots—assumptions that are no longer valid, false beliefs, or unreasonable expectations about the future? People act, as I've said before, in accordance with "The Truth" as they believe it exists. Thus a belief that a serious recession or mini-depression is imminent will cause a cautious competitor to rein in, change priorities, and play a more conservative game in the marketplace.

Hot Buttons. Many business competitors have what I call a *hot button*, a stimulus that will provoke a predictable response. These responses are often irrational. As an example, a Texas distributor lost his lead salesman to a key competitor, in retaliation, he offered the competitor's sales manager a 50 percent salary increase if the sales manager would defect to the distributor's company. The successive retaliations designed to disrupt each other's staff were predictable, and the adverse impact that both companies suffered over the ensuing year could have been avoided if the owners of both firms had not provoked a situation that brought their egos into play.

Significant Events. What has happened in the past that would significantly affect the way a competitor operates? Here I'm interested in significant emotional or personal events such as a unionization attempt, a near bankruptcy, the introduction of a product line that bombed or exceeded expectations, the loss of a key employee in a dispute, all of which I have seen happen in a way that changes the operating style of a business.

Remember, the primary purpose in profiling a competitor is to improve your understanding of how a person thinks and hopefully to enhance your ability to predict how that person will act in the future.

HOW TO PROFILE A COMPETITOR'S STRATEGY AND VULNERABILITY

In the movie *Patton*, when George C. Scott blunted the German advance in a pivotal battle, he proclaimed: "Rommel, I read your book!" Business and military leaders do, in fact, instinctively repeat what has worked for them in the past. Therefore, clues regarding the future directions a business may be taking are often found in the historic moves a business has made.

At any given time, a competitor may be in one of four strategic postures:

- *Holding* — continuing operations as in the past, more or less sticking to the status quo.
- *Retrenching* — reducing the scope of operations in the market or the market segment.
- *Expanding* — aggressively penetrating a market segment, extending market coverage, or perhaps adding complementary products that will be cross-sold to the same customer.
- *Repositioning* — leaving the market or changing the past emphasis placed on a market segment.

Each of these competitor positions presents its hazards and opportunities depending upon the strength of the competitor.

How might you predict with reasonable accuracy the strategies and plans one or more of your competitors may be following? Here's how:

Review the Past Few Years. Have there been changes in the competitor's sales force or workforce in terms of increases or decreases? I encourage clients, for example, to regularly read the want ads in order to spot any hiring activity among their competitors. Has a competitor opened or closed a branch office, and if so, where? Have there been changes in plant or facility size, or changes in the number of trucks used to deliver products? On one occasion, I had a client station one of his employees in a car on a public road outside of the warehouse of a key competitor. His assignment was to count all incoming trucks from suppliers and all outgoing company trucks delivering product. Since we knew that trucks arrived fully loaded to avoid surcharges and that outgoing trucks were similarly loaded, we were able to estimate the level of units the competitor was purchasing and selling, which was an acceptable surrogate for sales level.

As another example, a client in Alabama moved out of a rundown facility and into a new facility constructed with industrial revenue bonds. The new facility represented a threefold increase in manufacturing space. It was well known that the owner had installed a MAPICS system (a computer-driven manufacturing system). And it was hard to hide the fact that two new Peterbilt tractors had been added to the delivery fleet. An alert competitor might have concluded that this company was gearing up for a major expansion in its business. It was.

I use these two examples to demonstrate a point. While we talk about "privately held" companies, there is little that they can really do in private. Every time a business purchases an asset and borrows money to pay for it, a smart lender will file a Uniform Commercial Code (UCC) form. These filings are an important index of the company's fixed assets, indicating the lender, the borrower, and sometimes including a financial statement. In many states, UCC filings are recorded with the Secretary of State. Others states record them at the county courthouse. Check with your lawyer to find out which is the case in your state. A list of UCC filings appears on every Dun and Bradstreet report. Moreover, property owned or leased by a business is recorded at the county tax assessor's office, something that's open to public scrutiny.

The location of each store in a retail chain is usually listed in the telephone directory Yellow Pages and is a clue to a store's trading area. It is also a clue to the location of customers, who can be surveyed by ZIP code for further competitor intelligence, such as name recognition of various competitors, buying patterns, average size of purchase, gripes—anything you might want to know if you are a retailer's competitor. Similarly, the location of regional sales offices is an important clue to market coverage, and, therefore, market strategy.

Industrial revenue bond (IRB) filings reveal financial information and sometimes the plans—the rationale for the IRBs—of the company. This information must be made public through the local Industrial Development Authority office.

A number of computer databases allow you to retrieve published data by company name or subject. Selective Dissemination of Information (SDI) is offered by several database services such as DIALOG. This service allows you to automatically receive information every time the database is updated.

The fact is, information is available to anyone who is willing to dig for it, and it can be retrieved in ethical and legal ways. As I have mentioned before, you should keep a competitor intelligence file to collect information worth noting about a competitor's movements in the marketplace—plans, problems, announcements—or any other information that allows you to interpret the historic moves a competitor has made.

What Do Competitors Say About Themselves? I am amazed at the amount of information small business owners reveal about themselves. At trade conventions I have heard competitors talk openly about their business plans in explicit detail (especially after a few drinks), although not everything can be taken at face value.

Competitors sometimes allow each other into their plants or places of business, thus providing an opportunity to judge activity levels, such as the number of employees, the number of machines, the number of trucks, the number of cars in the employee parking lot, and floor space, that can be translated into measures of output. Several years ago, while working with a small manufacturing company that sold products to the automotive aftermarket, I remarked that it would certainly help our planning if we knew how many production machines the leading competitor had in operation. My client said, "That's no problem; I will be at the Riverside race next week and will stop by his plant on the way back to Atlanta." Remarkably, he was given a Cook's tour, and was able to count the number of production machines in operation, allowing us to estimate the sales volume of this "privately held" company.

What Do Others Say About Them? One small business owner I know calls his sales force "my in-house CIA." That's not far from the truth. Your salespeople are in the marketplace every day with endless opportunities to observe what your competitors are up to. They are in touch with your competitor's new product offerings, sales force changes, territorial reassignments, orders that are being won or lost and to whom, key management changes, and a variety of other facts that are quite useful in fleshing out the competitor's game plan. Unfortunately, few companies tap into this intelligence arm effectively, or when they do, the effort is sporadic and unorganized. If you have not already done so, you should develop a system for capturing this information from the marketplace and having it fed back to you so that it can be used as an effective competitive tool.

I helped a company develop such a system several years ago. This company has branch offices in eight major southeastern markets, and in each of those markets my client was up against national, regional, and tough local competitors. He had an excellent sales force, probably the best in the industry, and very little went on in the way of order activity that these salesmen didn't know about. Every week they were required to complete the customary sales activities reports, but I also required them to furnish the details of every sale they made—quantity, price, terms, and so forth—as well as the same details on every order lost to a competitor. This information was collected in the corporate office where it was processed through a computer program and added to a database. The value of the insight we have gained through the use of this information is incalculable: shifts in market share, sales campaigns under way, and weaknesses in a competitor's market coverage all became evident when this information was analyzed.

In addition to your own salespeople, the sales force of your suppliers is also a valuable source for competitor information. Suppliers frequently service competing firms. If that is the case, it never hurts to ask the supplier's salesperson about a competitor, although you may not get a straight answer. But on one occasion, based on feedback from his sales force, a business owner suspected that a local competitor was in trouble, and he wanted to confirm that the competitor's sales were suffering. When a mutual supplier visited him, he nonchalantly remarked, "I heard that XYZ's sales are up 50 percent from last year." The supplier's salesman without thinking responded, "You couldn't prove it by me; their purchases from us have been down for the past six months." We believed him. Of course, information flows both ways, and if the competitor didn't know that my client's sales were up, it was his own fault.

Mutual customers can also be quizzed for clues about the competition. As mentioned in an earlier chapter, a San Francisco construction company interviewed the architects and designers who used their services, asking them what were the worst features of their competitors. The answers they were given were bad manners, workers who track dirt across office carpets, and beat-up construction trucks (high-class clients objected to having them parked in their driveways). This information fueled a repositioning effort that enabled the construction company to become the preferred contractor for the high-end market. New trucks were purchased, estimators wore jackets and ties, the workforce was trained to be polite — in fact, invisible — and runners were always laid down over carpets. There is a lesson here. It makes sense that if you treat your customers as "members of the team," you will be able to serve them better, and you will also preempt the competition from exploiting a blind spot.

I have worked with a number of retail businesses, and we always comparison shop the competition. It's not a new idea; however, our shoppers do more than inspect the merchandise and monitor the pricing. Acting as customers themselves, they talk to customers, using leading questions that provide insight into the loyalty of the competitor's customer base, service levels, return policies, and other information necessary to profile the strengths and weaknesses of the competitor.

WHERE IS A COMPETITOR VULNERABLE?

Obviously, you profile a competitor's personality and assess his historic moves for the purposes of developing a plan of attack. As Wee Willie Keeler, the baseball star, used to say, "Hit'em where they ain't!"

Where Are the Competitor's Blind Spots? Have you ever dented a fender on a car and shuddered every time you saw it? But in time, assuming you did not repair the fender, it no longer bothered you — because you no longer saw it. That is a perceptual blind spot. We all have them, and businesses have them too.

Why was the San Francisco contractor able to capitalize on such obvious competitive blunders as the ones that I mentioned? Because his competitors had developed blind spots regarding service quality. If one or more of these competitors had snapped out of their scotoma, they could have neutralized their perceptive contractor by imitating his strategy. But they didn't. You can't fix what you don't see.

Where Do the Competitor's Systems Break Down? Sometimes a business's greatest strength is its greatest weakness. Here's an example. The rental car counters are at the top of the exit escalator stairs at the Atlanta airport. Predictably, the lines are long at the Hertz and Avis counters—the market leaders who advertise heavily—and also at the National car counter, which is the beneficiary of the spillover. But there is no line at the Budget Rent-A-Car counter. The market-wise Atlanta Budget franchisee, Roger Gilder, discovered a way to capitalize on the "success" of the market leaders (long lines) and transferred all of the Budget sign-up operations to the rental yard where the cars are kept. To the public, Budget appears to have its act together, whereas, the other major competitors appear conspicuously disorganized (long lines). To which counter would you go if you had a choice, particularly if you were in a hurry? Where the line is shortest—to Budget Rent-A-Car. And there you would be greeted by a polite attendant who would invite you around the corner where a waiting bus will take you to the rental yard.

Study Your Competitors and Look for Their Weaknesses. Sales organization effectiveness? Product quality or consistency? Service and response time problems? But, if you find a soft spot, make sure that it's exploitable. A weakness is only a weakness if it is important to customers. Federal Express built a business around reliable, on-time package delivery—an attribute important to its customers. It failed miserably with ZAP mail, a two-hour document delivery service, apparently because existing document transmission quality was acceptable to customers and because neither ZAP nor fax reproductions are legal documents. Legal document originals still had to use some form of express mail—like Federal Express.

What Constraints Is Your Competitor Subject To? Historic decisions may have committed a competitor to a limitation that can't be easily circumvented in the short term. For example, does a competitor have a cost structure, such as facility costs or overhead, that can't be divested easily? Is the competitor using up-to-date methods, technology, or equipment? Does the competitor have a conservative management style? Does he lack management depth? What competitive or market trends is the competitor ill-equipped to handle?

I have a client who competes head-on against a publicly held company in a classic David and Goliath confrontation. As a public company, the competitor has a constraint that my client doesn't—it must protect its stock price by turning in good quarterly earnings and earnings forecasts. This forces it and all public companies to take a conservative approach in seizing opportunities that would make good long-term sense but would adversely affect the short-term bottom line. But then, the future never has sold well on Wall Street. At any rate, the client is beating the competitor by rapidly exploiting an emerging market opportunity that the competitor has more resources to develop. We swing between marginal profitability and marginal unprofitability, and the struggle to find development capital is endless, but Goliath has happy stockholders and security analysts—for today, at least. Even though it's mortgaging its future by its preoccupation with quarterly earnings. I love it! Ain't private enterprise great?

BEFORE CLOSING . . .

Determining what the competition is up to is a beginning, not an end. It allows you to plan an attack, defend against your competitor's attack, use your resources more effectively, exploit a competitor—the list is endless, but do something with what you learn. Don't become absorbed in just collecting intelligence.

The pursuit of a better understanding of your competitors should also lead to a better understanding of your own company. If you can gather information on other companies, they can gather information on your company. This should stress a need for internal security. But more importantly, it should stress the need for self-examination. I cannot think of a statement that is more appropriate to self-knowledge than one articulated twenty-five-hundred years ago:

If you know the enemy, and you know yourself,
You need not fear the result of a hundred battles,
If you know yourself, but not the enemy,
For every victory gained, you will also suffer a defeat.
If you know neither the enemy nor yourself,
You will succumb in every battle.

— Sun Tzu

CHAPTER
TWELVE

UPPING THE STAKES

Fighting Back When the Competition Gets Tough

Plato tells a story of a ship's crew that was quarreling because each thought he should be at the helm. Despite the fact that none of them knew anything about navigation, they continued milling about the captain, demanding that he give them the wheel, having no idea that a true navigator must know the seasons, study the sky, read the stars, and use the wind if he is to be fit to control the ship. Plato observes, "In these circumstances, are not the sailors on any such ship bound to regard the true navigator as a stargazer of no use to them at all?"

Arthur Jones, the inventor of the Nautilus machine, which has been called "the thinking man's barbell;" and Fred Smith, who created a system that was originally intended to assure overnight delivery of checks within the Federal Reserve System—hence the name Federal Express; and Jim Hindman, who created the fast lube industry as it exists today; and others like these entrepreneurs are all stargazers. They saw what others could have seen—but didn't. Like the sailors of which Plato spoke, the "sailors" in the industries in which Jones, Smith, and Hindman appeared were also milling around, engaged in activities that had little to do with directing their companies into the future—activities that were more oriented to where they had been, than where they were headed.

In my experience, most businesses spend too many of their resources to enhance current products and services and fend off competitors instead of paying attention to what's putting them out of business. Here are some disc examples: Compact discs (CDs) obliterated the record industry, and digital tape—if it is ever allowed to be sold in the United States—may replace CDs—all in the space of a decade. Transistors, which replaced vacuum tubes, were themselves replaced by microchips and microprocessors. Videotape replaced a large segment of the theater-going audiences by allowing them to see movies in their homes. Finally, fax machines are replacing couriers as they exist today and probably will force them to be redefined as package and large document couriers—a much smaller market.

So it's safe to say something is replacing your business as it now exists. What is it? Do you even think about it? Quite likely, what will threaten your firm's future isn't a better "X" —it will be a *different* "X." In other words, fax isn't a better courier service—it's a different way to transport letter-sized documents—namely, instant delivery. Like the true navigator of whom Plato spoke, whose knowledge of seasons, of the sky, winds, and stars were signs that enabled him to guide his ship, you must be watchful of signs that tell you to change course or get out of the business you are now in when the trends are against you. How to do that is the subject of this chapter.

THE FUTURE ISN'T LINEAR

Change occurs in a business environment as a combination of evolution and revolution. Change first occurs incrementally in an evolutionary progression—often as logical improvements to current products and services. Then, almost overnight, an explosive, revolutionary metamorphosis occurs. Industries are replaced. The demand for a product or service disappears. Production equipment, work procedures, even selling practices can become suddenly obsolete. It's this morphogenic change that catches everyone off guard.

There are reasons for this pattern of change; the most significant is the natural phenomenon called *diminishing returns*. No resource in business or nature can continue to be improved on. An acre of ground will grow a certain amount of corn. Properly fertilized and cultivated, the production of corn on that acre of ground will increase. But at some point, more fertilizer, more cultivation, or more of anything else will not increase that acre's output of corn. Perhaps someone could go to a research lab and come up with further enhancements—synthetic soil, for example—that would marginally increase production, but the benefits would not justify the expense of doing so.

In the period following World War II, the military continued evolutionary improvements on aircraft in an attempt to increase flying speeds. They experimented with six- and eight-engine designs, but the fundamental limitation was that of the piston engine itself. The ramjet engine was a German World War II invention, and it provided the solution—not a better piston engine, but a different form of propulsion altogether. Revolutionary change. The current fanjet engine—an evolutionary change—replaced the early ramjets. In order to accommodate the higher speed capabilities of the jet engine, aircraft design was itself forced to change in the form of slicker fuselage shapes, swept wings, elevated horizontal stabilizers on the tail—none of which was necessary or would have worked with the piston-powered engine.

Change often occurs because the time is right. Congress has tried many times to pass real tax reform and failed. But in 1986, an election year, the media messages on tax reform were positive, the public supported it, and legislation passed. Sometimes change occurs because the availability of something creates the demand for that "something." Health care procedures and treatments, for example, are available today that were not offered in the past—cosmetic surgery, substance abuse, and preventive medicine—and their availability has created the demand for these new medical services. People once lived with crooked teeth; today they will not. Advances in technology and research have enabled patients to live when heretofore they may have been expected to die. Americans have probably lost their tolerance for physical or psychological discomfort of any kind because of the ever-increasing supply of health care services.

Fifteen years ago mobile telephones were available for vehicles, but they were essentially radios beamed to a central operator who dialed up the party being called and made the connection. For whatever reason, the demand for an automobile telephone simply wasn't there. I had one of those early "radio telephones," and I suspect their failure was a combination of poor transmission quality and the lack of privacy (I sold a washer and dryer to an eavesdropper who overheard my wife and me discussing buying new units over my car phone). But today, the story is different. With the development of the cellular network, car telephones are not unlike home telephones and will likely become a commodity in the future.

Other examples where the intersection of timing and availability produced market change and opportunity include: small black and white kitchen TVs, overnight small package and letter delivery, and VCRs. When products and services become "winners," we call them trends. And trends they may be, but timing and availability created the demand.

It's often difficult to see what the future demand for something will be — because the future isn't linear, and our view of the world is always smaller than it should be because we are looking at the world the way *it is* rather than the way *it will be*. For example, the classic miscalculation of the future demand for a product was IBM's mid-fifties forecast of the world demand for computers — a scant fifty-two of them! IBM had employed fifty-two experts in various industries and asked them to determine the world demand for computers — a device that was then more of a laboratory curiosity than a business tool. Undoubtedly, none of the fifty-two experts wanted to say that there was no demand for such a contraption, but to commit themselves to more than one would have been a risk. Therefore, one per expert — fifty-two in all — was the estimated world demand for computers — forever! And we know how that has turned out. Once available, computers, like office copiers, created their own demand.

But availability isn't always the beginning of a market. CB radios fizzled. HMOs, once heralded as the beginning of a new millenium in health care cost containment, have run into serious financial problems as their enrolled population grows older. And remember quadraphonic sound? — hardly. How about video discs? When products and services flop, we rationalize it by calling them fads. That's one way of dismissing their lack of success. But as Peter Drucker said in his book, *Innovation and Entrepreneurship*, "Leonardo da Vinci conceived of the submarine, the helicopter, and the automatic forge, not one of which could have been created with the technology and materials of his time — nor would the society or economy of the 1500s have had any interest in them."

So, we can dismiss the flops as fads, and accept timing as critical in the determination of revolutionary versus evolutionary change. To be a viable product, the small computer had to await the development of the microchip and a usable operating system. Outpatient surgical techniques had to await the exigencies of cost containment before they would be practiced routinely. The video camera had to await a widespread installed base of VCRs, decades after Polaroid had tried unsuccessfully to introduce an instant movie camera that used essentially the same technology as a Polaroid still camera.

A replacing product or service may go through several format changes before the right one sticks. For example, CB radios gave way to radio telephones, which gave way to cellular phones—all different formats for accomplishing essentially the same thing. Video discs gave way to the betamax videotape format, which lost out to the VHS videotape format (which has stolen a large segment of the pre-video tape era movie-going public). We've seen these changes happen before, and they will happen again. So how can you keep from being blindsided by revolutionary change? Be well-read regarding recent developments in your industry—change isn't instantaneous. Don't drag your feet when change is clearly underway. Act boldly in repositioning yourself in the marketplace or in getting out of markets altogether. A Taoist proverb says, "The leader sees things almost before they happen." You, too, can read the early trends before everyone sees them and the opportunity to act has passed.

Which brings me to my next point.

KEEP YOUR EAR TO THE GROUND

Wilson Harrell was the developer of Formula 409, a cleaning agent that enjoyed great market success a number of years ago. By keeping his ear to the ground, Harrell learned of plans by Procter & Gamble to test market a product called Cinch in Denver. Have you ever heard an announcement that a product was to be test marketed? Of course you have. And so have I. Big companies in particular are wild about their great plans. They announce them publicly. They issue press releases. And that's how Harrell got wind of Procter & Gamble's plans.

His response? He selectively neglected the Denver market. I don't mean that he refused to ship products to that market, but he did allow some empty shelf space to appear. Predictably, in the absence of Formula 409, consumers began to try the competitive product

Cinch, with the result that the Denver test market was a resounding success. That's precisely what Harrell wanted to happen. Because, as Procter & Gamble was planning a national rollout for Cinch, Harrell packaged a sixteen-ounce bottle of Formula 409 together with a half-gallon package and sold the combination for $1.48 — not as a price-cutting move, but rather to load up consumers nationwide with a six-month supply of cleaning agents at a bargain price. When Cinch hit the market, there wasn't a market. Within a short time, Cinch was recognized as a flop by Procter & Gamble executives and was removed from their product line. It's a classic David and Goliath story where the small company with few resources beats the big company with lots of resources. But it wouldn't have been possible if Wilson Harrell hadn't kept his ear to the ground.

Read industry publications. Belong to industry associations. Read as many business publications as you can. Ask questions. What do mutual suppliers say about your competitors? What do mutual customers say about your competitors? What does your sales force say about your competitors? Do a little detective work. What actions are competitors taking that reveal their probable future directions, such as a plant closing, sales force increases, or management changes?

Library databases are becoming quite sophisticated. Now you can easily do a subject search on virtually any topic for which you're interested in gathering information. Learn your way around a major library, particularly a business university library. Know what it offers. Devote a day a month to keeping yourself informed. This is good advice, but it's almost always ignored. However, if you have the discipline to do it, keeping informed will pay dividends.

Keep yourself informed.

ATTACK YOURSELF

No one knows the chinks in your armor better than you. Better that you repair them or shield them than to let the market or competition do it for you. So what threatens the way you are doing business today?

Three companies I have worked with asked that question, and each concluded that their futures were seriously threatened — two of them by their limited access to capital. The first sold out to a larger competitor who provided capital to acquire competitors. The result? — revenues are up 400 percent in three years. The second formed a strategic alliance with a supplier who wanted an exclusive channel to the marketplace and who also provided growth capital that the firm couldn't have otherwise obtained. The third foresaw a weakening market in its principal market line. Rather than clinging to the line, as many small companies would have done in hopes that things would get better, the owner had the discipline to sell out, take the money, and get into a different — though not totally unrelated — business. The company to which he sold out couldn't make a go of it with the business and has now shut it down.

See yourself as if a competitor knew all your secrets. Ask yourself what you would do. Then do it! If someone would buy you out for what your business is really worth — not a "smoke and mirrors" price, but its true worth — would you reinvest your proceeds in the kind of business you're now in? Your answer will be yes if you see a bright future. But if it's no — get out. Start shopping for a buyer.

Profile your company. Attacking yourself begins with a company profile. Would your management staff be capable of handling a serious downturn in the economy or a foray by a competitor into your market? Do you see weaknesses in your sales force, market coverage, or service level? Are your products and services up-to-date, representing good quality and value? Are sales trends and margins headed in the right direction for all products? Are facilities and equipment up-to-date and used near capacity?

These questions are the questions that any good manager should ask, you say? Certainly they are. But they aren't asked. Companies develop a curious kind of blindness to their inadequacies and failures. It's not that problems can't be seen, it's that people learn not to see. Let me give you an example. I replaced the gutters on the front of my house. The color didn't match the color of the siding. Initially, it bugged me every time I saw the difference, and I was determined to repaint the gutters as soon as I could get around to it. Which never came. After looking at the color difference long enough, I didn't see it anymore. While you and your people may have learned not to see your problems, your competitors don't suffer from that affliction. So attack yourself. Profile your company. Honestly appraise its strengths and weaknesses. (I might add that one of the values of using outside advisers and consultants is that they don't have the blind spots that you and your people quite likely have acquired.)

See yourself as your competitors see you.

CREATE, DON'T COMPETE

Competition means trying to be better than someone else. Creation and innovation mean trying to be different from someone else. Federal Express didn't try to compete with Emery Air Freight. Federal Express did things differently. They owned the airline on which their packages moved and processed them through a hub-and-spoke system, whereas, Emery Air Freight was a freight-forwarder using commercial carriers to transport their packages.

Sometimes it's necessary to see things from a different perspective, that is, to see the problem solved in different ways in order to create rather than compete. For example, the Ratheon Radarange used the heat from its magnetron to cook food, whereas the Amana microwave oven used the microwaves generated by the magnetron to cook the food. Both ovens used magnetrons but in different ways with different objectives. Amana became the industry's early leader.

Post-it Notes™, probably one of the most successful office products of the decade, is a contradiction in terms—it is permanently temporary. It's temporary in that it can be removed and reapplied at any time, but it permanently adheres to a surface until it's removed. And it's an ideal product—like an office copying machine, the use of the product becomes addictive. What did Post-it Notes compete against? Nothing. It created a market that wasn't there.

Dick Duke also created a market that wasn't there—ChemLawn™, the national lawn service leader. Duke owned a lawn and garden business and listened to his customers. They asked questions like "How much fertilizer should I put on my lawn?"; "How often should I apply it?"; "What type should I use?" So, for an extra dollar a bag, Duke applied the fertilizer for his customers and created a multimullion dollar business.

Doug Sheley was a Wendy's franchisee in Knoxville, Tennessee, who also owned a health-fitness center. His Wendy's customers were often his health-fitness customers, and they asked questions expressing concern over the amount of cholesterol, calories, and sodium in fast food. The result? D'Lites, a fast-food restaurant for diet-conscious consumers. Its subsequent failure was related to management rather than to its creative concept.

Creation requires you to think about your customers. Competition involves thinking about yourself or your competitors. In competition, the customer becomes a byproduct. A creator will cannibalize his own product lines by introducing new products in the interest of serving customers better. A competitor, on the other hand, defends existing product lines with a vengeance.

Be a creator, not a competitor.

MAKE EVERY CUSTOMER A MARKET

The idea of market segmentation isn't new. Upping the competitive stakes by treating *each* customer as a unique market is new. Customer needs may be similar, but they aren't identical. You must sell to the right customer in the right way in order to treat a customer as a market unto itself.

For example, customers who represent low benefits to your company—that is, the loss of that particular customer wouldn't be critical—should be serviced in a more standardized way than customers whose loss would be devastating. Similarly, customers to whom your company provides valuable benefits
- Will attach the highest value to your services.
- Will pay you more accordingly.
- Will be more loyal.
- Are more important to your firm's success.

These kinds of customers are the kinds you would serve with some "high-touch" approach. I have a client whose company sells a security service that every business can use. But he personally makes the sales presentation to key customers—and he's so good that he closes most of his prospects. He has a sales staff that calls on medium-sized businesses. Their closing rate isn't as good as the owner's, but if they were as good as he is, they'd start their own businesses. Dealers sell everyone else. From "high-touch" to "low-touch," each customer gets the service level justified by the value of the customer to the company and the perceived benefits of the service to the customer.

If a customer is to be treated as a market, be a stargazer. Do market research. Look for new products and services or opportunities that will allow you to sell more to each customer. Know your customer's plans by using your sales force as an intelligence-gathering arm. How do those plans include you? How do they exclude you? Know the customer's market trends if the customer isn't the end user. That way, neither you nor the customer will be caught off guard by either positive or negative trends.

Don't lose touch with a customer simply because the sale has been made. Manage the after-sale relationship, continuing to look for new needs that you can fill as those needs develop. Demonstrate the ongoing benefits that the customer enjoys by using your product or service and by continuing to maintain a relationship with your company. Research has shown that the most common reason for losing a customer—in fact, the reason customers are lost two-thirds of the time—is *Neglect*.

Develop each customer as a unique market.

TURN YOUR ENTIRE ORGANIZATION INTO A SALES FORCE

You don't get a second chance to make a first impression. Who usually makes the first impression in any company? The receptionist—often over the telephone. Customers that are put on hold for long periods of time, who are disconnected, whose messages are botched, who are told that the party they are calling isn't in (and the receptionist doesn't volunteer to take a message)—these customers aren't likely to come back.

I have a client who turned his entire organization into a sales force. Instead of having parts men who sell, he has salesmen with parts expertise on the counter. They may look the same, but the customer can tell the difference. In the same company, a secretary or receptionist can write up lease agreements if a salesman is tied up or out of the office. The controller can buy and sell used equipment if the equipment broker is unavailable.

Another client in Baltimore is a small distributor. The first time I visited his company, he introduced me to everyone we encountered— beginning with the receptionist—as we headed back to his office.

Somehow, the word got out that I was in the office, and others stuck their heads in his door and introduced themselves. Still others walked up to me as I was being shown around the warehouse and introduced themselves. One wrote me a note after I returned to my home city and told me how much he appreciated the opportunity to meet me. This was a sales organization! Right down to the office staff. Predictably, the company is growing at the annual rate of about 50 percent.

Make everyone a salesperson — even the office staff.

GOOD IDEAS CAN COME FROM ANYONE

New ways to do something, new ways to solve a problem, aren't the exclusive domain of managers and owners. A good idea can come from anyone.

Small companies have a real advantage in upping the stakes on big competitors because small companies can listen if they want to. Because of their size, they can listen to their customers better, and they can listen to their employees better. They should be able to spot change faster and respond to change faster because they don't have the bureaucratic baggage that big companies have. Big companies overmanage, and they don't listen well from the bottom up. They take too long to make decisions. That's one advantage Wilson Harrell had in the Procter & Gamble rollout of Cinch. He knew Procter & Gamble would be slow in studying the test market results — giving him time to load up consumers. I remember reading once about a small microprocessor manufacturing company that devised and implemented a strategic redirection of its company in a weekend. Its principal competitor, Motorola, learned of this, and one of its executives simply shook his head and said Motorola people couldn't have agreed on a place to hold a meeting in a weekend.

People — your people — who do their jobs day in and day out know where the breakdowns and bottlenecks are and know how these can be improved. Nurture these people. As I've said before, people do creative things in their own personal lives, but they're often treated like robots in their business lives. Teach your people to be stargazers. A small contract manufacturing business owner tells his people that if they have an idea, go ahead and try it, don't ask permission. If it fails, he won't know; but if the idea works, he does learn of it and passes out $50 bills. In another company an employee devised a tool that virtually eliminated scrap waste. When the owner was shown the tool, he told the employee to take the next week off and go to Hawaii with his wife, all expenses paid. Couldn't have done that in a big company, could he? That's what makes working with small companies so much fun.

Nurture creativity.

STARGAZERS CHANGE THE RULES OF THE GAME

As I've mentioned before, Wendy's was a fast-food Johnny-come-lately started by Dave Thomas. He *changed the rules* of the fast-food game. Thomas entered the maturing fast-food restaurant industry and set it on its ear with the successful introduction of the drive-thru window—a format change that created a new basis for competition. In time, 40 percent of Wendy's sales went literally out the window, enabling them to operate with smaller dining rooms requiring smaller building lots—both distinct cost advantages. A successful format change is most dreaded by the competitor who has the greatest number of units in operation—in this case it was McDonald's. If a restaurant has not been built with a drive-thru window in mind, it's a nightmare to add one. The building is too far back on the lot to allow traffic to pass behind it, the kitchen is in the wrong place, the dining room must be rearranged, and on, and on. No fun. As McDonald's found out.

Domino's also changed the rules in the pizza industry by providing home delivery—in thirty minutes! Not much longer than it takes to get service in a restaurant, and a whole heck of a lot more convenient. Who would have thought that a twenty-three-year-old upstart, with no college degree could build a $2 billion business operating in fifty states and six foreign countries in just over twenty-five years? Nobody, except Tom Monaghan, the founder of Domino's Pizza. The systems and procedures used to provide home-delivered pizzas aren't the ones that are used for restaurant-prepared pizzas. The rules of competition in the sale of pizza have been permanently changed. And if home-delivered fast food is the wave of the future—and every indication is that it is—what does a competitor do with all those restaurant buildings?

Remember "Bugs" Burger, the guy who's in the pest extermination business—*not* the pest control business. "Bugs" resigned from the National Association of Pest Controllers because they wouldn't change their name to the National Association of Pest Exterminators. He is a real stargazer. Like Arthur Jones, "Bugs" is the industry upstart—a true maverick. He changed the rules. "Bugs" deals exclusively with restaurants, and he warrants his service. Find a bug or other pest in a restaurant he services, and the meals that day are on him. A warranted pest *elimination* service? Whoever heard of such a thing? An executive in one of the biggest pest control companies in the industry told me that "Bugs" sure gives them headaches with his service guarantees.

When the rules of the game are successfully changed, the big guys usually lose big time. Then it costs something for competitors to catch up—if they can.

Change the rules and up the stakes to create a competitive edge.

BEFORE CLOSING . . .

I read recently of a wealthy New Englander who died and deeded his estate to his heirs exclusively in the form of common stock—in streetcar companies. Under the trust agreement, the heirs were prevented from selling these stocks. It was 1925, and the benefactor couldn't imagine a world without streetcars. No stargazer here.

Businesses large and small seem intent on coping with evolutionary change—keeping up—and many do it well. But a revolutionary replacement is hiding in a niche somewhere, and it almost always whipsaws the industry when it comes out into the open.

By attacking yourself, converting your entire business into a sales organization, and by having everyone in the company keep a collective ear to the ground, it's possible to minimize the damage of explosive change. It also helps combat another danger. When the economic cycle turns down, as it most assuredly will in the future, markets shrink and overcapacity mounts. Typically, service levels drop as companies scramble to cut expenses. Be a "contrarian." Stay close to your customers, expand your sales efforts, listen to your people, and you'll likely outperform naysayers.

Philosophizing five hundred years before Christ was born, Lao-tzu, the author of the *Tao Te Ching*, said:

> To know how other people behave takes intelligence,
> but to know yourself takes wisdom.
> To manage other people's lives takes understanding,
> but to manage your own takes true power.
>
> If your goals are clear, you can achieve them without fuss,
> if you are at peace with yourself, you will not spend
> your energy in conflicts.

Be a stargazer.

CHAPTER THIRTEEN

THE GATHERING STORM

How to Get Through the Coming Recession

On May 18, 1980, at 8:30 in the morning, seventeen feet of the top of Mount St. Helens blew off with a force equivalent to five hundred times that of the bomb which destroyed Hiroshima. Smoke and ash rose ten miles into the sky. Mud and rubble to a depth of fifty feet spread out over a five-mile area from the base of the mountain. Everything within 150 square miles was flattened—including Harry Truman.

Harry was a caretaker at a lodge on Spirit Lake, just north of Mount St. Helens' vengeful peak. Unlike the tourists, hikers, and residents who had heeded the warnings to clear the area—after seismic readings indicated that an explosion was imminent—Harry and his sixteen cats carried on life as usual. His neighbors' pleadings and even a sister's telephone call attempting to talk some sense into the old coot failed to budge Harry. He boasted to a national television reporter, fascinated with Harry's indifference to danger: "Nobody knows about this mountain more than Harry, and it don't dare blow up on him." Today Harry's face decorates T-shirts, his name punctuates folksongs, and he is lionized by the local folk as a symbol of a curious form of grittiness that destroyed him.

On Monday, October 19, 1987, the stock market continued a free-fall that begun the previous Friday, closing down 508 points for the day. A trillion dollars in paper value vaporized as completely as the top seventeen feet of Mount St. Helens had seven-and-a-half years earlier. But, unlike Mount St. Helens, whose visitors escaped disaster, the economic warning signs had largely gone unheeded by much of the financial community. A shift in monetary policy in the summer of 1982, which allowed Mexico to reschedule its debt, also flooded thirsty financial markets that had been restricted by Federal Reserve Chairman Paul Volker's draconian measures. Interest rates fell, and investors dumped interest-rate-sensitive instruments in a scramble to enter the stock market, a flight not unlike the Oklahoma Land Rush nearly a century before. The Dow began to climb out of the 700- to 800-point range where it had been stuck for months. Interest rates continued falling through 1986, down to 7.5 percent, further boosting the Dow well above the 2000 mark. Everyone "in the know" was predicting 5 percent to 6 percent interest rates—something I'd not seen since the early sixties.

In the spring of 1987 interest rates suddenly turned up and continued to rise. Walking to a game field one Saturday that spring, I asked my assistant soccer coach, an economist with a major Atlanta bank, "What in the heck is going on with interest rates?" "It's a glitch," he answered. But the "glitch" was being driven by the need to entice foreign and domestic capital into debt instruments in order to help finance the accumulated federal deficit. From its low at 7.5 percent, thirty-year bond interest rates rose to 10.5 percent. Mortgage interest rates and the prime rate also rose.

But the Dow Jones Industrials disregarded the historic inverse interest rate/stock price relationship and continued its euphoric rise to 2700. In August 1987, one prominent newspaper ran three articles comparing the similarity of this bull market with the run-up that preceded the 1929 stock market crash. However, Robert Prechter, the stock market forecasting guru, continued to predict a 3000 Dow, using his Elliott Wave Theory model.

In September, then Treasury Secretary James Baker disengaged the dollar, allowing it to seek its own level against world currencies as a means to combat the mounting trade deficits. A nervous market, with its computerized trading programs primed and cocked, bit its fingernails down to the cuticles while stocks sold at price to earnings ratios (P/Es) of 20+ —twice the historic average—and the yield on the Standard and Poor's 500 fell below 3 percent. Then "something happened" (nobody knows exactly what it was in situations like this), and the house of cards caved in.

But the story doesn't end there—which is why I think the happenings in October 1987 should concern us even today. Stock specialists, strapped for cash after the October 19 free fall, again faced disaster after a 200-point bounce on Tuesday the twentieth turned into another selling rout. The Federal Reserve informed reluctant New York banks that they were backed on any loans they wanted to make to specialists who couldn't otherwise borrow to keep trading going. So, loans were made to the specialists, the rout was reversed, and the market closed up 102 points. On Wednesday, the twenty-first, the market was up again almost 200 points—a 300-point, two-day recovery that still left the Dow 300 points below the previous week. The Fed had averted a worldwide meltdown of financial markets. But that's not all.

When people are scared, what do they do? Hoard. They hoard food if food is endangered—they hoard money if money is endangered. And that's exactly what happened in the days following October 19—an exodus of capital left the stock market seeking safety, and thirty-year T-bill yields were forced down to 8.5 percent. Almost two years later, yields on two- to four-year treasury bonds were higher than long bonds—a sure sign of uncertainty about the future economic climate. Investors keep short accounts when they see mixed signals.

WHAT IF?

The United States saves about $10,000 per person, West Germany saves about $12,000 per person, and Japan saves about $20,000 per person. What if Americans get scared enough to put another $2,000 in savings? A half a trillion dollars—half of the amount that vanished from the stock market on October 19—will leave the consumer-spending segment of our economy. Of the four elements of the GNP—government spending, consumer spending, capital spending, and net exports—consumer spending is currently the only one that still has a pulse. The most likely candidates to save more of their incomes are people who are financially well off—those who also purchase high-priced goods and services such as vacations, luxury homes and cars, and similar high-ticket items, the producers of which employ nearly 15 million people. One researcher noted that if Americans do remove from consumption (which is the way they'll save) the equivalent of $2,000 additional per person, and if only half of this reduced consumption comes out of the hide of luxury industries, three million people will be put out of work. In turn, this could have a domino effect on other economic segments.

An outcome of the Great Depression was the Federal Deposit Insurance Corporation. The FDIC insures deposits up to $100,000 — a large sum at that time but a paltry amount today. But many depositors are corporate accounts, which have considerably more than $100,000 on deposit, and half the funds of the major overnight deposit banks come from foreign countries with deposits in the hundreds of millions of dollars — funds far exceeding the FDIC protection limit. What happens if these depositors get nervous? They pull out — by wire — overnight. Our banking system, learning that billions of dollars had escaped by wire transfer to foreign banks around the world, would be faced with the dilemma of covering obligations. Under current banking rules this would be impossible, and the entire American banking system could face collapse. In fact, on October 20, 1987, the Japanese banks, nervous in the face of what had happened on the previous day, threatened to stop lending to the United States. Which could have made a bad situation unmanageable.

Couple this scenario with the fact that foreign business organizations are much more debt-leveraged than U.S. organizations. American companies use debt/equity ratios to the tune of about 2:1. But, the debt/equity ratios in foreign companies give a new meaning to the word leverage — sometimes it's as high as 100:1. So, a shaky U.S. short-term outlook could cause foreign lenders to call in loans in order to pay their nervous creditors, particularly if their own shaky paper economies needed financial shoring up.

The Japanese stock market P/E ratios make our stock market's P/E ratios look conservative. For this reason, Japanese investors see more bargains on the American exchanges than on their own. But if Americans lose confidence in Wall Street, the foreigners will retreat too. And if the Japanese stock market collapsed under the weight of high P/Es, there could be bargains in Tokyo, triggering a Japanese sell-off on Wall Street to finance bargains on their exchange.

One more thread in this economic Gordian knot. Our interest rates are more attractive to the Japanese due to their people's higher propensity to save. Thus lower Japanese interest rates in constrast to our lower leverage, lower P/Es, and higher interest rates are the factors that make American financial markets attractive to Japanese and other foreign investors. But the performance of the European, London, American, and Japanese stock markets track pretty much in sync, so an autonomous perturbation in any one of these markets could trigger a sell-down in all of them. Witness October 19 and its effect on world exchanges. Until trade deficits, fiscal deficits, Third World debt, and closer alignment of the economic policies of the Germans, British, Americans, and Japanese occurs, we will all be steering a course between Scylla and Charybdis.

As you can see, we no longer live in a U.S. economy. We live in a world economy. Who's hurt worse in an economic downturn? The poor. In a world economy, a world economic downturn would hurt the lesser developed countries that have borrowed heavily and will default on their loans. They have already technically defaulted on them in the past, only to be resurrected by "magic money" from the United States and the World Bank. But a wide scale, unredeemable default by the lesser developed countries would force the major U.S. banks, which have lent lots of money to them, to write down those assets as uncollectible. This could erase the net worth of many U.S. banks, exacerbating the already nervous condition of foreign depositors.

Perhaps you're wishing you hadn't started reading this chapter. But I saw a cartoon in which a mythical Adam was saying to Eve on their expulsion from Eden, "My dear, we are living in a time of transition," and we too are living in a transitionary period. Be assured I am not a doomsday prophet. Foreigners have so many investments in American assets that the last thing they want to see is our economic collapse. That's our insurance policy. There will be temporary disruptions as we get through the transition period. But I think we will have a more tidy economy in the nineties, one based on tangible rather than ephemeral values. Possibly the Dow Jones Industrials will reach the elusive 3000 mark that Robert Prechter predicted for 1987. But it will have to occur with higher corporate earnings—not higher P/Es.

I also think the world economic leadership in the future will not be dominated by the United States, but, rather, shared by the United States, the United Kingdom, Japan, and Germany, whose fiscal and monetary policies currently are at odds with each other. (We want low interest rates to spur economic development, whereas the others, Germany in particular, have kept their interest rates high against ours.) And if you look at the cycles of human history, a world political and economic empire lasting longer than a hundred or more years is rare. The Roman Empire lasted three hundred years. The United States economic and political ascendancy began in 1775—over two hundred years ago—and I think it is realistic to expect that economic and political influence is shifting away from us. Particularly when we face two modern industrial nations, Germany and Japan, whose economies were obliterated by us in World War II and whose economic machinery is now less than fifty years old.

We are more than seventy-five months into the current economic expansion—longer than any other expansion in modern economic history. I personally believe that the world is transitioning to an economic period that will see, at least in America, a twelve- to eighteen-month recession beginning sometime in late 1989 or early in 1990.* In fact, during the summer of 1988, I conducted a survey of twenty-one thousand small business owners to coincide with the Democratic National Convention in Atlanta, and 60 percent of the responses were evenly divided in their opinion that the recession would begin in the first, second, or third quarter of 1989. In the period following the election of George Bush, there has been an uptick in optimism, which has delayed a recession. But I believe this optimism will be relatively short-lived. In late 1989, housing starts had been in decline for two years, interest rates had risen steadily since early 1988, the trade and fiscal deficits had not declined, help wanted ads had been flat for a year, foreclosures and small business failures had been rising for over a year—the fundamental problems were still there. Not to mention the spate of junk bonds issued to finance those silly takeovers and the effect that a business downturn

---

*Jesus said, "You will always have poor among you." I say, "You will always have recessions with you." How they start will be different, but a free market economy can't get rid of them. Therefore, this chapter will be as timely twenty years from now as it is today.

will have on paying their interest rates, or for that matter, paying the bond payments themselves.

FIFTEEN WAYS TO SURVIVE

What can you do as a business owner to get through this economic transition and emerge as a stronger company? Here are fifteen good ideas.

• *Give closer attention to all work.* Favorable economic conditions are a siren song—they tend to lure us into complacency, encourage us to devote more time to activities outside the business, and consequently pay less attention to what provides our livelihood. My recommendation, in order to get ready for the coming recession, is to reduce your outside activities so that you can pay attention to everything. How is your phone answered? How are orders being written up? How are your accounts receivable being collected? What's happening to your service levels? Where are the opportunities to operate smarter?

I've said it before, and I'll say it again—in business, you get not only what you expect to happen, but also what you *inspect* to see that it is happening. When you begin to inspect it, you may find that a lot of what you expected to happen isn't, and you'll find a lot of what you didn't think was happening is. Moreover, by paying attention to the details of your business, you will invariably produce a sharper image—something that will be critically important in the coming two years. Remember the old Gillette razor commercial—"Look sharp! Feel sharp! Be sharp!" It's a recommendation you should follow. Be sharp! Pay attention to your business, particularly because service levels tend to drop during times of economic softness. And a soft economy is a buyer's market. The reduced sales that are there will go to the company that has its act together.

There is an adage that says, "God is in the details." In other words, look to the little things. An English proverb makes a similar point: "Pay attention to the pence—and the pounds take care of themselves." Expect concerned suppliers, bankers, and customers to visit you, perhaps unannounced, but let them see a clean operation that is humming like a fine machine because the details aren't being sloughed off.

- *Expand or reposition your know-how.* As your primary markets contract, you will have to deal with surplus capacity. How can you apply your know-how to opportunities you are not now pursuing? For example, look at your aftermarkets. These are often ignored as low priorities because they often involve menial work, such as maintenance and repairs. However, these will be higher priorities in tougher times when people are looking for work to keep their equipment and employees busy and when customers will maintain what they have rather than purchase new durables. I have a client who produces fabricated canopies and convenience stores for gasoline dealers. At present, his production capacity is full—he's concerned with simply getting jobs out on time. But these buildings require almost continual maintenance beginning about three years after they are constructed, and from time to time their owners make major changes in the exterior facade. This is not the kind of business that a metal building fabricator wants to do—it is maintenance and rehab work, "sorta beneath our dignity." But when production shops are running at reduced capacity and field crews have less to install, what would be a better use of their time than maintenance and rehab work? The time to pursue that market is now, not a year or more from now when the competition for aftermarket work will be intense.

Another client sells and rents heavy industrial machinery. That market began to soften about a year ago. I encouraged him to get ready for a downturn and to shift his emphasis away from sales and rentals and more toward parts, maintenance, and general product support for the equipment that is already in the field. Although such a refocus has occurred, he delayed implementing it, and the opportunity passed for a quick sell-off of rental equipment that would be idled in a downturn. Unlike a year ago, when he would have been able to sell a rental unit in one month, it now takes about seven months to find a buyer because the market has contracted. The margins have too.

Anticipate what your customers will need in a depressed market and go after it now. At the same time, anticipate what they won't need and don't depend on their weakened demand. Sell out of what they won't need and get into what they will need.

Consider contracting out your services and surplus capacity to businesses that require operations you're able to perform. For example, a proprietary manufacturer might take on contract manufacturing — something that he wouldn't have done in better times. His production capacity then would have been used to produce his own branded products. A letter courier might take on the delivery of larger packages — something that is not as convenient to transport, but in the face of reduced demand for letter couriers (created both by economic conditions and the inroads that fax machines have made into the market), package delivery looks attractive. A landscape contractor who installs plant and other landscape materials might get into landscape maintenance, which uses the same equipment and people of the same skill levels. The work is not as technical or artistic, but it's money.

Expand or reposition your know-how — but do it now!

• *Reduce your cash break-even by at least 20 percent.* Good times cause break-evens to rise. But high break-evens are a killer in stable or declining markets. Lee Iacocca's real turnaround at Chrysler was a break-even turnaround — he reduced break-evens by 50 percent, resulting in the highest profits in the history of Chrysler at half the sales volume. You should anticipate a downturn in your sales over the next two years and begin to reduce your break-evens now so you'll be profitable with lower revenues.

Your projected earnings with reduced revenues should cover current interest charges at least ten times or at least cover principal and interest by one-and-a-half times. Break-evens can be lowered by reducing, eliminating, or avoiding nonliquidating debt. Loans made against accounts receivable and inventory are self-liquidating, since the sale of inventory or the collection of accounts receivable enables you to repay the loans against them. On the other hand, loans made to purchase equipment, facilities, or properties don't self-liquidate, therefore, they must be paid out of cash flow.

Since the end of 1983, total debt in nonfinancial corporations in this country has climbed from about a $1 trillion to almost $2 trillion, and through the middle quarter of 1988 interest payments were running at an annual rate of about a $100 billion — $30 billion more than net interest payments of two years ago. While some of this is due to increases in interest rates, interest payments have risen faster than interest rates; that is, business is using more debt capital. During the same period, the total debt of nonfinancial corporations in this country has grown at a rate of 13 percent compared with 9 percent over the previous twenty-five years! Currently, U.S. nonfinancial corporations use over 20 percent of their cash flow to service their outstanding debt. Revenues, reduced by a serious recession, will make that percentage rise quickly, because large companies can't reduce break-evens quickly. However, small companies can reduce break-evens quickly, and one sure way to make it through the coming recession is to anticipate its effects on cash flow and make those adjustments now.

Ideally, long-term debt should be no more than 25 percent of your capital structure, a debt/equity ratio of 1:3, insulating you somewhat from interest spikes, which could reach mid-teens in the next two years. Examine your capital structure and make the tough decisions now while there's time. The tendency of many small business owners is to say, "I can't cut anything." If your revenues fell by 10 percent — which means 10 percent of revenues are immediately erased from your bottom line — I suspect you would get quite creative in finding something to eliminate from your ongoing expenses while continuing to have a going business. You'd have to act quickly, so you would sell something to pay down debt and the associated negative cash flow connected with debt service. Do that now. Sell assets not absolutely required in your business over the next two years — planes, property, and idle or underutilized equipment that have accumulated in the good times.

Eliminate perks — cars, club memberships, and expense allowances other than reimbursement for actual expenses paid. And watch travel and sales expense outlays like a hawk. The elimination of perks will help lower your break-evens, and, in case you're thinking that you and your people will groan, think of the alternative — the elimination of salaries and the people who go with them. I think perk holders would prefer giving up perks to giving up incomes. The elimination of incomes in order to bring down break-evens is much more of a morale bummer than the elimination of perks. If your people can be made to "see the light" for the next two years, perks pale into insignificance.

Reduce sales guarantees. Otherwise, you will have to fire a salesman in order to lower your overhead—and this cuts your sales throat because you reduce your presence in the marketplace. High guarantees for commissioned salespeople are bad under the best of times, but over the next two years, if you need them, you're already in trouble. In one case, I had the sales manager of a client tell me that he'd lose his entire sales force if guarantees were cut, but his choices were either to cut the guarantees or cut some people. He cut the guarantees and, much to his amazement, nobody left. But then it was put-up or shut-up time—the good people didn't worry about the guarantee elimination because they earned well over their guarantees, and the others—well, they knew they had to go to work.

Install automation that pays back in twelve months or less. If automation pays back over a longer period than that, it won't matter. Assuming we will have a two-year recession, you've got to have automation that makes money for you in the second year. Big automation projects, such as a computer system, should make big savings—fast. Automation eliminates labor, which is a high cost in any business.

Subcontract support functions. For example, use a pickup and delivery service to eliminate company trucks or use payroll services to eliminate the person now performing that task in your accounting department. At a minimum, you can free up accounting time that can be absorbed by other bookkeeping activities. Maintenance services provide no value to your product, so don't do it with in-house personnel—use a janitorial firm and/or a fix-it company.

These may seem like draconian measures. They aren't. Remember when you began your company? Why, it took a meeting of the board of directors to spend $100. As you grew and there was more money available, you began to spend thousands with a lot less concern than you initially spent $100. You didn't feel deprived then; you were careful. Why not be as careful now when the margins for error may became as tight as they once were?

• *Become cash rich.* Omar Khayyám's *Rubáiyát* (XIII), says, "Take the cash and let the credit go, nor heed the rumble of a distant drum." Good advice. Too many small businesses are money rich and cash poor. They ignore the rumble of the distant drum—but they don't take the cash. In a depressed economy, cash is king. It's cash, not profits, that enables you to pay your bills.

You can become cash rich by selling and leasing back critical assets or undervalued assets. Selling and leasing back critical assets transfers the title from your company to the lessor. In the event—heaven forbid—that the recession takes you into Chapter 11 bankruptcy, creditors can't get at those assets because the lessor holds title to them. But you can continue to use the assets, which, since they are critical to your operation, enables you to continue doing business. If you don't feel good about selling and leasing back these assets to an outsider, sell them to yourself. Unless you're personally guaranteed on the obligations of your business, the asset will still be beyond the reach of creditors. However, make sure you have a lawyer review the transfer so it's a defensible sale/lease-back.

Undervalued assets should be sold and leased back in order to cash-out your equity. Why tie up cash in an asset when use of the asset is, in most cases, more important than owning the asset? Your company should only buy its assets when it has more cash to invest in the business than the business operation needs. What better investment can the business make than to buy an asset required by your business? You should lease assets when you need cash for operating the business rather than for owning its assets. Lease-backs can include an option to purchase the assets, provided the repurchase price is reasonable. This way, the lease payments are tax deductible. If the repurchase price is artificially low, the IRS could call the lease an installment purchase and void their tax deductibility other than a fair market interest charge and depreciation. As I've said before, get a lawyer to review the transaction so it's defensible.

Reduce and return inventory. Lower inventory frees cash and reduces your exposure to "dead" inventory. I know companies that would be debt free if they cut inventories in half. Return inventory that you can't sell within the next twelve months, even though your supplier might charge a restocking fee. Whatever the restocking fee is now, you can count on it doubling in tough times, because suppliers won't want inventory returned. In fact, in other recessionary periods, suppliers have charged such exorbitant restocking fees that they were in essence pawn brokers. Go through your inventory like a bloodhound and pull out everything that doesn't have a reasonable inventory turn, (and to me, a reasonable turn is at least six times a year). Once you've identified the slow-moving inventory, if it can't be returned to the supplier, have a "fire sale." You may make a smaller margin by dumping it, but most importantly, you'll have your cash.

Establish a bank credit line — probably receivable financing. You don't have to use it, but it's better to establish one now than in the midst of a recession when credit granting will be tougher. By selling assets you won't need over the next two years, and reducing inventory, you can transform some of your credit requirements from long-term debt to short-term debt (receivables financing).

• *Keep short accounts.* Avoid long payoff projects. I recently reviewed with a client a capital-spending project that had a payback period of five years. I was strongly opposed to it, despite its alleged efficiency improvements. I warned, "Within a five-year period, we could conceivably pass through two recessions, and I wouldn't want to be stuck with either this asset or its associated debt for that period of time." I was overruled. I wish him the best, but I believe he made a mistake because his industry is at the beginning of the distribution chain, and, as such, gets hit early when business "heads south." If a "savings" doesn't occur within twelve months, it will be an outlay rather than an investment in the face of the coming recession.

You keep short accounts by selling or leasing out space that your business will not need in the next two to three years. You don't want to enter an economic slowdown with overhanging capacity. If you currently need new space or equipment, don't buy it; lease it on short terms. Watch your capacity utilization — equipment, trucks, anything required to do business — and consider what the effect of a 10 percent downturn in sales would be on your current utilization of capacity. If you're not now using it fully, can you afford to carry idle capacity through a recession?

Terminate the employees you'd release if revenues dropped 10 percent. Unless your bottom line is immorally high, you can't live with a 10 percent revenue hit. So if these are the employees you'd cut, they're already marginal, and you simply haven't yet stepped up to the decision to dismiss them. It sometimes takes something as dramatic as an economic downturn to get business owners to face the fact that an employee simply isn't going to make it. But don't wait. Do it now!

• *Improve sales and product leverage.* If you carry a product that is used by one or a very few customers, get rid of it. If you have a customer who buys only one of the products in your total product line, get rid of the customer. These may not be one and the same. Why carry a product that only one customer uses? It kills your product leverage. Why have a customer who buys only one of the several products you sell in your business? It kills your marketing leverage. In order to get through the coming recession, your objective should be to eliminate all unnecessary inventory—by eliminating low-demand products—and to maximize the revenue per sales call—by eliminating single-product customers.

Another way you can increase the revenue per sales call is to become a distributor of complementary products you do not now carry. In good times, there may be justifiable reasons for not carrying these complementary products, but in tough times, you need as many potential bucks per sales call as you can assemble. "But that will increase my inventory investment," you might be thinking. You're right. But as I've already said, you need inventory that turns fast. So complementary products must pass that test too.

• *Manage value added.* Cost is a function of processes, methods, and materials. Revenue is a function of demand, which is less controllable than cost. Value added is the spread between cost and revenue.

Cost control is important—but value added control is more important. If costs go up or revenues go down, value added is reduced. Value added is your only source of continuous funding. Value added pays payroll, utilities, overhead, debt service, and every other expense of doing business. Manage it like cash.

• *Screen prospective customers.* With tough times ahead, screen customers who might end up in trouble or who might hide in Chapter 11. When you have the opportunity, be a secured creditor. Find out who previously supplied the prospect, and why you're now getting business. You may really be "getting the business." Could be the prospect was cut off by previous suppliers.

Remember that a customer who buys on open terms enjoys the privilege of paying later—it's not a right. Open terms put you in the banking business, so act like a banker in extending credit. Ask for financial statements for the last several years. If the prospect has been a marginally profitable company during the last few years, which have been years of economic prosperity, imagine what it will be like when the economy fizzles. With your own sales softening, it's a temptation to ignore the warning signs that a sales prospect's financial conditions might give. But using valuable resources to produce product that is sold to a slow payer or a no payer is immeasurably worse than taking the revenue hit. I'm frequently involved in helping clients find bank loans, and I can tell you that banks are "cherry picking" their loan candidates right now. You should be doing the same thing.

• *Work with slow payers.* Now is the time to scrutinize customers who have been traditionally slow payers. Again, if a company has stretched you out during the good times, imagine what it will do to you in the bad times. And it is inevitable that you will also find a slowdown in payments by customers who have historically been timely in their payments to you. Work with them, finance what's due to you without alienating them. Tough times produce personal stress, and under such conditions an irritated customer may unreasonably stretch you out in order to get even with overzealous collection attempts. A slow payer may have been a good and loyal customer in the past, and as such, when the economy and their business strengthens, their loyalty will also be strengthened by your willingness to work with them in the tough times. At least it doesn't encourage them to switch to a competitor when their options improve.

I'm not proposing that you should delay being paid, but rather that you find creative ways to get paid. For example, visit your customer and negotiate terms. The squeaky joint gets greased, so make sure that you squeak loudly. Stay on the telephone—people take your claims about as seriously as you do. So, keep the pressure up. I have a client who took a piece of property in lieu of a cash payment. Always come away with something other than a promise to pay in the future. You already have that.

Remember the four "C's" of credit:
- Character—that beats them all.
- Collateral—get it if you can get it.
- Capacity—thin in tough times.
- Conditions—you hope that's why the customer is a slow payer rather than a deadbeat.

• *Create a come-back team.* Surround yourself with winners. You'll need them to get through a recession. Intensify training and development. As times get tough, your competitors will invariably lay off quality employees including good sales people. Hire them. You want as much presence in the marketplace as you can get, and this means more salespeople. In the 1981-82 recession, a client hired good salespeople who had been cut by his competitors. As a result, his company's sales actually rose during those two years because he was farsighted enough to pick up the quality players when competitors "cut expenses" by laying off salesmen who were "making too much money."

A come-back team is what Lee Iacocca created to get Chrysler turned around. It doesn't require a lot of people to do great things — but it does require the right ones. A come-back team is a lot like airborne infantry — the team members are used to fighting while surrounded. A come-back team works through lunch and members eat at their desks. The team doesn't need to be told to come in on Saturday to catch up on paperwork so that work days can be used more productively. And, of course, no organization can rise above its leadership, so you're the critical example in determining how effective your company will be in making it through the recession.

• *Pay for performance.* Raises without productivity increases are dumb. In tough times they can be suicidal. Instead, install incentive-based compensation such as gainsharing programs or true profit sharing that pays off immediately rather than accumulates in a retirement plan. The last thing employees are thinking about during the heat of a recession is retirement. When one or a group of your employees pulls off a coup — getting a shipment out early, collecting a past-due or written-off account, or cutting costs — dole out some $50 bills as an immediate and visible reward.

• *Improve the acquisition of management information.* Information is the lifeblood of your business. Work now to improve the quality, quantity, and timeliness of feedback from every pressure point in your business. This is the only way that you will be able to make decisions in real time instead of with dead data. The acquisition of a computer system that will accomplish this is an investment, not an expense.

• *Know your cash position every day.* I'm not talking about knowing how much cash you have in the bank. That's just a number. You should know cash on hand, cash encumbered by past purchases, and cash receipts projections. Remember, cash is king in an economic slowdown. So anything that diminishes cash threatens the viability of your business.

• *Look for bargains.* There will be many of them, and cash is required to take advantage of them. Real wealth doesn't disappear in a recession—it just changes hands. Fortunes were made in the Great Depression by those with cash—not wealth. I have a relative, for example, who was not wealthy by any standards during the Great Depression. He was a postal worker and a frugal saver. As foreclosures came on the market in the form of land and housing, he had cash, and cash drove a hard bargain. So, while he wasn't wealthy *in* the Great Depression, he was wealthy *after it.*

Subscribe to *The National Bankruptcy Reporter* to learn of "fire sales" in your industry that represent bargains. You might find opportunities to acquire or merge with other companies that will make both of you stronger in and after the coming recession. A client with access to capital is doing just that—buying companies that are weakened by the slowdown in commercial building construction. These companies weren't for sale two years ago, and their weakness now is their lack of resources rather than a defective management team or marginal products. Predictably, my client is becoming a stronger company every day, his company will get through the recession without a hiccup, and it will be a dominant industry competitor when the economy returns to normal.

It is possible that a recession could be accompanied by a liquidity crisis such as occurred during the 1969 recession. If so, there will be bargains in abundance for those who have cash to seize them.

• *Keep the faith.* Watch your face. Worried looks, furrowed brows, and closed doors put everyone on edge. You must be steady at the helm and have unswerving faith that you will get through the coming recession. The importance of the morale of your employees in tough times can't be overstated. The companies that get into trouble will, to a great extent, be in trouble because they have lost faith in themselves. Many times, I have seen companies endure crises because their founders had bulldog tenacity and supreme confidence that they would get through the mess. Tough times stiffened their resolve. In one case, the owner of the company had a sign on his office door that said, "Yea, though I walk through the valley of the shadow of death, I can beat the (bleep) out of anybody in there." This kind of determination is infectious and steels the will to win in every employee.

BEFORE CLOSING . . .

Remember Harry Truman? The guy who heard and saw the rumblings of Mount St. Helens—and disregarded the warning? Don't be like him—act now.

There's a temptation when you're told that tough times are ahead to deny it. You rationalize yourself into inactivity. But denial is the first stage of a crisis. And at this phase of the economic cycle, it's like whistling in the graveyard to keep your spirits up. I've been put down by clients whom I have cautioned to enact the very things I've said here. Their comments go something like this: "I've been hearing that we were going to have a recession for the past three years, and one hasn't happened yet." But what *I'm* hearing is Harry Truman—"This mountain won't get me." Your spirits will be kept up not by whistling in the graveyard, but by being ready.

I don't know anyone who watches the evening news, and reads *The Wall Street Journal* and other business publications who isn't a bit nervous right now. It's a lot like being on a Caribbean island with a hurricane headed your way. You don't know when it will hit or if it will hit. You can't run away—so prepare. Preparation is a self-fulfilling prophecy. You assume an impending crisis and preparation avoids its consequences. So make *all* of the *right* changes—and do it now—and you'll be here two years from now to talk about it. And if the current mixed signals delay the inevitable economic downturn, look at how much more profitable you'll be in the interim if you do these things.

When William Saroyan died, he had written his own obituary. "I always knew a man had to die, but I somehow thought an exception would be made in my case . . . now what?" I suspect that there's a bit of gallows humor here, but the time for the "now what?" is coming.

> Confusion now hath made his masterpiece.
> — *Macbeth*

AFTER WORDS

When I took trigonometry in high school, the notation Q.E.D. was at the bottom of the page on which a theorem was worked out. It stands for a Latin phrase, *quod erat demonstradum*, an appendage to a math solution that means, "We have proved what we set out to prove." I wish I could say that I had accomplished my purpose of providing some practical ideas for managing your business by writing this book. But I'll never know. I would have preferred to speak these words to you. Speaking is a less formal way of communicating, so words and phrasing don't have to be chosen as carefully. Body language and emotion are part of a spoken presentation—an important part. Audience feedback is immediate. I can see how an audience is reacting, so adjustments can be made in my presentation: speed up, slow down, even stop and engage in a two-way conversation with members of the audience. But spoken words are for limited audiences, and my goal was to address a larger audience than is practical through speeches.

Writing, on the other hand, requires more creativity than the spoken word as a medium for communication. Lacking audience feedback and the inability to use body language and emotion, written words must be chosen carefully, phrased perfectly in order to get meaning across. In a speech I can cover a topic in one hour that would take ten hours to deliver in writing. Moreover, speeches are delivered to and governed by the needs of the audience. Writing—books and articles—is governed by the needs of a publisher—deadlines, length, and content. Because writing is such a creative activity, it balks at deadlines and rebels against a writer's pressures. Sometimes ideas refuse to come. Other times, the ideas are there, but the words are defiantly illusive. It's an imperfect process because a writer's ideas and experiences are intangibles, made of a different material than are words. It's hard to translate the stuff of one substance into the stuff of another. As all writers have experienced, I have spent hours bludgeoning into line a few dozen uncooperative words so they will say what I want them to say, the way I want it said. That's why I wince when someone speaks of "causal reading." How can someone casually read something that wasn't casually written?

Writers write not because they want their words to be read, but because they want their ideas and experiences to be understood. In that respect, the motives for starting a business and writing a book probably aren't that different. If you start a business in order to make a lot of money, chances are you won't. But if you start a business because you know how to solve a problem better than anyone else, then the money will follow. Similarly, books that are written for fame or fortune will achieve neither. The writer must believe he has something valuable to say. Many don't. Consequently, the reader doesn't make it past the first few chapters, and the book goes nowhere—like a business that offers nothing new to the market. A writer's raw materials are his experiences, and those that lack experiences that are valuable to others are writing in a vacuum. Their pages have words on them, but they are otherwise empty.

But there are many books that have much to say. Regrettably, what they have to say is never fully communicated because of the casualness with which most people read—they read a book and think they've learned what it has to say. But if a book has something to say it must be studied, not read. When you first read a book, you see its idea "through a glass darkly," to borrow a phrase from the Apostle Paul. Research into cognitive learning shows that on a first reading you'll only grasp the tips of the writer's most salient points and will lose all but a shadow of that new knowledge without reinforcement. A first reading of a book creates no more than a context within which subsequent rereadings provide the real opportunity to learn what the writer is trying to communicate. Some people understand this and do it instinctively—they will read ahead in order to get a sense of the writer's message and then drop back and reread for content and understanding. That's the difference between reading, and studying.

So if you want to get value out of this book that far exceeds the price you paid for it, here's how to do it.

Pencil into your calendar within the next two weeks a time to completely reread this book—cover to cover. Why two weeks? Because a first reading, as I've said, is ephemeral, a contraction of two Greek words, *epi* and *hemera*, which literally translates "for a day." The context of a first reading will attenuate quickly. Your first reading of this book, which hopefully you've now completed, has prepared you to begin learning what I've tried to communicate in these thirteen chapters. Because you and I have different processes by which we think and learn, having discovered in your first reading where I was going, a quick rereading of the book by you will put my ideas into the context in which they existed in my mind when I wrote them, a context that couldn't possibly have existed in your mind, because you and I haven't experienced the same things in life. The communication of ideas that have been transformed into words in an effort to produce understanding in another person's mind is a kind of alchemy—converting one substance into another—with a lot lost in the process. On your second reading, you'll help your understanding of the ideas in this book if you'll use a highlighter pen or underline and write margin notes to yourself. That's what I do, and for that reason I never give away a book because after reading and rereading and making notes, I've shaped the book's ideas to my needs.

Next, pencil in a third reading into your calendar about three months from now. You may be thinking, "What! . . . three readings of the same book when I could have read three different books during that time?" Well, that's all you would have done—read three books and gotten very little lasting value from them. Whereas, you can study one book, and it could change the way you think and work. If I didn't believe that, I wouldn't have taken the past year to write it. Having read and quickly reread this book, a third reading ninety days from now will enable you to discover new ideas that were missed in the previous readings. And new business experiences will occur in the next ninety days that will make a third reading of the book more relevant to your needs as a business owner and manager.

Finally, pencil into your calendar a fourth reading twelve months from now. Now before you say, "you're kidding," think about this. There is a Chinese proverb that says, "No man steps into the same river twice." Like most proverbial expressions, the statement has practical and symbolic meanings. In a practical sense, if a person steps into a river, steps out, and steps back in, the part of the river into which he first stepped has now moved downstream so that he steps into a *new* river. The symbolic sense is that things are always changing — including you and me. Thus, an experience at one point in your life isn't like the same experience at another point in your life. For that reason, when you reread this book a year from now, you will read it as a different person. Hopefully the book will have changed you. But certainly life will have made you a different person. Of course, the same rationale could be given for reading it two years from now, five years from now, and ten years from now — which I hope you'll do, because you'll be a different person then also. I have reread books that I first read twenty-five years ago and have discovered new meanings and messages that I hadn't seen as a younger, less "streetwise" businessman.

Give copies of this book to key employees, key customers, and key suppliers. Don't give *your* copy away. It has the investment of your notes and underlining. "Aha! . . . you're trying to sell more copies of your book!" Not so. I can assure you a million copies of this book would have to be sold before it would have any economic impact on my wallet. Besides that, I didn't write it with economic motivations. I wrote it to share ideas and consulting experiences of more than fifteen years with you, and if those ideas have been helpful to you, why not share them with others? But in a more practical sense, and assuming this book has had an impact on the way you work and manage your business, it is a way to communicate with people who see a different world than you do.

As I said at the outset, my preferred medium for communication is speaking. I relate better to an audience I can see, but such is the defect in writing versus speaking. But I will give you a way to talk back to me if you want to. Send your comments, or questions, or ideas about what I've said here to my home address or call me on my business phone:

William H. Franklin
3464 Hidden Acres Drive
Atlanta, Georgia 30340
(404) 934-1047

If you call and I'm out of my office, I'll call you back. Just leave your name and number and mention the book, so I'll know why I'm returning the call.

Incidentally, when I wrote three sample chapters of this book for my publisher, he said I would need eighteen chapters in order to make an average-size book. I gave him nineteen. Then he called me and said, "I've got enough material here to almost make two books . . . give me six more chapters, and I'll publish those and the surplus chapters as a second book—a follow-up to *Street Smarts*." I'll be doing that, and if you're interested, you can look for it soon.

So long. And do let me hear from you.